1-00 .

1-00

GARDENER'S CALENDAR

GARDENER'S CALENDAR

A MONTH-BY-MONTH GUIDE

ROY HAY

Based on the television series

BOOK CLUB ASSOCIATES
LONDON

Granada Publishing Limited
Frogmore, St. Albans, Herts AL2 2NF
and
36 Golden Square, London W1R 4AE
515 Madison Avenue, New York, NY
10022, USA
117 York Street, Sydney, NSW 2000,
Australia
100 Skyway Avenue, Rexdale,
Ontario M9W 3A6, Canada
61 Beach Road, Auckland, New
Zealand

This edition published 1983 by Book
Club Associates
By arrangement with Granada
Publishing Ltd.

This book was edited, designed and
produced by Grub Street, London

*British Library Cataloguing in
Publication Data*

Hay, Roy
    Gardener's calendar.
    1. Gardening
    I. Title
    635 SB450.97

ISBN 0-246-11955-1

Printed and bound in Germany by
Mohndruck,
Graphische Betriebe GmbH, Gütersloh
Origination by Newselle, Italy

Photoset by Sackville Studio,
Billericay.

CONTENTS

INTRODUCTION

THE GARDENING YEAR

FOREWORD

The Royal Horticultural Society's garden at Wisley in Surrey is unique. There is no garden which contains such a variety of features – rose garden, rock garden, hardy borders, heather garden, model fruit and vegetable plots, a garden for the handicapped and disabled, greenhouses and so on. It was a splendid idea for Granada television to collaborate with the RHS and produce a regular 'Gardener's Calendar' programme of work to be done in the garden each month. Everything is there to see at Wisley and there too is the expertise of the staff in charge of the various departments – all this has been made available and well used by Granada.

This book has been based on the year's series of the 'Gardener's Calendar' television broadcasts. Obviously you cannot cover the whole of gardening in a half-hour's broadcast once a month, so the book offers a more complete and balanced summary of the gardening year; and its detailed practical information is an excellent complement to the undoubted attributes of television.

The broadcasts have followed advice contained in the Royal Horticultural Society's two excellent books, *The Fruit Garden Displayed* and *The Vegetable Garden Displayed.* So naturally I have relied heavily on these books and am grateful to the Society for permission to reproduce the vegetable rotation cropping plan from the latter. I would also like to thank the staff at Wisley for their kind cooperation and help in putting this book together.

My thanks also go to Baco, Walter Blom, the Bulb Information desk, Samuel Dobie & Son, ICI, Murphy, Sutton seeds and Unwins for their valuable assistance.

Finally, my special thanks are reserved for my wife Frances Perry, without whose help and advice this book may not have been possible.

Roy Hay

Weather variations

1. The average date at the Royal Horticultural Society, Wisley is about the third week in March. In extreme years it can be up to 1 month earlier or some 3-4 weeks later.

Spring comes later to higher ground, the delay being about 1 day for every 33 ft (10 m) increase in height above sea level.

2. The average date at RHS Wisley is about the first week in December, but can be earlier in years when November is cold.

Winter comes earlier to the higher ground, the advance in date being about 7-10 days for every 330 ft (100 m) increase in height above sea level.

3. Frost is very local in its incidence, and it can occur much later in frost hollows, river valleys, and over light dry soils such as those at Wisley.

The year-to-year variation in date of the last spring frost is about 30 days either side of the average. Last frosts are always later in years with dry springs. (Data for high hills and mountains have been omitted on this map.)

4. The length of the frost-free period is greatest on the coasts and least in areas well inland. Variations in the average can occur within small areas according to the site.

The first autumn frosts may arrive up to three weeks earlier or later than the average date. In some years gardens on the south and south-west coasts can be frost-free. (Data for high hills and mountains have been omitted on this map.)

5. In the 'Dry' area, garden watering will be needed almost every year.

In the 'Intermediate' area, watering will be needed in the drier years, but only infrequently in the wetter years.

In the 'Wet' area, watering will only be needed in occasional dry spells or in exceptional drought years.

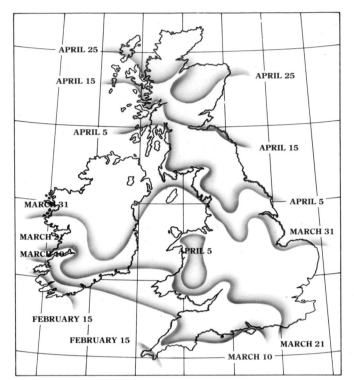

1. Average date of start of spring growth

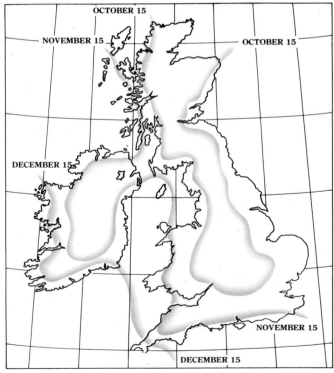

4. Average date of first autumn frost

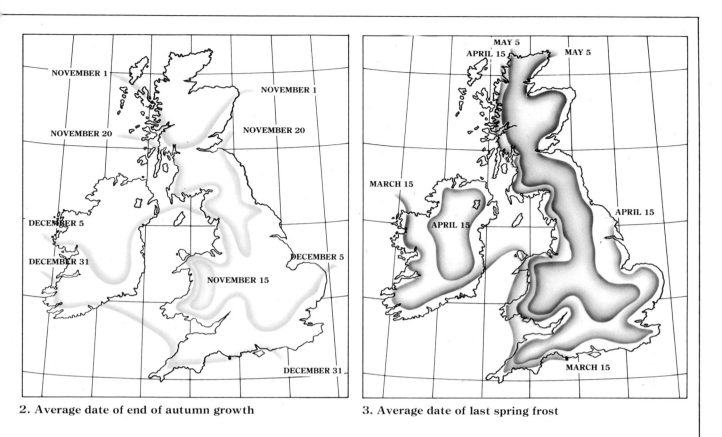

2. Average date of end of autumn growth

3. Average date of last spring frost

5. Soil moisture regimes

9

Garden planning

When first taking over a garden – virgin or existing – there are two main things to check. Firstly, the aspect of the garden, where and when it gets shade, sun, wind and frost. These factors will all affect your plant's performance and therefore the decision as to what and where to plant.

For example, if shelter is required, consider how best to provide this – by a fence, hedge or maybe by planting shrubs in a border of say 2 m (6 ft) wide.

Secondly, find out whether the soil is acid or alkaline. A cheap soil testing kit will settle this point and determine the range of plants you can successfully grow. If necessary, you can then see what can be done to improve it (see pp 14-16).

Many books have been written about garden planning and thousands of plans have been published, yet all these well-meant suggestions only offer ideas which may or may not help you to design the garden you want. Doubtless, it is a good idea to go to the local library, borrow a book or two about garden planning and see if you can pick up some ideas to help you plan your own garden.

Alternatives

But a better idea, before you try to work out a plan on paper – to lay out a garden on a virgin plot or to replan and re-arrange an already existing garden – is to sit down and think out with your family what you really want from your garden. It is essential to plan your garden to your needs and limitations.

Do you want a lawn, flowers, fruits and vegetables, with maybe a rock garden and a pool – an ambitious layout which will require a lot of work every week?

If you are young and strong and have a young family or older and willing to work such a garden would make a lot of sense. But if you do not want to spend hours digging and hoeing – or perhaps you are not really physically capable of such regular hard work – it might be a bad idea to be too ambitious. So you maybe want a labour-saving garden – a lawn, perhaps even long grass cut two or three times a year where the vegetable garden used to be, beds and borders of perennial plants and shrubs. You will also need ground cover plants to suppress weeds. Vegetables would be reduced to a minimum; salad crops, perhaps, a row or two of peas, runner beans and maybe an asparagus bed.

Or you may decide a fair-sized area behind the house can be paved over leaving spaces here and there for small plants to break up the bare expanse of paving. Tubs and other containers make such an area a real joy. The rest of the garden could consist mainly of rough grass to be mown only two or three times a year.

There is another aspect to be considered when planning a garden. Many people sell their house when their children leave home, or when they retire because they do not need or cannot afford such a large house and garden. So they may acquire a new and smaller property.

It is important in this case to think ahead a few years and plan the garden accordingly – pulling it apart, over a period if necessary, and reorganizing it – so that you will be able to cope with it as your physical strength diminishes.

Elderly people know what jobs they find difficult and eventually impossible – such as digging, hoeing, and hedge trimming. Eliminate these if you are heading for what you hope will be a gentle and happy retirement!

Basics

But let us return to the basics. It is sensible to make a plan of the garden on graph paper.

This helps to give you some idea of how much space you can allow for various features and therefore how many you can pack in, whether they be roses, shrubs, herbaceous plants or whatever.

Always try to deal with the front garden first – to make that at least respectable. Then concentrate on the back garden and here you should really try to decide on a work programme. Basically if construction, reconstruction or reclamation work has to be done, concentrate on the area nearest to the house and stop this kind of work by the end of April. After then concentrate on keeping the front garden and the reclaimed or developed part at the back tidy. Let the rest wait until the autumn when reclamation and construction can begin again.

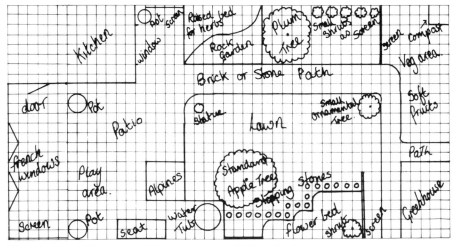

Planning a garden on graph paper : a rough first draft.

This garden is a mixture of the formal and informal, but in early summer is very colourful.

These colourful borders are full of spring flowers — daffodils, tulips, primroses, *Alyssum saxatile* and saxifrages.

A charming informal garden with lawn surrounding a pool and an interesting variety of foliage colours .

A bright display of summer flowers — African marigolds, nicotianas, geraniums, fushsias and scarlet busy lizzies.

A restful garden with many shades of colour provided by armerias (thrifts), oriental poppies, asters and shrub roses.

An intriguing garden with surprise features succeeding each other. Very informal, few straight lines.

Preparing the ground

'It is not lavish expenditure that I preach – it is thoroughness, thoroughness, thoroughness. Thoroughness, that cheapest and best of investments; thoroughness, the gardeners' richest capital; thoroughness in preliminary preparation, his easy, perfect insurance against all the woes that afflict the little flock in his charge.'

I cannot do better than start this section by endorsing Reginald Farrer's homily to rock plant enthusiasts, for it expresses succinctly the best advice a gardener can possibly receive whatever the nature of his interests.

The plants' basic requirements are air, light, water and food; all of which gardeners more or less take for granted. Nevertheless an understanding of the soil is essential in order to get the best out of the garden.

In the past plantsmen often knew such things instinctively; they had a 'feel' for a plant's requirements so that people referred to them as 'green-fingered' or 'sons of Adam'. Today, the work of research stations, reports from various scientific bodies, articles in the horticultural press and talks and demonstrations on radio and television do much to spread a knowledge of soil science to a wide field – so helping all gardeners.

Fortunately most hardy plants are not fastidious; on the contrary they are reasonably adaptable and thrive in most soils. Nevertheless it is in the well fed, properly managed gardens that one finds the strong flower spikes, the rich colours and large blooms, the crisp, succulent vegetables and the luscious fruits associated with good husbandry. Everything begins with the soil; its make up, how you feed and treat it – and later on how and what you plant in it.

All soils are composed of mineral particles – and it is largely the disposition and quantities of these which determine its nature, making it for example a sandy soil or a clay soil. Additionally soil contains water, air, various amounts of organic material known as 'humus', which is really decomposing animal or vegetable matter, and a host of creatures, many of which are microscopic. All these are necessary and have a part to play in making soil fertile.

Although one constantly hears about good loamy soil there is no such thing in nature. Rather it is a condition brought about by understanding and good cultivation and therefore possible to produce in most gardens.

The main soil types are clay, sandy and chalk. Peat soils exist but are not common and have to be drained before much can be grown in them.

Clay soils

Clay soils are usually quite fertile if properly treated, retaining fertilizer and water better than lighter soils. Pure clay is impossible to cultivate, but if clay particles are incorporated with other constituents such as sand and humus it becomes workable; the degree of fertility is related to the quantity of these other materials that are present.

Clay soils are notoriously heavy, sticky and slow to drain. This is largely due to the smallness of their individual particles, to the preponderance of these in relation to the other ingredients and to the nature of the spongy substances which surround each clay fragment.

Known as colloids these absorb moisture and swell when there is water about, but in dry weather lose moisture and shrink – and so form the characteristic cracks associated with clay soils.

The stickiness and plastic nature of clay is associated with this property as well as the fineness of its particles. If clay soils are worked when wet the colloids swell, the particles become more and more closely packed down and eventually water cannot drain through.

It is rather like making a clay pot. When a potter kneads clay he constantly dips his hands in water to keep it moist. Eventually by means of shaping and pummelling he fashions the shape required and because the colloids swell the pot holds water.

Similarly, when you work or tramp about on clay when it is wet this emulates the potter and can temporarily spoil the soil texture.

However clay possesses another property called flocculation. This means that the particles can, under certain conditions, coagulate or clot together, the effect of which is to create larger soil groupings, so that air spaces form. This results in better aeration and drainage and can occur naturally as a result of 'weathering'.

By digging the soil in autumn and leaving it rough in large clods the alternate wetting and drying, freezing and thawing, plus the various changes of temperature it will experience during the winter months, will cause a certain amount of spontaneous flocculation. Then in spring, provided the gardener picks a good day when the soil is reasonably dry the clods will crumble to a fine tilth when raked or otherwise cultivated.

Certain chemicals can artificially induce flocculation, the most important from the gardener's point of view being lime. When this is applied to clay soil it becomes converted to carbonate of lime, some of which goes into solution as bicarbonate of lime – a salt possessing powerful flocculating properties.

Although potash and other minerals are naturally present in clay they are only released slowly, as a result of cultivation.

To increase food in the soil it is therefore important to add man-

Different soils and their plants

Typical weeds found in clay soils. From the left, *Primula vulgaris, Ranunculus arvensis* and *Dipsacus sylvestris.*

Typical weeds found in sandy soils. From the left, *Centaurea cyanus, Chrysanthemum segetum* and *Cytisus scopiarus.*

Typical weeds found in chalk soils. From the left, *Clematis vitalba, Fagus sylvatica* and *Viburnum lantana.*

Clay

Plant indicator

Daucus carota, wild carrot.
Dipsacus sylvestris, teazle.
Genista tinctoria, dyer's greenweed.
Mentha arvensis, field mint.
Primula vulgaris, primrose.
Ranunculus arvensis, buttercup.

Plants suitable

Aesculus, chestnuts.
Alnus, alders.
Aucuba japonica.
Bamboos – most.
Berberis – most.
Chaenomeles, Japanese quince.
Cotoneasters.
Crataegus, hawthorn.
Forsythia.
Ilex, holly.
Laburnums.
Lonicera, honeysuckle.
Pulmonarias, lungworts.
Pyracantha, firethorn.
Rosa.
Salix, willows.
Viburnums.

Sandy

Betula – all, birch.
Castanea sativa, Spanish chestnut.
Centaurea cyanus, cornflower.
Chrysanthemum segetum, corn marigold.
Cytisus scoparius, broom.
Papaver dubium, poppy.
Potentilla anserina, silverweed.
Pteris aquilina, bracken.
Scleranthus annuus and
S. perennis, knawel.
Spergula arvensis, spurrey.
Ulex europaeus, gorse.

Acer negundo.
Berberis – all.
Castanea – all.
Calluna vulgaris and cultivars.
Cistus – all.
Cotoneaster – all.
Erica – all.
Ilex (hollies) – all.
Kerria japonica.
Lonicera (honeysuckle) – all.
Robinia – all.
Ulex – all.

Chalk

Cichorium intybus, chicory.
Clematis vitalba, traveller's joy.
Cornus sanguinea, dogwood.
Echium vulgare, viper's bugloss.
Fagus sylvatica, beech.
Fumaria officinalis, fumitory.
Geranium molle, dove's foot cranesbill.
Lotus corniculatus, bird's foot trefoil.
Scabiosa columbaria, sheep's scabious.
Silene inflata, bladder campion.
Viburnum lantana, guelder rose.

Armerias, thrift.
Buddleia (butterfly bush) – most.
Bulbs – most.
Campanula species, bellflowers.
Centranthus ruber.
Cheiranthus, wallflower.
Cotoneaster – most.
Crambe cordifolia.
Dianthus, pinks and border carnations.
Gypsophila paniculata, chalk plant.
Helleborus orientalis, Lenten rose.
Iris germanica and varieties, iris.
Prunus, flowering cherries.
Salvia – most.
Scabiosa caucasica, scabious.
Romneya coulteri, tree poppy.
Verbascum species, mullein.
Viburnum – most.

ures, preferably bulky organic materials since these also help the drainage by forcing the soil particles apart.

If lime is added apply it on some other occasion or it will cause the manures to rot away too rapidly. If manure is dug in during the autumn digging, use the lime as a spring dressing. In very wet soils the addition of sand, brick rubble or old weathered ashes also helps drainage and makes cultivation easier.

Sometimes very tenacious and heavy clays are almost impossible to dig, in which case it may be advisable to build up the topsoil by mulches and top dressings. Tree and shrub roots forcing their way downwards will also help to open up clay soils but of course it takes a long time for virgin clay to become crumbly and easy to cultivate.

Treatment

Clay soils are cold so take time to warm up in spring but once under control are very fertile. They are also naturally acid.

Dig clay soil in the autumn and keep off it when it is wet or there is snow or frost on the ground.

Pick a fine dry day for spring cultivation.

Don't apply lime and manure together.

Use bulky, well rotted, organic manures.

Sandy soils

One of the commonest minerals found in the earth is quartz, which breaks down into flints and sands. Sand is practically pure silica, insoluble and quite devoid of plant food, yet beneficial in soils because its comparatively large particles make for free drainage and aeration.

Consequently sandy soils are lighter to work and also warmer than clays. However when too much sand is present soils become poor and hungry and also dry out too quickly for the welfare of most plants.

When there is 60% or more sand in any soil it is useless for growing and reclamation becomes a slow, laborious – even expensive – task. Sandy soils also become weedy and there is a shortage of potash, lime and soluble mineral salts.

When cultivating sandy soil therefore it is important to increase its water retaining capacity. This is achieved by adding bulky organic manures such as farmyard manure, garden and mushroom compost, hop manure, leafsoil, spent hops and the like, all of which serve as a source of humus and act like sponges in retaining water and soluble salts.

As the humus-forming material rots down it also slowly releases nitrogenous and other salts and gradually the soil quality improves. Lime then plays an important part in bringing out its fertility but it is important not to apply it at the same time as manures. Also on light soils use a slow acting form, such as carbonate of lime or hydrated lime.

Treatment

Sandy soils are excellent for early crops but tend to dry out later in the year.

Add organic manures during soil cultivation, also as mulches in order to feed the plants and to conserve moisture.

Potash manures will be needed.

Weeds are likely to be a problem.

Piped water will be particularly advantageous on light soils.

Chalk soils

These soils are variable, their fertility depending to a great extent on the depth of soil overlying the chalk strata. Where this is shallow good growth cannot be anticipated, unless heavy mulches of organic material are frequently applied.

On the credit side chalk soils are warm and well drained and often rich in phosphates.

But they do tend to dry out rapidly and can also lose organic material (humus) because of the action of the lime. Conversely, lime is sometimes necessary for certain crops, even when the subsoil is chalk.

However too much soluble lime creates a condition known as chlorosis, which causes the leaves of plants like lilac, camellia, hydrangeas and soft fruits to turn yellow and drop. This is because the lime interferes with the plants' intake of iron – associated with nitrogen in the green colouring matter of leaves – so that growth becomes stunted.

Some plants need lime, others seem indifferent to its presence while a few dislike it so much that they die where it is present. Such plants are known as calcifuges or lime haters. Examples are *Erica cinerea, E. ciliaris, E. tetralix* and their hybrids; *Gentiana ornata, G. alpina, G. sino-ornata, G. verna* and others; *Nertera depressa;* many rhododendrons; *Daphne blagayana* and most dodecatheons.

Treatment

Build up the topsoil with plenty of rotted compost or other bulky manures. When deep and sheltered chalk soils can be very fertile.

Go in for shallow digging.

To treat chlorosis apply dressings of chelated iron with magnesium and manganese (sold as sequestrene) to counteract the effects of the lime. Apply annually to affected plants in spring.

Weed constantly.

Loams

As clay soils are worked and improved they may contain enough sand or grit and humus to permit reasonable drainage, yet retain sufficient moisture near the surface to prevent drying out. They then make very good clay loams. However, when the proportion of sand is higher, yet fertile through good cultivation with plenty of humus it will be known as sandy loam.

Digging

Of all the tasks in the garden digging is the most arduous, but it is essential and when well done, very satisfying.

There are a number of digging methods suggested by the experts. But firstly, there is the 'no digging' school who work on the principle that if compost is continually added to the surface soil there is no need to dig. This is a complex and contentious theory which works well enough on some soils but not so well on others and requires an awful lot of compost. So for the purposes of this book it is best to dismiss it.

Plots intended for planting fruits and vegetables, and also for herbaceous plants, trees, shrubs, or roses are normally double dug. The top spit or spadeful of soil is removed, the lower spit is forked over thoroughly, and maybe manure or fertilizer is incorporated with it; then the top spit is returned into the trench or planting hole. Again manure or fertilizer may be worked in as the top spit is replaced.

Digging in manure. Late autumn and early winter is a good time to do this. Fork into the top spit of soil, well decayed dung, garden compost, hop manure or other organic material.

Large plots

Sometimes a fairly large plot has to be dug. This may be a virgin plot covered with turf, or a plot that has been dug over before.

With the grass-covered plot, one method is to dig out a trench 1 ft wide across the plot; skim the turf off with a spade and stack it to one side of the plot, then dig out the soil to the depth of the spade and pile this next to the turf. To make a thorough job it is worthwhile loosening the soil in the bottom of the trench to the depth of a fork.

Then skim off the turf from the next 1 ft and shovel this into the trench, face down. Scatter a good handful of sulphate of ammonia to each square yard of the inverted turves. This will help the turf to rot down quickly and avoid any denitrification problems.

Then turn the top spit of soil over into the trench and if any well rotted manure or garden compost is available, work some of this in with the soil. Carry on like this until you reach the end of the plot and then barrow up the turf and soil you removed from the first trench to fill the last trench.

There is another and better way of digging a rectangular plot, however. Divide it down the middle. Take out the trench across the top of the left-hand half and place the soil (or turf and soil) by

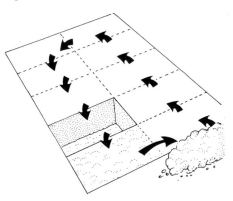

Digging a large rectangular plot. This is probably the best method of digging such a plot, as it is labour saving.

Tipping soil over. After rose pruning has been completed and all prunings, fallen rose leaves and other debris raked up for burning, fork the soil over lightly.

the right-hand half (at the same end).

Then dig down to the end of the left-hand section, and fill the last trench from soil from the bottom end of the other half. Continue to dig back up the right-hand half and at the end, the soil is ready and waiting to fill in the last trench.

There are various powered machines which will cultivate the top spit of soil quite efficiently. If large areas are to be cultivated these are very worthwhile.

Even on smaller areas, the smaller powered cultivators are extremely useful to gardeners who find digging arduous.

Handy Hint: For those who find digging hard work – there is the Wolf Terrex spade. This is a spade which you never lift off the ground.

You tread it in with the foot, and then pull it smartly towards you; the lever at the back of the spade resting on the ground acts as a fulcrum and the spadeful of soil is thrown forward and turned over into the trench.

The spade is then angled gently to the next position – never leaving the ground, so no lifting is involved. With a little practice you can become very skilled with this tool and do hours of digging without fatigue or straining.

Mulching

Many people are puzzled about the meaning of the word 'mulch'. According to the Concise Oxford Dictionary a mulch is 'a mixture of wet straw or leaves etc to protect roots of newly planted trees etc'. Actually this only gives half a definition. A better description of a mulch is a layer of organic material not less than 1 in (2.5 cm) thick, spread over the ground among plants. This will suppress weeds, help to conserve moisture by reducing loss by evaporation, and with a number of materials enrich the soil when at the end of the season the mulching material is dug in. In fact, gardeners do not make nearly enough use of mulching materials because, when properly used, mulches are of the greatest benefit in a garden.

Types of mulch

There are many mulching materials. Indeed, you can keep a mulch of an inch or so of loose soil over beds and borders by regular hoeing and this will conserve moisture in the ground and check the growth of seedling weeds. But it will of course involve a lot of labour.

Among the many materials that may be used as a mulch well rotted farmyard manure, if you can find it and afford it, is probably the

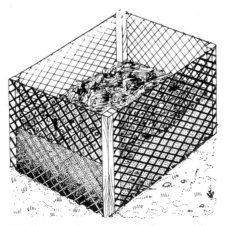

Making garden compost. One way is to surround the heap with wire meshed panels.

A compost heap needs to be turned from time to time, kept moist but protected from excessive rain.

best. Mushroom manure – the residue of the horse manure used on mushroom farms – is also very good. In fact, its manurial value is about half that of fresh horse manure.

Mushroom manure is splendid for spreading over beds, borders and among vegetables or fruits. It is best to get it direct from a mushroom farm as if you buy it in bags it is obviously quite expensive.

Sawdust can also be a great help in the garden. It may be spread on the ground say up to 2 in (5 cm) thick. It is important, however, to scatter a handful of sulphate of ammonia over each square yard of the mulch. This is to counteract the effect of denitrification caused by the soil bacteria which will be breaking down the sawdust. Peat, straw, bracken or leaves are all excellent materials as mulches but if they are dug in at the end of the season when they are only partially decomposed then the sulphate of ammonia should be applied as recommended above.

If you have large quantities of leaves in the autumn these will make marvellous mulching material. Stacked in the autumn they will, in their half decomposed state, make a splendid mulch to spread under roses, shrubs, fruit bushes, herbaceous plants, or under fruit trees or vegetables.

Home made garden compost is of course ideal mulching material if it is properly made and well rotted. Pests, and weed seeds should have been eliminated and it should be free of diseases, if diseased material is burnt in the first place and not put in the heap.

In recent years thin plastic sheeting has been introduced as mulching material. It is laid on the ground and anchored by soil or stones. Slits are made at required intervals and plants planted through them but so far these plastic mulches have not proved popular with amateur gardeners.

Normally most mulching materials are dug in about the end of the year during the autumnal cutting down and clearing up of beds, borders or fruit and vegetable plots. However, an exception can often be made with sawdust which can be applied (if available cheaply enough) up to 4 in (10 cm) deep and this is not disturbed.

Soluble feeds can always be applied through the mulch. When it is necessary to irrigate a mulched area allow at least 4 gallons (15 litres) of water to the square yard/metre to wet the mulch and then carry on watering to supply another 4-6 gallons (15-23 litres) to the square yard for the crop.

Normally you should not put on a mulch of any kind before mid-April when the soil has begun to warm up. A mulch is like a cellular blanket. It prevents the warmth of the sun penetrating easily during the day and also prevents the stored up warmth in the soil from rising and warming the air around the plants and fending off late frosts. Thus if put on too early, a mulch will retard the growth of many plants in spring.

Finally, it is important to apply a mulch to clean ground – hoe off any seedling weeds, or apply a weedkiller such as glyphosate before applying the mulch.

Watering

For most gardeners watering is a time-consuming nuisance. You have to carry cans or haul hose pipes about – all of which is a huge bore. But there is always some period in every year when in most parts of Britain we do not receive enough rain. It may be in spring – in 1980 many parts had virtually no rain in April, May and the first half of June – but sometimes the shortage of rain occurs in mid-summer or autumn.

Water applied at crucial times (when seedlings have just appeared or when young plants have been planted out) can be of enormous value.

Old gardeners often say you should never start watering because if you do you have to keep on. This is wrong. Watering should be started before the plants suffer any kind of stress from water shortage – even before they show signs of stress by wilting.

Begin to think about watering in April. If there are about 10 days without any appreciable rain from early April onwards be prepared to put on about a gallon (4.5 litres) of water to the square yard for any plants that you want to really look after well. These would include all plants, trees or shrubs planted in the past few months, seedlings of flowers or vegetables raised from seed sown in the spring, or planted out.

Later vegetables such as summer cauliflowers, peas, beans, marrows, sweet corn, potatoes and soft fruits will all benefit from regular watering.

The golden rules are water early and adequately. Just sprinkling the surface is no good. If you have to carry water to plants in cans, do a small part of the garden

Oscillating sprinklers which deliver fine gentle droplets of water may be adjusted to water borders of narrow widths.

each day – the evening is the best time as it is cooler and the water will not evaporate as quickly as it would in the heat of the midday sun. Never apply less than a gallon or a gallon and a half to the square yard.

Sprinklers

The easiest way to apply water is by a sprinkler attached to a hose. There are several types:

1. The simple circular type on a spike which you push into the ground and which waters a relatively small circle of up to about 27 ft (8.2 m) diameter.

2. The rotating sprinklers with two arms which fling out a jet of droplets and according to size and the water pressure may cover a circle up to 38 ft (11.5 m) in diameter.

3. The oscillating sprinkler – a metal bar with tiny holes which deliver fine rain-like droplets and which swings back and forth.

It can be adjusted to water a rectangle, or part of a rectangle – useful, for example if a border is to be watered and you do not wish to

waste water on a path or drive. Again according to the water pressure available there are oscillating sprinklers capable of covering areas from 48 ft by 32 ft (14.6 m by 9.7 m) up to about 52 ft by 49 ft (15.8 m by 15 m).

4. The so-called flip-flap or pulsating or pulse-jet sprinklers. These will water a circle up to around 60 ft (18.3 m) diameter given sufficient water pressure.

5. There are also models which can be adjusted to water a full circle or part of a circle. These sprinklers are very useful where it is desired to water an area (for example, in the vegetable garden where there are fruit bushes, or runner beans) because they can be mounted on a pole above the crops.

The easiest way to do this is to buy a pulse-jet sprinkler mounted on a plastic spike, acquire an 8 ft (2.4 m) length of old water pipe, drive this in the ground and stick the spike in the top. Clip the hose pipe to the water pipe with a few twists of wire.

6. There are also 'lay flat' hoses punctured with small holes

which are useful for applying water in fine droplets to a long border or for watering irregularly shaped areas.

7. A final method of applying water is by means of a kind of 'leaky hose' system which you can lay between rows of plants or on a border and the water seeps out from the hose.

Water pressure

Choosing a sprinkler suitable for your garden can obviously be a bit of a puzzle especially if you do not know what water pressure you have. The manufacturers usually state what kind of pressure is needed for their various models – low, medium or high.

But you can easily obtain a rough idea of what pressure you have in your water main by timing how long it takes to fill a two gallon bucket from the end of your garden hose. It is necessary to fill it from the hose and not direct from the tap as there is always loss of pressure – the longer the hose, the greater the loss.

If the bucket fills in 20 seconds you have high flow or pressure; if it takes 25-30 seconds you have medium pressure and if it takes 35 seconds you have low pressure.

One way of making the best use of water in dry spells when it is necessary to irrigate trees or shrubs, is to scrape away the soil to make a shallow depression of 1-2 in (2.5-5 cm) for about 12 in (30 cm) all round the shrub.

Apply the water to this slight hollow and then push the dry soil back over it. This helps to slow down the rate of evaporation.

If planting has to be done in dry weather it is always desirable to water the planting site thoroughly some hours before planting – overnight perhaps. You can take out holes ready for the plants and fill these with water. It is also most desirable to water pot plants well before planting as it is very difficult to wet a dry ball of soil once it has been planted.

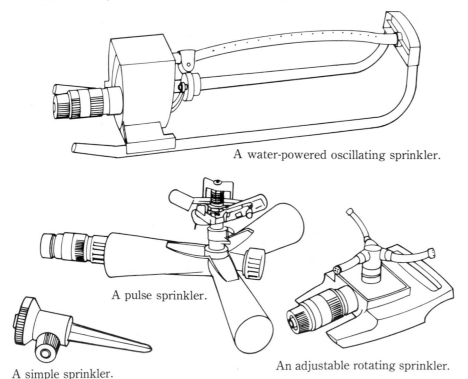

A water-powered oscillating sprinkler.

A pulse sprinkler.

A simple sprinkler.

An adjustable rotating sprinkler.

Propagation

Perhaps the most fascinating aspect of gardening involves reproducing plants from living pieces of an original specimen. This is called vegetative reproduction, or propagation.

Of course seed represents the natural means of increase and we see evidence of nature's fecundity all around – particularly in the way weeds spread and the use gardeners make of seeds for growing hardy and half-hardy annuals, vegetables and other plants. Nevertheless seed sowing has certain limitations.

Natural species, that is plants occurring wild, produce seedlings which look very much like their parents. So one may sow seeds from species plants with every expectation of a uniform result, but occasionally one seedling may produce a distinctive form, perhaps with flowers of a different colour or double, or with variegated leaves. These are known as sports or mutations and if the break is attractive you may wish to increase this new form.

It is here that difficulties can occur for the seedlings from sports are always variable and more often than not revert to the type species.

Again, when two species are crossed, the resultant offspring (known as hybrids) will show much variation. Some will look like one parent, some like the other, while a few may display characteristics of both. Occasionally some of the hybrids may be good enough for naming and then one naturally will wish to perpetuate them.

Seed sowing from hybrids will still prove chancey however, although when the strain is good, as for example in a good selection of delphiniums, or Brompton stocks this may not matter. Constant rogueing by seedsmen over a long period keeps certain strains of flowers and vegetables pure. Consequently gardeners are able to grow named varieties of vegetables and flowers in the confident anticipation of a uniform result.

Uniformity and also high quality can be expected from the varieties marked in a seedsman's catalogue as F_1 hybrids. The seedlings from these produce 'look alike' plants, but with specific improvements over their parents, such as greater cropping potential, larger flowers or a sturdier habit.

They are obtained from first generation crosses made between two selected forms of a plant, carried out under controlled conditions. The improvement is due to what is known as *hybrid vigour*. Unfortunately seeds saved from F_1 hybrids do not breed true, nor will the seedlings carry these desirable qualities a second season, so the cross has to be duplicated every year. As a result seeds of F_1 hybrids are naturally more expensive.

Seed sowing

Seeds are sown in various ways at various seasons. Most vegetables, perennials like lupins and geums and many hardy annuals and biennials are sown in drills – taken out with a draw hoe – outdoors. Because all seedlings will die if the roots cannot reach water soon after germination, the soil must be raked down as finely as possible so that there are no large air pockets and the soil particles are in close contact.

Soil moisture is then passed on from one particle to another. The smaller the seeds the more important is this initial preparation.

Vegetable seeds are usually sown in straight rows, following a line stretched from one end of the plot to the other. Small seeds require shallow drills usually around ½ in (1 cm); peas and beans will need 1½ in (3.8 cm).

Always sow thinly and afterwards cover the seed by lightly raking the soil or else scuffle the soil into the drills with the feet – first the left foot, then the right.

Flowers in cutting beds, wall-flowers and the like will be sown in the same way and later (like all seedlings) must be thinned according to the instructions on the seed packet.

In the case of annuals sown where they are to flower, informality is important. Straight lines are not desirable in flower beds. Consequently the seed may either be broadcast within predetermined areas and then lightly raked in, or shallow drills can be made with a pointed stick. These drills can be as irregular as you like provided they fit within their allotted confines.

After sowing cover the seeds and smooth the soil, using the rake in an upright position so as not to bury the seeds too deeply. Label each group of plants and grow on as recommended.

Half-hardy annuals and small quantities of perennials or alpines are usually raised in pots, boxes, pans (half-pots) or Jiffy 7's. The latter, being made of peat, have to be soaked beforehand and the seeds inserted in their tops.

Potting soil (proprietary or home made) will be required for the other receptacles. Clay pots and pans will need crocking but not plastic pots since these have adequate drainage holes across their bases. After filling the containers with compost, smooth the tops, sow the seeds very thinly and cover them with a light sifting of soil or sand. Very fine seeds – such as begonias – will not need covering; place a sheet of glass over the pot to retain the humidity.

When the seedlings are large enough to handle they are pricked off into seed trays – or into old tomato trays which can easily be obtained from your greengrocer.

Use a proprietary seed or potting compost. You should normally prick off about 50 seedlings into a standard seed tray – rather more into a tomato tray.

The ordinary amateur gardener does not need a large quantity of seed sowing, pricking off or potting composts. There are two types; the loam-based John Innes composts and the peat-based composts, each with its own devotees.

Young seedlings should not be exposed to hot sun, especially through glass, so lay sheets of newspaper over the pots when necessary, but remove them immediately the sun goes down.

Division

A safe and easy method of increasing plants, particularly herbaceous perennials with fibrous roots and plenty of shoots is by division.

Sometimes pieces can be cut from the sides of an established plant, without lifting the parent, for example with paeonies. However, Michaelmas daisies, heleniums, bearded irises, erigerons and many others may have to be lifted first and the roots shaken free of soil.

They are then cut up into pieces and the segments replanted. Very stubborn roots can be prised apart by inserting two garden forks, back to back in the clump, then levering the handles outwards.

Division is usually practiced in the spring or autumn.

Cuttings

Plants root from a variety of places, such as young shoots, pieces of stem, slices of root, and even individual leaves. The gardener needs to know which methods suit particular plants and can then exploit the appropriate techniques to make what are known as cuttings – leaf cuttings, stem cuttings and so on.

The chief advantage of cuttings is that a quantity of plants, alike in every respect, can be obtained from a single individual plant. It is the nurseryman's main method of increase but easily practiced by amateur gardeners, particularly if arrangements can be made for warmth at the rooting area.

Placing soft, leafy shoot cuttings in a propagating case, or rooting them in sand or light compost on a greenhouse bench or in an outside frame with soil warming cables provides ideal rooting conditions, although the leaves must be kept turgid meanwhile. Occasional overhead sprays of water and shading from hot sun will take care of the latter, or a mist propagation unit may be installed.

With a mist propagator you do not have to spray or shade, since a fine misty spray is ejected from raised nozzles on a soil warmed bench, as and when this is needed.

Hardwood and half-ripe (heel) cuttings on the other hand will root outdoors under cloches, in cold frames or at times even in the open ground as will root cuttings.

Dipping the cut ends in a rooting compound accelerates the rooting of woody stemmed cuttings and is commonly practiced in the case of shrubs and many other plants.

Soft cuttings

This is a method of propagation to be adopted during the growing season and usually practiced in spring and summer.

Sturdy shoots of young growths are taken from the plant, not too long and preferably with several pairs of leaves. The lower leaves are then taken off and the stem cut cleanly across with a sharp knife or razor blade immediately below a node (joint).

This is the area of greatest rooting potential, except in the case of hydrangeas and clematis which often root more successfully from internodal (between joint) cuttings.

The cuttings should then be inserted with a dibber or pointed stick into a vermiculite or peat and sand compost (one part sharp sand to 3 parts peat or vermiculite) in boxes, pans, pots or on open benches where there is a mist unit.

Label the cuttings and, apart from mist unit benches maintain a moist atmosphere by closing propagating cases and frames except for brief periods each day and protect the glass from sunshine.

When only small numbers of cuttings are rooted indoors, for example in a pot on a window sill, insert several canes or a bent piece of wire in the pot, and slip a polythene bag over the top, tucking the ends under the pot. Once rooting has taken place all cuttings should be lifted and potted.

Among a wide range of plants propagated by soft cuttings are dahlias, pelargoniums, calceolarias, Michaelmas daisies, herbaceous and alpine phloxes, salvias, various house plants and many alpines.

Half-ripe or heel cuttings

Half-ripe cuttings, as the name implies, are normally taken around July and August. They are made from pieces of the current season's growth 3-4 in (8-10 cm) long pulled from the plant – usually a shrub – with a sliver or heel of the older wood attached.

After these side growths have been pulled from the branch, the bases are trimmed and the cuttings are inserted in a propagating medium, as recommended for soft cuttings.

As the weather is normally warm at that time of year, heel cuttings often root satisfactorily outdoors, under a cloche or in a frame. Plants which can be propagated in this manner include lavender, rosemary, santolina, weigela, brooms and ceanothus.

Hardwood cuttings

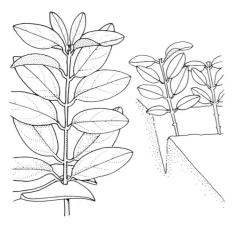

Hardwood cuttings are made from ripened shoots of the current season's wood. Naturally the year is well advanced before the growths are sufficiently tough and rigid for them to be made into cuttings, so the method is only practical with woody plants, such as shrubs, roses and fruit bushes.

Straight sturdy stems are removed from the plants with secateurs around September and October, then cut across immediately below a node. By that time deciduous shrubs will usually have lost their foliage. The unripe tips of these are also removed, but left intact in the case of conifers. The length of the cuttings will vary up to 12 in (30 cm) or so, depending on the normal growth of each plant.

When plants with a short 'leg' are required, as with gooseberries and red currants, the basal buds are picked out with the finger nail;

otherwise leave the shoots intact.

Next take a spade and make a slit trench about 6 in (15 cm) deep in a sheltered part of the garden and insert the cuttings for two thirds of their length and 4-6 in (10-15 cm) apart.

Such deep planting is necessary in order to obtain a vigorous root system. Return the soil, firm it with the foot and leave them to root. After heavy winter frosts check that none of the cuttings have lifted; if they have tread them back again.

Plants which can be propagated from hardwood cuttings include forsythia, privet, yew, cornus, shrub roses, willows, gooseberries and currants.

Root cuttings

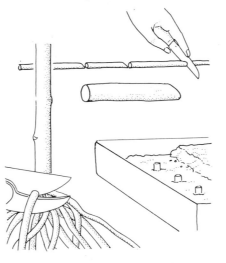

Root cuttings may be taken at various seasons of the year, even in the depths of winter. It is usual to lift the plant to be increased and cut its roots into segments of 1-2 in (2.5-5 cm). Fairly thick roots are cut horizontally at the top and slanting at the base, so that one can then avoid planting them upside down.

They may then be inserted (like other cuttings) in deep boxes or pots of gritty compost to root; their tops covered with a 1 in (2.5 cm) layer of coarse sand. Stood in a cold frame or against a shed wall with a protective covering of ashes

or leaves, in winter only, they soon start to sprout.

Certain forms of root cuttings are too slender to 'plant' upright. The herbaceous phlox is a good example. Such cuttings may be laid horizontally on half-filled seed trays of soil, then covered with sand, or they may be tied in small bundles and inserted upright in the normal way. It is essential to separate and pot them up as soon as shoots appear, otherwise the new roots will become hopelessly entangled.

Plants which may be propagated by means of root cuttings include oriental poppies, seakale, anchusas, acanthus, Japanese anemones, *Primula denticulata*, and echinops.

Leaf cuttings

These usually need warmth in order for rooting to take place. Very little preparation is required; some plants – like African violets – will even produce small plantlets from a leaf kept indoors in an egg-cupful of water.

In other cases a severed leaf may be pegged down into gritty soil, the right way up, after incisions have been made with a sharp knife across the veins, or a leaf may be cut up into segments and rooted in a propagating frame.

Plants to increase in this way include *Begonia rex*, streptocarpus, saintpaulia, ramonda and gloxinia.

Frames and cloches

With the production of the most welcome and the most valuable crops in mind, it is well worth considering the purchase of some cloches, or a cold frame or two. Cloches may be of glass or plastic and they come in a variety of shapes and sizes. It pays to spend a little time comparing the costs of the different types of cloches. Glass cloches if carefully handled should last for many years but are the most expensive.

Types

There are various types of plastic in use for cloches, from the very thin sheeting which with care may last two seasons and is very cheap – to the semi-rigid and rigid types of clear plastic. Evaluate cloches by comparing the cost per square foot of growing area covered.

A cold frame is most useful. It need not be anything elaborate – any handyman can knock one up quite cheaply. There are of course various metal frames with glass or the latest clear plastic claimed to last for many years.

Cloches or frames placed in position in January will warm the soil quite appreciably and towards the end of the month in the southern and milder parts of the country, you can sow a quick growing variety of carrot such as 'Amsterdam Forcing', 'Nantes Express' or 'Early French Frame Rondo'.

Sow the seed very thinly on a bed of good garden soil enriched with a little peat and a dressing of general fertilizer applied according to the maker's instructions.

You can also sow salad onions such as 'White Lisbon' and a radish such as 'French Breakfast', 'Cherry Belle' or 'Saxerre', all broadcast thinly among the carrot seeds. The radishes will mature first followed by the spring onions and tender

The grow frame with virtually unbreakable clear plastic guaranteed for 12 years.

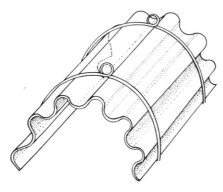

A plastic cloche.

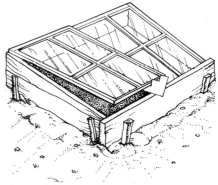

A rough home-made cold frame.

A glass cloche. A net can be used in place of a top pane.

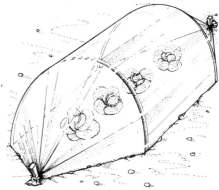

A polythene tunnel is very useful protection for seedlings.

young carrots.

Cloches or frames are also invaluable later on for protecting summer cabbage seedlings, sweet corn, runner and dwarf beans and other vegetables raised in heated

glass, until they may be planted out when the danger of frost is past. Frames of course are very valuable to accommodate young flower seedlings, for forcing bulbs and other purposes.

The greenhouse

In our unpredictable climate a greenhouse is almost a necessity. Even one that's unheated is an undeniable asset, providing sanctuary for countless plants – and their owners – throughout the year.

A greenhouse can certainly keep out wind and wet, if not frost, making it easy to dry off onions and gladiolus corms in autumn; rest bulbs in their dormant season; give an early start to seedlings including vegetables like celery and leeks; raise a crop of early strawberries and even grow choice fruit trees in pots.

Tomatoes and early chrysanthemums are other plants which can be grown without damage from wind and rain; choice rock plants may be flowered and viewed from a convenient waist-high bench and various types of propagation carried out to increase stock.

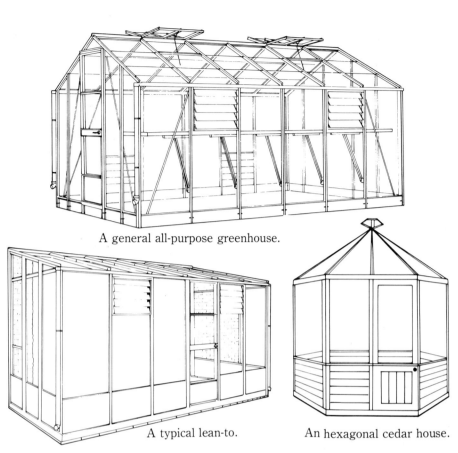

A general all-purpose greenhouse.

A typical lean-to.

An hexagonal cedar house.

Cold Greenhouse

Admittedly some form of heating increases the potential of a greenhouse greatly – even if this is only a soil-warmed propagator, but if for various reasons this is not possible, a cold greenhouse is still very worthwhile.

If possible build it close to the house, possibly as a lean-to on a warm wall. This avoids long walks to fetch water or having to go too far to tend plants in the dark or inclement weather. It can be constructed of wood or metal, but bear in mind that wooden greenhouses have to be regularly painted or oiled, and metal does not.

Again it can be partially glazed with its lower half built of brick or wood; or have glass all the way down to the ground – which is particularly useful if you aim to grow tall plants like tomatoes and chrysanthemums.

Size is relative to requirements and how much you want to spend, but, bearing in mind the need for a

path down the middle, it should be about 8 ft (2.4 m) wide by 10 ft (2.7 m) long or bigger. Since even unheated greenhouses can get very warm when the sun shines, ventilation from top lights is essential and side lights are desirable as well. One other point; before putting up any glasshouse check with local byelaws that there are no obstacles to its erection. Better be safe than sorry, rather than having to remove or modify any structure.

Even if artificial heat is not installed, there are tremendous advantages in laying on piped water. You will need it constantly – for watering, damping down, washing pots, spraying and cleaning.

Other desirable additions include a raised bench or benches, watering cans, sprayers, a maximum/minimum thermometer, pots of various sizes, compost materials, blinds or materials which can be painted on the glass in summer to reduce the glare of the sun, a propagating frame or box with a

glass top in which to root cuttings and an outside garden frame (see p 24) for hardening off bedding plants and accommodating plants that have finished flowering.

Cool Greenhouse

A frost-proof greenhouse is one which can be sufficiently warmed in winter to exclude frost, that is to prevent the temperature from falling below 34-35°F (1-2°C). A cool greenhouse aims at a temperature which will not fall below 40-45°F (4.5-7°C); consequently some form of heat may be necessary between early October and mid to late May (according to season and the part of the country), although the gardener can rely on sun heat for the rest of the year. A much larger range of plants can be grown in cool houses than in cold or frost-proof greenhouses, and it will also be possible to have flowers in bloom throughout the year.

There are various types of heating; firstly electricity, the cleanest, easiest and most reliable – although it can be expensive if high temperatures are maintained. With thermostatic control the systems become automatic and waste is eliminated as the current switches off when the temperature rises above the setting.

There are various methods of application, such as tubular heaters, immersion heaters (used to boost an existing boiler) and fan heaters. The latter entail no installation costs other than bringing the electricity supply into the house to a switch and socket, and work by driving warm air round the house. They are thermostatically controlled.

Small amounts of heat can also be brought to specific points, by means of soil warming cables. These should be laid on a bed of sand on a bench and covered with more sand. Pots stood on top will feel the benefit of bottom heat. There are also electrical propagators which enable gardeners to root cuttings or raise seedlings in a cold or frost-proof house.

Gas and fuel-oil burners are only practical when existing central heating units can be tapped, possibly for a small lean-to greenhouse on a south wall of the house.

But the cheapest heating for a small house can be provided by an efficient paraffin heater. This must be of modern design however; do not use an old throw out model as this can be dangerous. Also it must be kept scrupulously clean and the correct fuel (blue paraffin) used. Under extremely cold conditions oil heaters are invaluable, keeping the temperature just above freezing in a frost-proof greenhouse, but, one important point; always leave a chink of air while the lamp is burning.

Another aid to conserving heat is a lining of translucent polythene round the sides of the house and the lower part of the roof. It is unwise to cover the whole of the inside as moisture droplets form, due to surface tension and then run

down the material and drip onto plants. Leaving part of the roof free of polythene overcomes this to some extent and also allows the roof ventilators to be used.

Annuals to flower in a cool greenhouse

Antirrhinum (Snapdragon). Sow early spring or late autumn. Flower in 6 or 7 in (15 or 18 cm) pots, blooming in summer.

Campanula medium (Canterbury Bell). A biennial, so sow seeds in May or June in a cold frame. Prick out and pot on keeping them outdoors until spring. Flowering in early summer in 7 or 8 in (18 or 20 cm) pots.

Clarkia. Sow seeds September or March for flowering in summer. Tolerates cool conditions in winter 45°F (7°C).

Nicotiana affinis (tobacco plant). Sow March and again in June for a succession of flowers. Little or no heat required once seedlings are potted. They flower in 6 in (15 cm) pots in summer and autumn.

Petunia. Various kinds, some double; F₁ hybrids the best for greenhouse work. Sow March in a temperature of 55°F (13°C); grow on and flower in 5 in (12 cm) pots. For autumn flowers sow again in July.

Reseda odorata (mignonette). Sow February or March and prick out in threes in each 5 in (12 cm) pot. Stake carefully and leave to bloom in summer.

Senecio cruentus (cineraria). Flowering in 5 in (12 cm) pots in early spring. Sow May or June, leave in a cold frame until October then bring into a cool house.

Schizanthus (butterfly flower). Sow August or September, prick out into 3 in (8 cm) pots and leave in the cool 45°F (7°C) until early spring. Pinch out tops to make bushy plants, then pot on carefully into 5 or 6 in (12 or 15 cm) pots; stake carefully and leave to flower in spring.

General management

Whichever type of greenhouse you install there are certain basic principles which must be observed.

Cleanliness: Essential to keep down pests and disease. Ideally houses should be washed down with a disinfectant (like Jeyes fluid) once a year and any walls limewashed.

Rubbish, dirty pots and boxes should never be allowed to accumulate, understaging should be raked over – it is a common fault to use the greenhouse as a dumping ground for tools, sprays and a miscellany of things which should be kept in a garden shed – or probably discarded.

Plant hygiene: Avoid overcrowding and regularly remove dead leaves and flowers from pot plants. Don't overpot (ie, use a pot larger than necessary), as this can cause soil sourness and induce algae and moss growth.

On the other hand keep young plants moving into slightly larger containers until they reach maximum size or are planted out. Keep a watchful eye for pests and diseases and take appropriate measures.

Shading: Newly pricked out seedlings, ferns, primulas, and cinerarias cannot tolerate hot sun shining through glass and concentrating on the leaves.

Blinds, a proprietary glass shading on the outside of the greenhouse, limewash with a little flour and milk similarly applied, or even newspaper laid over plants are all effective in breaking up the direct rays of the sun and reduce transpiration losses and plant scorching.

The proprietary material Coolglass sprayed or painted on the glass will not wash off even in the heaviest downpour but is easily brushed off when dry.

Watering: Water plants according to their needs, bearing in mind

Good crops of tomatoes may be grown in the greenhouse and a little heat is best.

water is very hard and have to water a few plants which resent alkalinity, it may be necessary to install a tank or water butt where it can collect rainwater from roofs and gutters. When in doubt about the advisability of applying water to a pot plant, lift it and feel the weight. This will tell you a great deal about its needs.

In principle, it is generally better to water from below than to spray over plants, particularly if you live in an area of hard water. The latter method soon causes a white deposit to settle on the leaves and spoils their appearance. It can also cause rotting of hairy foliage such as saintpaulias and gloxinias.

A mixture of bedding petunias.

the need to rest some of the bulbous rooted kinds (particularly) at certain seasons. In general most water will be needed in summer, when a moist atmosphere should also be maintained by spraying the floor and staging with water in the mornings and afternoons during hot or dry weather.

Standing pots on sand or fine gravel and watering into the base (automatically or by hand), keeps the base of pots damp and if plastic pots are used or a plug of glasswool is pushed into the drainage hole of clay pots, the plants inside take up water as and when they need it.

If you live in an area where the

A good strain of antirrhinums.

Mixed clarkias.

The rock garden

The term 'alpine plant' should strictly only be used to describe plants from alpine or mountainous regions. But its wider use to include plants suitable for a rock garden but not native to the mountains is now acceptable.

Growing alpines is a fascinating hobby; true, it is fairly time-consuming and to grow many of them successfully requires a good deal of skill and experience. Against this however, is set the undoubted advantage that you can find something to do with alpines and enjoy them practically the whole year round – if you have a cold greenhouse or the facility to bring them indoors in winter.

A frame or two or some cloches are essential for protecting the more demanding alpines before they are brought indoors or into the greenhouse. These need not be anything elaborate and a good handyman can knock one up quite simply.

Clear plastic sheeting may be used instead of glass lights – frame tops covered with this plastic are easy for one person to handle. Being so light of course they blow away easily but may be anchored quite simply with a hook and eye at each end. A sheet of plastic is placed on the ground and when pots or pans are stood on this they are packed round with sand or peat. This is done to keep the pots from drying out and so reduce the frequency of waterings.

Most alpines are happy in a neutral, slightly acid or even slightly alkaline compost, although some must have acid soil and some need alkaline soil.

But for pots and pans, John Innes Compost No 2 with the addition of about one part of coarse grit or shingle to three parts of compost is suitable for most plants. The peat-based, loamless composts are not suitable for alpine plants.

Alpines, obviously, may be grown in a rock garden – but the construction of such an area can be impractical as rock garden stone is now relatively expensive. However, there are many equally acceptable ways of growing alpines so whether you intend to grow alpines in a rock garden, a raised bed, or in stone sinks choose a site in full sun away from trees which not only cast unwelcome shade but shed leaves which are a nuisance in the autumn.

They may be grown in flat beds, with a few pieces of rock here and there but the beds must be well drained; or many may be grown in the gaps between flat stone walls. Plants that revel in acid soil may be grown in a raised bed made with peat blocks and filled with a mixture of half moss-peat, a quarter lime-free soil and a quarter sharp sand or grit (parts by bulk).

Another excellent way to grow alpines is in stone sinks raised on some bricks to a height where they may easily be cared for by people who cannot bend or stoop, or even by those who are unfortunately confined to a wheelchair.

Some plants, of course prefer a shady or semi-shady position which is another reason for growing them in stone sinks as these can be placed in a suitable spot.

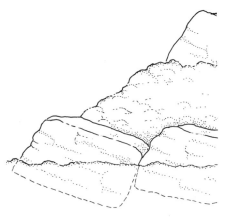

Build ground-level rocks into the soil to resemble an outcrop. Tilt them backwards to direct rainwater towards the rock garden.

Making a rock garden

If the garden slopes it is easy to make a rock garden. If it is flat, you have to dig down a little here and there and use the soil to build the ground up slightly.

Be careful not to bury the topsoil; remove it carefully before digging out the hollows and replace it. Do the same for the higher parts, using the sub-soil from the hollows to create the mound and put the topsoil back over it; or merely set rocks in place on a level site.

If you are using natural rock try to site the rocks so that they form a series of level pockets one above the other and so that as they connect with each other their horizontal lines of stratification match up. You can place a plant where the rocks join each other which will soon hide the join.

A good rock garden should consist of a series of shallow beds each fronted by rock which is not obtrusive so that the whole area resembles a natural rock formation on a gentle slope of a hill or mountain.

Stone sinks

Genuine old stone sinks are now almost collectors' items and are therefore expensive. A good imitation is the glazed sink, thousands of which are being discarded by householders each year.

The glazed sink can be camouflaged to look like an old stone sink very simply. First, scrub it clean inside and out. Then paint it with a bonding agent such as Polybond or Unibond going down a short way inside the sink.

Mix up 2 parts peat, 1 part sharp sand and 1 part cement (parts by bulk). Do not make it too sloppy; then press the mixture on to the sink and allow it to set. To make it look more like old stone it may be worthwhile scoring it lightly with an old kitchen fork before it has set solid.

Fill the sink with a soil mix as advised for a raised bed (see p 45).

Making a rock outcrop — a simple way to grow alpines — placing the stones in position.

Having completed laying the stones, the gaps are filled with soil.

Plants are carefully inserted in the gaps between the stones.

When planting is complete the surface is given a top dressing of stone chippings or gravel.

The finished outcrop planted with alpines.

The same outcrop has weathered nicely after a year.

29

Vegetable varieties

There are now hundreds of varieties of vegetables on offer to the amateur gardener. Seedsmen's catalogues give a great deal of useful information about the different varieties and it is well worthwhile writing off for them and choosing your seeds accordingly.

In catalogues you will find a number of varieties with the symbol F_1 in front. This means that they are first generation hybrids between two specially selected parent strains and they will have certain valuable attributes – they may produce earlier crops, heavier yields or be resistant to a disease.

For whatever reason F_1 varieties, even if they are more expensive, are very worthwhile – always go for them.

The varieties listed below will perform well under any good garden conditions:

Beans, broad: Dwarf types good for growing under cloches are 'The Sutton' and 'Bonny Lad'. Longpod varieties: 'Hylon', 'Imperial Longpod' and 'Colossal'.

Beans, climbing, French: 'Largo', 'Blue Lake', ('Earliest of All') and 'Garrafal Oro'.

Beans, dwarf or French: 'Sigma Cropper', Tendergreen', 'Sprite' and 'Daisy'.

Beans, runner: 'Sunset', 'Fry', 'Enorma', 'White Emergo', 'Mengoles' and 'Red Knight'.

Beetroot: 'Boltardy', 'Crimson Globe', 'Little Ball'; and long variety 'Cheltenham Greentop'.

Broccoli, sprouting: For early autumn picking (calabrese), 'Express Corona' and 'Mercedes'; for later, 'Green Duke', 'Green Comet' and 'Corvet'. For winter and spring: 'Early White', 'Early Purple', 'Late Purple' and 'Late White'; 'Nine Star Perennial' produces numerous small cauliflower-like heads.

Brussels sprouts: Early, 'Peer Gynt' and 'Lancelot'; maincrop (October–December) 'Cor (Valiant)' and 'Perfect Line'; late (January–March) 'Rampart' and 'Sigmund'.

Cabbages: Spring varieties, 'Durham Early', 'Offenham Compacta', 'Offenham – Flower of Spring' and 'Wheeler's Imperial'. Summer varieties: 'Hispi', 'Derby Day' and 'June Star'. Late summer and autumn varieties: 'Green Diadem', 'Hispi', 'Golden Acre' and 'Minicole'. Late winter varieties: 'Christmas Drumhead', 'January King'. Savoys: 'Ice Queen' and 'Celtic'.

Carrots: Early and for forcing under protection: 'Amsterdam Forcing' and 'Nantes'. Maincrop: 'Chantenay'. Late maturing: for winter storage – 'Autumn King' and 'Berlicum'.

Cauliflowers: Early summer varieties: 'All the year round' and 'Dominant'. Late summer: 'Dok' and 'Nevada'. Autumn: 'Barrier Reef'. Winter: 'Snow's Winter White' and 'Northern Star'. Spring (overwintered plants): 'St. George', 'Walcheren' and 'Winter Thanet'.

Celery: Trench varieties: 'Giant White' and 'Giant Red'. Self-blanching: 'American Green' and 'Golden self-blanching'.

Kales: 'Tall Green Curled' (Scotch), 'Cottagers', 'Fribor', 'Frosty' and 'Pentland Brig'.

Leeks: Early: 'Autumn Mammoth'. Mid-season: 'Argenta' and 'Lyon'. Late: 'Snowstar', 'Giant Winter Cataline', 'Musselburgh' and 'Yates Empire'.

Lettuce: Early sowings under glass: 'Unrivalled', 'Little Gem', 'Tom Thumb' and 'Winter Density'. Sowing in the open ground: 'Avondefiance', 'Great Lakes', 'Webb's Wonderful' and 'Windermere'. For growing to overwinter: 'Lobjoit's Green' and 'Winter Density'. For picking as 'leaf lettuce': 'Lobjoit's Green Cos', 'Paris White Cos' and 'Salad Bowl'.

Marrows and courgettes: Bush types: 'Early Gem', 'Emerald

Broad bean, 'The Sutton'.

Beetroot 'Boltardy'.

Sprouting broccoli 'Express Corona'.

Carrot 'Amstel Amsterdam Forcing'.

Leek 'Winter Crop'.

Cauliflower 'Barrier Reef'.

Celery 'Unrivalled Pink'.

Lettuce 'Unrivalled'.

Spinach 'Jovita.'

Kale 'Pentland Brig'.

Pea 'Little Marvel'.

Sweetcorn 'Kelvedon Sweetheart'.

31

Sowing and planting guide for vegetables

	Sow	Plant	Rows apart	Distance apart in rows	Harvest
Beans: Broad Open ground Under cloches	March-July Nov-Dec Feb-March		24-36 in (61-90 cm) or in double rows 6 in (15 cm) apart, 30 in (75 cm) between each pair of rows	6-9 in (15-23 cm)	June-Sept June-July
Beans: French dwarf	April-July	May	18 in (46 cm)	10-12 in (25-30 cm)	July-Sept
Beans: Runner and climbing French	May-June	May-June	Double rows 24 in (61 cm) apart 5 ft (1.5 m) between each pair of rows	9-12 in (23-30 cm)	July-Sept
Beetroot	March-July		12 in (30 cm)	4-6 in (10-15 cm)	July onwards
Broccoli (Calabrese)	April-May	May-June	12 in (30 cm)	6 in (15 cm)	Aug-Sept
Brussels Sprouts	March-April	May	24-36 in (61-90 cm)	24-36 in (61-90 cm)	March-April Oct-Feb
Cabbage: Under glass Open ground according to variety	Jan-Feb March-Aug	April-Sept	18-24 in (46-61 cm)	18 in (46 cm)	June Aug-Oct Dec-March
Carrots	March-July		12 in (30 cm)	4 in (10 cm)	July-Nov
Cauliflowers: In the open	March-May	May	24 in (61 cm)	24 in (61 cm)	Aug-May
Celery: Under heated glass Under cold glass	April April	May-June	In block 9-11 in (23-28 cm); in trench 18 in (45 cm)	In block 9-11 in (23-28 cm); in trench (9-11 cm)	Oct-Dec
Kale	April-May	July-August	24 in (61 cm)	24 in (61 cm)	Nov-March
Leeks: Under glass Open ground	Jan-Feb March-April		15 in (38 cm)	6-9 in (15-23 cm)	Sept-Nov
Lettuce: Under glass Open Ground For under glass	Jan-Feb March-Aug Sept	March-April	9-12 in (23-30 cm)	9-12 in (23-30 cm)	June June-Oct May
Marrows	April-May	Late May-June	24 in (61 cm)	24 in (61 cm)	July-Oct
Onions: Seed Sets	March-Sept	March-April Sept-Oct	12 in (30 cm) 10 in (25 cm)	3-4 in (8-10 cm)	Aug-Sept Aug-Sept June-July
Parsley	March-July				July-Dec
Parsnip	Feb-May				Oct-Dec
Peas: Under cloches Open ground	Oct, Nov, Feb or March March-July		18 in (46 cm)	2-3 in (5-8 cm)	June-July July-Sept
Potatoes: Early varieties Late varieties		March-April	18 in (46 cm) 30 in (76 cm)	15 in (38 cm) 15 in (38 cm)	Late June -October
Radish	March-Sept				May-Oct
Shallots		Jan-March	8 in (20 cm)	8 in (20 cm)	July-Aug
Spinach Perpetual or spinach beet	Feb-Aug March-July		12 in (30 cm)	9 in (23 cm)	May-Oct July-Aug
Swedes	May		15-18 in (38-46 cm)	9-12 in (23-30 cm)	Oct-Dec
Sweet Corn: Under glass Open ground	April April-May	Late May-June	24-36 in (61-90 cm)	15 in (38 cm)	July-Sept
Tomatoes: Sown under Glass	Jan-May	Late May-June	24 in (61 cm)	24 in (61 cm)	June-Oct
Turnips	April-July		12 in (30 cm)	4-6 in (10-15 cm)	Aug-Nov

Cross', 'Golden Zucchini' and 'Table Dainty'. Trailing varieties: 'Long Green' and 'Long White'.

Onions: For spring sowing and pulling as spring onions: 'White Lisbon'. For pickling: 'Barletta', 'Paris Silver-Skin' and 'Quicksilver'. For bulbs for storing: 'Ailsa Craig', 'Bedfordshire Champion', 'Hygro' and 'Rijnsburger Wibo'. For autumn sowing: 'Reliance' and 'Express Yellow'. Planted as sets in spring: 'Sturon', 'Coronado' and 'Stuttgarter Giant'. Planted as sets in the autumn: 'First Early'.

Parsley: 'Bravour', 'Moss Curled' and 'Spartacus'.

Parsnip: Short-rooted: 'Avonresister' and 'White Gem'. Long-rooted: 'Lisbonnais' and 'Tender and True'.

Peas: Early: 'Hurst Beagle' and 'Feltham First'. Second early: 'Early Onward' and 'Kelvedon Wonder'. Maincrop: 'Onward' and 'Hurst Greenshaft'.

Potatoes: Early varieties: 'Foremost', 'Maris Bard' and 'Pentland Javelin'. Maincrop varieties: 'Desirée', 'King Edward' and 'Maris Piper'.

Radish: 'Cherry Belle', 'French Breakfast', 'Red Prince', 'Saxa' and 'Sparkler'.

Spinach: Summer spinach: 'Long Standing', 'Sigmaleaf' and 'Symphony'. Perpetual spinach (Leaf beet): New Zealand spinach for sowing under glass in April and planting out in late May or June, or sowing in the open in May.

Swedes: 'Best of All', 'Mancunian' and 'Marian'.

Sweet corn: Early varieties, specially suitable for northern districts: 'Earliking', 'Sundance', 'North Star' and 'First of All'. Later varieties for milder districts: 'Aztec', 'Kelvedon Glory' and 'Northern Belle'.

Tomatoes: For growing outdoors, bush varieties: 'Sleaford Abundance', 'Sigmabush', 'Alfresco' and 'Arla'. Tall varieties for growing outdoors: 'Ailsa Craig', 'Alicante', 'Ronaclave', 'Marmande' and 'Golden Sunrise' (yellow fruits). For growing in a greenhouse: 'Ailsa Craig', 'Big Boy', 'Golden Sunrise' and 'Eurocross A'.

Turnips: For early sowing under protection: 'Snowball', 'Milan White' and 'Purple Top Milan'. For outdoor sowing: 'Golden Ball', 'Golden Perfection'; also 'Green Globe', specially for 'turnip top greens'.

Unusual Vegetables

Most seed catalogues include a number of exotic or unfamiliar vegetables. Many are well worth growing, partly for interest but also for the unusual flavours they provide. It is a good plan to grow one or two new ones each year alongside the plantings of runner beans, carrots and other universally grown crops.

Taking salads first, American cress is similar to watercress but much easier to grow. It does not need running water.

Among brassicas, Chinese cabbage has a delicate flavour and no unpleasant smell when cooked. And why not try calabrese, a delicious early-autumn sprouting broccoli.

As a substitute for spinach, Good King Henry (also called poor man's asparagus) is a native British plant. It will grow in quite poor soil.

Asparagus peas live up to their name, having a delicate asparagus flavour. As with sugar peas, or *mangetout,* the pods as well as their contents can be eaten.

Soya beans are another crop little-grown in this country. Both pods and beans can be eaten if picked young, otherwise the pods are discarded.

Tree onions save work, being a perennial plant that not only survives from year to year but is also easy to grow. Its bulbs are produced both under and above ground.

Finally, consider growing Chinese artichokes, which produce delicately-flavoured white tubers.

Herbs

Three favourite herbs. From the left, mint, rosemary and thyme.

The establishment here of many foreign restaurants and the vast increase in tourist travel abroad have led many British people to appreciate the value of herbs in cooking. Apart from their uses in the kitchen or for drinks, many herbs are attractive garden plants and a herb bed or border can be made into quite an ornamental feature.

Also a varied collection of herbs makes an interesting talking point to entertain visitors by inviting them to smell the crushed leaves of the various types. Some herbs, notably mint, tend to be rather encroaching and are best planted in a small bed of their own.

Alternatively, a part of a herb bed or border may be sectioned off by inserting some old tiles or even a piece of asbestos or corrugated iron vertically in the ground to confine the roots.

Here is a selection of the most popular herbs

Perennials: Mint, several varieties; apple mint is best for mint sauce, spearmint is strongly flavoured.

Sage; thyme, also available in several varieties, lemon scented, caraway and the ordinary type.

Balm, chives, fennel; these are available as young plants, or most may be raised from seed.

Other herbs normally raised from seed each year are parsley, borage and marjoram.

33

JANUARY

Fruit: Finish pruning; spray against pests.

Vegetables: Plan vegetable plot; order seeds. Finish digging and manuring; inspect stored crops. Sow peas and broad beans. Plant rhubarb and force established plants; plant shallots.

Flowers from seed: Order seeds.

Alpines: Take plants into greenhouse. Water plants in frames.

Cold greenhouse: Water and ventilate alpines. Order seeds and prepare for sowing. Bring in bulbs.

Cool greenhouse: Check and propagate late flowering chrysanthemums; prune climbers.

Dahlias: Check dahlia tubers in store.

Chrysanthemums: Check early flowering chrysanthemums. Watch for pests. Take cuttings of late flowering types.

Hardy border flowers: Take root cuttings.

Bulbs: Bring bowls from plunge beds indoors or into a greenhouse. Check bulb corms and tubers in store.

Trees and shrubs: Tidy shrubberies; prune greenhouse climbers.

Fruit

Complete top fruit pruning this month.

To rid apple and pear trees, particularly of aphids and scale insects overwintering in bark crevices as well as moss and lichens, spray top fruits with tar-oil wash.

Choose a still, frost-free, windless day and prepare the material according to the maker's instructions. It is a good idea to spray wooden fences and walls behind the trees as well – but not if they are carrying ornamental climbers.

Vegetables

If there is space and time available, growing some of your own vegetables makes a lot of sense. They are not cheap any more nor are they likely to become any cheaper; also they are so much nicer when gathered fresh from the garden and in prime condition.

Planning

A lot of thought must be given to the kinds of vegetables that are best to grow at home and January is a good time to plan ahead. As with most things, common sense should prevail. Obviously if space is limited there is no point in growing parsnips if the family do not like them.

Nor is it worth while growing, for example, main crop potatoes or carrots which the farmers and the market gardeners can grow quite cheaply. Early potatoes and carrots are a different proposition.

The crops to concentrate on are those which are the most expensive to buy – the early and the late crops and those like peas and beans, sweet corn and tomatoes which can be a bit of a gamble in the shops as far as quality is concerned.

Shop tomatoes are mostly picked half ripe and they never taste so good as those left to ripen fully on the plant; indeed millions of people have no idea what a really ripe tomato tastes like.

The pattern of planting may also be varied if you have a deep freeze. It may well be that it would pay you handsomely to grow a large quantity of runner beans which freeze well and give an excellent yield per foot run of row; instead of say, carrots or cabbages which are cheaper in the shops and normally come in excellent condition.

Rotation

Where space is limited there is the problem of proper crop rotation. Ideally one should not grow the same type of plants – such as the cabbage family which of course includes kales, cauliflowers and Brussels sprouts – on the same ground more than once in every three years. The same goes for onions, root crops like potatoes, carrots and beetroot; and also peas and beans.

But if you restrict the number of kinds of vegetables grown obviously it becomes more difficult to carry out a proper rotation – which is very important.

Plants grown on the same soil year after year take particular plant nutrients from the soil and they may suffer from pests or diseases which build up if a change of crop is not carried out.

Some people, however, who frequently grow very large onions (perhaps for showing) do grow them on the same well manured plot for many years. This is obviously fine unless, or until, some disease or pest appears and the onions must then be moved to another plot. (The rotation problem can be helped a little, if, for example, you grow some strawberries on the same plot.)

If a new row is planted every year, the oldest row that has carried its third crop may be discarded. Thus one small section of ground is available for a vegetable.

(You can use flowers in this way too if you wish to grow say a batch of chrysanthemums, dahlias, gladioli, sweet peas, or other flowers for cutting.)

Obviously the larger the plot or plots available the easier it is to plan a proper rotation. The main points to remember are:

1. Grow root crops on ground that has been manured for a previous crop; fresh manure may cause some root crops to produce mis-shapen roots.

2. If you cannot manure all the rest of the plot each year concentrate on the part reserved for peas, beans, onions, leeks, etc.

3. Do not grow related crops such as cauliflowers, kales, Brussels sprouts – indeed any of the brassicas (cabbage family) which includes turnips and swedes – on the same ground for at least two years.

4. Where space is limited it is important to try to keep the ground always occupied by a crop. This of course is not always possible because there are bound to be times when, for example, a plot has been cleared of root crops in the autumn and will remain empty until it is time to sow peas, or broad beans and to plant the successional crops in the spring.

With a little thought it is possible to keep much of the vegetable plot productive over a long period. One way is to sow short rows of such vegetables as lettuces, beetroot, carrots and radishes and pull these young when they are at their most succulent and, as many gardeners believe, most nutritious.

Another way of keeping up a succession is to sow packets of mixed lettuces or mixed radishes. They contain several varieties which take different times to mature. So if you sow a fairly long row and start cutting the lettuces and pulling the radishes while they are quite small, you can go on cutting lettuces for a month and pulling radishes for three weeks.

A simple three-year rotation of principal crops

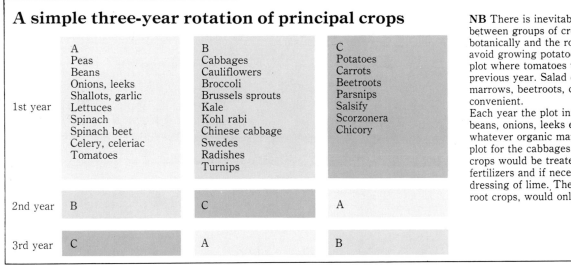

	A	B	C
1st year	Peas Beans Onions, leeks Shallots, garlic Lettuces Spinach Spinach beet Celery, celeriac Tomatoes	Cabbages Cauliflowers Broccoli Brussels sprouts Kale Kohl rabi Chinese cabbage Swedes Radishes Turnips	Potatoes Carrots Beetroots Parsnips Salsify Scorzonera Chicory
2nd year	B	C	A
3rd year	C	A	B

NB There is inevitably some overlap between groups of crops related botanically and the rotation groups. Try to avoid growing potatoes on the part of the plot where tomatoes were grown in the previous year. Salad crops, sweet corn, marrows, beetroots, can be fitted in where convenient.

Each year the plot intended for the peas, beans, onions, leeks etc is manured with whatever organic manure is available. The plot for the cabbages and other brassica crops would be treated with general fertilizers and if necessary given a dressing of lime. The third plot, for the root crops, would only receive fertilizers.

This helps to overcome the glut problem when the hot weather comes and lettuces tend to bolt to seed and radishes grow fast and become tough and hollow in the middle.

Separate, of course, from the rotational plots are the permanent crops such as asparagus and herbs. Asparagus beds may last and remain productive for 20 years.

Herbs are best grown in a plot as near as possible to the back door to be easily accessible for gathering a few sprigs of mint, parsley, thyme, chives, tarragon, rosemary or any of the many other herbs when needed for cooking.

Vegetable seeds can obviously be bought in garden shops or garden centres or ordered from a mail order seed catalogue. A wider choice is available in the catalogues and much guidance is given regarding times of maturing, resistance to disease and other points of interest.

Once the vegetable plots have been planned continue to dig over any vacant ground in January and work in manure or compost. If the ground was dug over in the autumn, manure worked in, and the surface left rough, the action of winter frosts should have made it easily workable. Clods break up easily with a rake and the surface may be raked down to create a layer of fine soil suitable for sowing or planting.

It is most important for seed sowing that this fine tilth is obtained and you have to wait until the soil is fit to work – if it does not stick to your boots it is probably in a state where it can be raked down for sowing or planting.

If digging has been left until the New Year the sooner it is done the better.

Seed sowing

To give seeds a fair chance to germinate and produce strong seedlings it is important that the soil is broken up really fine. The seeds (especially small seeds) must be in actual contact with the soil so that their roots can go down in search of water and food and are not perched above little air pockets where they will shrivel up. After raking the surface it is wise to tread the surface down and then to give it the final raking.

When sowing rows of vegetables in drills always use a garden line to keep the drill straight. Keep one foot on the line as you move backwards to keep it from moving as you draw the drill with the corner of a 'swan neck' or draw hoe.

Most seeds are sown in shallow 'V'-shaped drills but peas are usually sown in flat drills about 1½ in (3.8 cm) deep and 2 in (5 cm) apart. The drill may accommodate a single row or if it is made about 9 in (23 cm) wide, the seeds may be scattered thinly or placed 2-3 in (5-8 cm) apart in three rows with 4½ in (16 cm) between the rows and 18 in (45 cm) between the drills.

Broad beans are usually sown in a double row, staggered, leaving about 30 in (75 cm) between each pair of rows.

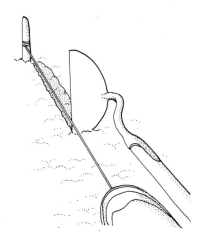

Making a 'V' trench. With one foot on the line take out a shallow drill with a draw hoe.

General tasks

Inspect crops in store and remove any that are showing signs of rotting.

In the milder parts of the

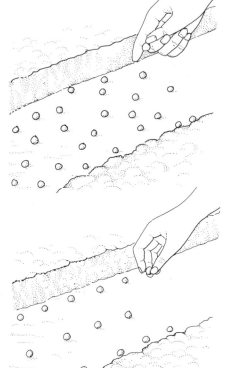

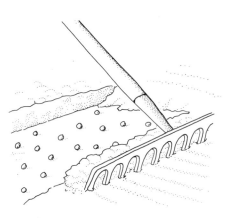

Sowing peas. This may be done by scattering them in a wide flat drill taken out with a hoe (top), or placing them in three rows. Draw soil over with a rake.

country – broadly in the south and west – if the ground is in a fit state sow an early variety of pea and broad bean.

In less mild districts broad beans may be sown under cloches, provided the soil is workable, but in the north delay sowings until February or March.

Seeds of various vegetables – radishes, spring onions and carrots – may be sown direct in a cold frame. Cover with a sifting of fine soil.

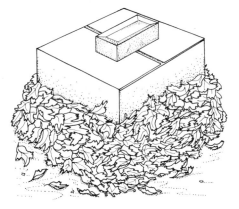

Rhubarb must be well protected when first planted and this can be done by covering it with an old box and packing it round with leaves.

To help the soil dry out a little and be in a fit condition for seed sowing, place cloches in position over the rows now. You may then be able to sow the seeds next month.

Rhubarb may be planted now – about 3 ft (91 cm) apart. Do dig in plenty of manure or compost as

it is important to give rhubarb a good start and it is going to remain in one place for many years.

Cover some rhubarb plants with a foot thick layer of straw or leaves. Or put an old pail, a large drain pipe or an old box over the crowns and pack leaves or straw around it to encourage the growth of early young succulent sticks.

Plant shallots in the mild districts if the soil is workable. Cover them with soil so that only the tip is showing above ground. In the north and in cold districts elsewhere do not plant shallots until late February or March.

Flowers from seed

Many flowers are easily raised from seed and January is the time to order seeds to start sowing next month. Some, hardy annuals, biennials or perennials may be sown in the open ground. Others (half hardy flowers) may be sown in a cold greenhouse; in a frame or under cloches; or outdoors later but of course they will flower later and their flowering period will be that much shorter.

Others such as begonias and annual rudbeckias need a long growing period and they need a greenhouse temperature of 55-60°F (13-15°C). It may be possible to maintain these temperatures in a greenhouse, or perhaps in a part of a greenhouse sectioned off with a wall of plastic sheeting.

Again an electric propagator may be used to provide the required amount of heat to germinate the seeds but there must be somewhere where the seedlings – after they have been pricked off – can be accommodated at temperatures around 45-55°F (7-13°C) until they can be moved into a cold frame or placed under cloches.

Broadly speaking, seedlings of half hardy and tender annual flowers must be kept free from frost until they may be safely planted out at the end of May in the south of England or early in June in the north and in Scotland.

It is usually possible to keep these plants free from frost in a cold frame in April or May if it is covered with some kind of matting – old carpet, hessian or even one or two layers of plastic fertilizer bags to conserve the heat.

You may have an electric propagator in the greenhouse or in a room in the home in which to germinate seeds. Sow in the early months of the year as mentioned above but remember it is no use sowing seeds in a propagator unless there are facilities for accommodating the seedlings once they have been pricked off.

Lewisia 'Comet'.

Rhodohypoxis baurii.

Alpines

Take plants grown in pots in frames or under cloches into the cold greenhouse if you have one.

Water plants in frames sparingly – do not let them dry out but do not over water them.

Cold greenhouse

Even in the depths of winter a cold greenhouse need not be dull or empty. Given a solid bench of handy height with a layer of pea-sized shingle all over its base (prevented from falling off by a narrow board around the edges) various plants can be induced to flower better and earlier than in the open.

Naturally these will have been planted in pots or pans beforehand and either grown along in a cold frame or under cloches in the case of alpines or kept in a plunge bed outdoors if they are bulbs.

Some alpines, notably those with downy or woolly foliage like species of androsace, ramonda and the cushion saxifrages, dislike water on their leaves and crowns. If they have to be watered from the top use a small can with a curved spout and a small aperture.

As another precaution against

Iris histrioides 'Major'.

the stems rotting at their base top-dress the pots or pans with washed granite chippings or gravel. This prevents water lying on or near the crowns of plants, yet conserves moisture, deters slugs, prevents mosses and liverworts from growing and also gives a finished appearance to the containers.

Plenty of ventilation is essential if alpines are grown, so open the top lights whenever the weather permits, but close them if frost is forecast. Laying white tissue paper gently and in successive layers over very special plants does much to safeguard them in severe frosts. Polythene house linings also help.

However should unseasonal warmth be experienced, as sometimes happens in winter, open both top and side ventilators. In foggy weather all apertures should be closed.

Plant types

Plants suitable for cold greenhouse (alpine house) treatment include the following:

Anacyclus depressus, purple-backed, white daisies.
Androsace – most kinds.
Aquilegia discolor, blue and cream.
Asperula suberosa, pink.
Asarum europaeum, red.
Calceolaria darwinii, yellow and chocolate.
Campanula – most small rock garden sorts.
Cassiope lycopodioides, white.
Codonopsis clematidea, blue.
Cyananthus lobatus, rich blue.
Cyclamen coum, crimson, *C. libanoticum,* rose-pink.
Dianthus – small kinds.
Erica carnea, winter forms, red or white.
Gentiana saxosa, white, *G. verna,* blue.
Gypsophila aretioides, white.
Helichrysum frigidum, white, *H. coralloides,* yellow.
Hypericum aegypticum, yellow, *H. cuneatum,* yellow, *H. empetrifolium,* deep yellow.
Lewisias – all.

Sempervivum marmoreum rubrifolia.

Sedum spathulifolium. 'Cappa Blanca'.

Lithospermum diffusum 'Grace Ward', rich blue.
Omphalodes luciliae, blue.
Oxalis – several.
Pernettya pumila, white, pink or white fruits.
Pleione – all.
Primula – many.
Ramonda myconi, deep blue.
Ranunculus calandrinioides, white.
Raoulia australis, silver foliaged.
Rhodohypoxis rose and white – all.
Saxifraga – many.
Sedums – many.
Sempervivums – many.
Valeriana supina, white or pinkish.
Viola cornuta, purple.

Small bulbs suitable for mixing with alpines include the following:
Winter aconites (eranthis) yellow.
Anemone blanda, blue, pink or white.
Chionodoxas, blue.
Crocuses, yellow, white, purple or mixtures.
Erythroniums, pink, yellow.
Galanthus (snowdrops) white.
Ipheion, light blue.
Iris danfordiae, yellow, *I. histrioides,* blue, *I. reticulata,* various shades of blue and purple.
Muscari (grape hyacinth) blue or white.
Narcissi (dwarf forms) yellow.
Scillas, blue or white.

Order seeds and prepare pans or pots and compost for sowing.

Bring in bulbs from the plunge bed, particularly hyacinths and narcissi grown from prepared bulbs.

Cool greenhouse

Chrysanthemum cuttings of late flowering kinds can be taken as soon as the young shoots are a few cm high (see p 41). Root in light soil.

Bring in early bulbs.

Watch the weather and cover tender plants such as calceolarias, cinerarias and schizanthus with newspaper when the weather is very cold.

Do not allow water to fall on primulas and plants in bloom.

Ventilate whenever possible.

Dahlias

Check dahlia tubers in store to see that there is no rotting. If there is cut away the affected parts and dust the wounds with flowers of sulphur. If the tubers have begun to shrivel place the whole root in a bucket of tepid water in a warm place for 24 hours for the tubers to plump up again. Dry them off thoroughly before placing them back in their tray or box. Cover the tubers with soil or peat again but of course do not cover the crown of the plant.

Chrysanthemums

There are hundreds of varieties of chrysanthemums and these fall into two main groups: first, those grown in the open ground and which flower outdoors without protection before the end of September; these are called early flowering chrysanthemums.

Second, the varieties which are grown in pots outdoors or even in the ground during the summer to be brought into a greenhouse in September or October to bloom with a little heat if available when the flowers are just approaching their best. These are called intermediate or late flowering chrysanthemums.

They will flower in a cold greenhouse but if a little heat can be provided to keep the temperatures around 50°F (10°C) so much the better as it will maintain air circulation and avoid spotting of the flowers.

In January look at plants of outdoor or early chrysanthemums that were lifted and stood in a cold frame. Keep them moist but not too wet. Cover the frame with sacks or hessian in bitter weather. Watch for pests in a frame or a greenhouse and spray if necessary.

Take cuttings of late flowering chrysanthemums. Those that grow from the base are the best, although if there are not many of these you can use the young shoots that appear on the old stem.

There are also hardy chrysanthemums, varieties of *Chrysanthemum rubellum* and Korean varieties. These make excellent border flowers, grown naturally as sprays.

The following is a recommended selection of varieties:

Early flowering garden varieties:

'Apricot Kingston Improved'. Light bronze; reflexed; 4 ft (1.2 m) tall.
'Ann Dixon'. Light bronze; incurving; 4 ft (1.2 m) tall.
'Bronze Eve Gray'. 3 ft 6 in (1 m) tall.
'Cornish'. Cream; medium-sized incurving; 3 ft (0.9 m) tall.
'Gambit'. Purple; reflexed; 4 ft 6 in (1.4 m) tall.
'Ginger Nut'. Light bronze; incurving; 4 ft (1.22 m) tall.
'Mac's Delight'. Waxy golden florets; incurving; 4 ft (1.22 m) tall.
'New Stylist'. Lemon yellow; reflexed; 4 ft (1.22 m) tall.
'Oyster'. Peachy cream; incurving; 4 ft 6 in (1.4 m) tall.
'Peter Rowe'. Yellow; incurved; 5 ft (1.5 m) tall.
'Rosedew'. Pink; intermediate; 3 ft (0.9 m) tall.
'Timmy Gray'. Purple; medium reflexed; 3 ft (0.9 m) tall.
'Venice'. Vivid clear pink; 3 ft 6 in (1 m) tall.
'Yellow Cornish'. Clear yellow; incurving; 4 ft (1.22 m) tall.
'Yellow Ginger Nut'. Yellow; incurving; 3 ft 6 in (1 m) tall.

Late varieties for the greenhouse:

'Beechwood Flame'. Bright red; reflexed; 4 ft (1.2 m) tall.
'Corngold'. Golden amber; incurving; 4 ft (1.2 m) tall.
'Enid Whiston'. Purple; reflexed; 4 ft 6 in (1.4 m) tall.
'Fairweather'. Light purple; incurved; 3 ft (0.9 m) tall.
'White Fairweather'. White sport of above.
'James Hall'. White intermediate; 4 ft (1.2 m) tall.
'John Hughes'. White; incurved; 4 ft (1.2 m) tall.
'Yellow John Hughes'. Sport of the above.
'Regency'. Purple; medium-sized reflexed; 4 ft 6 in (1.4 m) tall.
'West Bromwich'. White; reflexed; 4 ft (1.22 m) tall.
'Xenia Noelle'. Red; reflexed; 5 ft (1.5 m) tall.

Hardy border flowers

Take root cuttings of oriental poppies *(Papaver orientale)*, anchusas, *Phlox decussata* varieties, perennial verbascums, gaillardias and perennial statice *(Limonium latifolium)*. For method see p 24.

Bulbs

Bring bulbs from outdoor plunge beds into the house at intervals in order to obtain a succession of flowers.

Examine bulbs already inside for signs of aphids (greenfly). These often appear on crocuses and tulips, having survived the winter underground or on the stored bulbs.

Check gladioli in store, removing any with evident signs of rotting.

Lily seeds can be sown in pots of seed compost, barely covering the seeds. Keep them cool in an unheated greenhouse or frame to germinate.

Protect early flowering dwarf irises like *I. danfordiae* and *I. histrioides* against snow and icy rains by propping a sheet of glass on bricks over the blooms.

Trees and shrubs

Tidy up shrubberies, remove fallen branches and check recently planted specimens. Tread the latter back firmly after frosts to prevent subsequent frosts damaging the roots. Shake snow from evergreens and conifers .

Greenhouse climbers such as plumbago, bougainvillea, passion flowers and roses can be pruned. Remove weak shoots and in the case of plumbago and passion flowers reduce last season's growths to within a few inches of the old wood.

FEBRUARY

Fruit: Protect trees and bushes against birds; cover strawberries; prune raspberries; spray peaches outdoors.

Vegetables: Finish digging; set seed potatoes to sprout. Set out cloches for early sowings; make early sowings in cool greenhouse.

Flowers from seed: Make first sowings of annuals in cool greenhouse.

Alpines: Transfer pots or pans from frames to cold greenhouse. Watch for pests particularly slugs in and under cover or in the open.

Cold greenhouse: Water sparingly. Ventilate when possible.

Cool greenhouse: Sow tomatoes and onion seed; start fuchsias into growth and prune; set potatoes to sprout; check dahlias; start begonias and gloxinias into growth. Force sprays of forsythia, flowering currants and other shrubs in water to flower early. take and root carnation cuttings. Water sparingly, ventilate on mild days. Check roots in store.

Dahlias: Check old roots in store.

Chrysanthemums: Watch for pests; continue taking cuttings of late varieties.

Hardy border flowers: Lightly prick over soil among plants.

Bulbs: Pot lily bulbs; check gladioli in store; bring in bulbs for forcing.

Trees and shrubs: Prune various shrubs. Cut back clematis.

Fruit

In areas where bullfinches and other birds damage fruit trees by picking out the buds, spray the trees with a deterrent, or cover branches within reach with a teased out nylon 'spiders web'. Scaraweb is one such material, available in black or white; it rots away in a few months and cannot trap birds.

Plums, cherries, red currants and gooseberries are also vulnerable.

Spray outdoor peaches with a copper spray of mancozeb to check leaf curl and with a suitable spray for red spider mites (see p 184).

Tip the summer fruiting raspberry canes this month. Cut back the autumn fruiting canes like 'Zeva' and 'September' to ground level.

Cover strawberry plants with a polythene tunnel (see p 24) or cloches in order to produce an early crop. Pot grown strawberries in a cold greenhouse will also fruit earlier than outside.

Stages in the growth of fruit trees when the application of sprays is most effective. Top: bud burst, green cluster and pink bud. Bottom: petal fall and fruitlet stage.

Vegetables

If the ground is workable press on with any digging that remains to be done.

If cloches are available set them out to warm the soil a little ready for sowing broad beans, beetroot, Brussels sprouts, carrots, cauliflowers, lettuces, onions, radishes, spinach and turnips for early crops. In the south an early variety of pea may be sown.

If a heated greenhouse – or a part of it which can be heated – is available sow summer cabbages and cauliflowers, onions and leeks.

Set seed potatoes up in trays to sprout with the 'rose' or 'eye' end uppermost. The rose end shows the tiny embryo shoots. Set the trays in a light airy frost-free place – on a shelf in a heated greenhouse, on a window sill in a kitchen or spare room, in a heated sun lounge – anywhere that can be guaranteed to be frost-proof and in full light.

Set seed potatoes to sprout with the 'eye' uppermost.

Flowers from seed

Some annual flowers need a long growing period and should be sown in a heated greenhouse this month. Lobelias, antirrhinums and begonias should be sown this month provided they may be kept in a temperature of around 64°F (18°C).

If it is not possible to maintain such high temperatures in a greenhouse, an electrically heated propagating case may be the answer (see p 26).

The seeds may be germinated in such a case and the seedlings pricked out into boxes, but they must then be grown on in a greenhouse or sun lounge where the temperature does not fall below around 50°F (10°C) at night.

Handy Hint: Millions of paper cups or beakers are poured out every day from drink vending machines, used once and thrown away. If you can get hold of a supply of these used cups they are extremely useful for sowing seeds such as beans, marrows, lettuces, all the cabbage family and sweet corn and for pricking off seedlings or rooting cuttings.

All you have to do is drill a ½ in (12 mm) hole in the bottom – which is easily done by packing say a dozen together upturning them over a block of wood and drilling from the bottom.

As the plastic cups are rather deeper than is necessary for seeds, seedlings or cuttings, you can economize on the seed or potting compost by filling the bottom third of the cup with sand, vermiculite, perlite, or even peat.

Alpines

Continue to transfer alpine plants in pots or pans from the frame to the cold greenhouse.

Watch for signs of slugs or snails in frames, under cloches or

Raised beds are excellent for growing alpines.

shingle or sharp sand (parts by bulk).

A double handful of bonemeal worked in to each square yard/metre will be all the food alpine plants will require. After the rock garden, raised bed or stone sinks have been planted cover the surface with stone chippings, or pea gravel of a colour that will as nearly as possible match the rocks.

Put on a generous layer 1 in (2.5 cm) thick tucked well round the plants. This is important as many rock plants are killed not by the cold but by excessively wet conditions at the base of the plants.

Most true alpine plants pass the winter under a cosy cover of snow and dislike the wet conditions they have to endure in Britain. So for many of them a sheet of glass propped up over them, or a small cloche to keep off excessive water is essential. For such plants, of course, a cold greenhouse (if you have one) provides the ideal conditions.

Handy Hint: For handicapped people who have to do their gardening from a wheel chair, and those who cannot stoop or bend very much, raised beds are a necessity. These may of course be of stone, encased by concrete slabs or old railway sleepers cut to length or cheapest of all, old car or lorry tyres.

Old tyres can be laid one on top of the other; for a child that cannot stand, one or maybe two tyres will make a bed they can manage. For a person in a wheelchair, four tyres would be about right.

As the tyres are filled with soil one can push some plants like aubrieta, *Campanula portenschlagiana*, arabis and *Alyssum saxatile* or thyme between each tyre and these will help to camouflage them. If the tyres are painted white they will look much smarter.

Alpine varieties
There are so many plants from high alpine regions which can be

indeed on the rock garden. If there are signs of damage, or their slimy trails, put down slug bait, slug powder or water on a liquid slug killer. Look out for slugs in the cold greenhouse also.

A raised bed
If the soil is heavy, liable to be waterlogged in winter, too acid, or too alkaline, alpines may be grown very successfully in a raised bed. Dig out the topsoil to a depth of 12 in (30 cm) and stack it to one side. Fill in with broken brick or concrete – anything that will ensure quick drainage.

Build a low wall about 6 in (15 cm) of bricks or flat stones around the area – no need to set them in concrete. Alternatively, you can encase the area with old railway sleepers or tree trunks. Fill the bed with 2 parts good garden soil mixed with one part of leaf mould or fine moss-peat and one part grit, grown under the artificial conditions and lower altitudes of gardens, that to make a selection can often be perplexing.

The golden rule, as always, is to start with easy kinds and progress with experience to some of the rarer or more difficult kinds. If cost is a factor remember many species can be raised from seed.

Some attractive yet reliable plants suitable for rock gardens, and in some cases for planting between crazy paving stones or in sink gardens or dry walls (as well as growing in pans in unheated greenhouses) are included in the following list. Unless otherwise stated, all are spring flowering.

Adonis vernalis. Gleaming gold, many-petalled flowers; ferny foliage; 9 in (23 cm) tall.

Aethionema armenum 'Warley Rose'. Clear pink; 8 in (20 cm) tall.

Alliums (ornamental onions). Many, including the 9 in (23 cm) golden *A. moly* and bright blue, grassy leaved 6 in (15 cm) *A. cyaneum.*

Alyssum saxatile (gold dust) and forms. Various shades of yellow; silvery leaves; 9 in (23 cm) tall.

Anemones (wind flowers). Low growing kinds like *A. blanda;* blue, white or pink; 4 in (10 cm) tall; also *A. coronaria;* red, blue, violet or yellow; 3-9 in (8-23 cm) tall.

Arabis alpina (snow in summer). White, single and double also one with variegated leaves; 9 in (23 cm) tall.

Armeria maritima (thrift). Pink; 8 in (20 cm).

Aubrieta deltoidea. Mat forming, mauve, blue and red; 6 in (15 cm) tall.

Bellis perennis cultivars (daisy). 'Dresden China'; pink; 4 in (10 cm) tall.

Campanulas, many. Mostly blue and summer flowering; 4-9 in (10-23 cm) tall.

Cyclamen coum crocuses all spring flowering and *C. neapolitanum,* autumn. Both in pink and white; 3-4 in (8-10 cm) tall.

Dianthus (pinks). Many species and varieties; summer flowering often fragrant; 3-4 in (8-10 cm) tall.

Eranthis (winter aconite). Large, gold, buttercup flowers on 3 in (8 cm) stems.

Galanthus (snowdrop). White; 4-12 in (10-30 cm) tall.

Gentiana (gentian). Many, some difficult, mostly blue, trumpet-shaped flowers, spring and summer flowering; 3-6 in (8-15 cm) tall or higher.

Gypsophila repens (chalk plant). Showers of white or pink starry flowers; summer flowering; 6 in (15 cm) tall.

Helianthemum nummularium (rock rose). Varieties, yellow, orange, pink, red, white, singles and doubles; June flowering; 9 in (23 cm) tall.

Helichrysum bellidioides. Mat-like, white everlasting flowers; summer flowering; 6 in (15 cm) tall.

Iberis semperflorens (candytuft). White; evergreen; 4-9 in (10-23 cm) tall.

Iris. Any small kinds especially *I. danfordiae,* yellow; 3 in (8 cm) tall and *I. histrioides,* blue; 6 in (15 cm) tall.

Lewisia species and cultivars. Showy white, pink, apricot or striped flowers; sun loving, succulent leaves; summer flowering; 3-6 in (8-15 cm) tall.

Lithospermum diffusum. Deep blue; dislikes lime; summer or autumn flowering; 6 in (15 cm) tall.

Mimulus (monkey flower). *M. cupreus* varieties, copper, yellow and scarlet; summer flowering; 6-9 in (15-23 cm) tall.

Muscari (grape hyacinth). Blue or white; 6-8 in (15-20 cm) tall.

Narcissus, dwarf species.

Onosma taurica (golden drop). Yellow, tubular, scented flowers; grey hairy foliage; 8 in (20 cm) tall.

Oxalis. Various colours; usually bulbous; all summer flowering; 3-9 in (8-23 cm) tall.

Penstemon. Any small shrubby kinds like *P. menziesii;* violet blue; 6 in (15 cm) tall and *P. rupicola;* crimson; 4 in (10 cm) tall.

Phlox subulata varieties (moss

Adonis vernalis.

Anemone coronaria.

Aubrieta deltoidea.

Saxifraga burserana.

Dianthus 'Sprite'.

Phlox subulata 'Temiscaming'.

Sedum acre.

Lewisia 'Weald Strain'.

Tulipa tarda.

47

phlox). White, pink, red, mauve; 6
in (15 cm) tall.
Polygala chamaebuxus (dwarf box).
Cream and yellow flowers; evergreen, pea-shaped; 6 in (15 cm) tall.
Primula (primrose). Many
including *P. auricula* (auriculas); 9
in (23 cm) tall, *P. denticulata* (drum-
stick primrose); round mauve to
purple flower heads on 9 in (23 cm)
stems, *P. sieboldii*; white, rose or
purple; 6-8 in (15-20 cm) tall.
Pulsatilla vulgaris (pasque flower).
Purple; 10-12 in (25-30 cm) tall.
Ramonda myconi. Mauve, also
white and pink; for north facing,
rock crevices; early summer
flowering; 4 in (10 cm) tall.
Saxifraga. Many kinds; mat-
forming or rosettes; 2-5 in (5-13
cm) tall.
Scilla tubergeniana. Pale blue with
deeper streak; 6 in (15 cm) tall.
Sedum acre (stonecrop). Bright
yellow; summer flowering; 1-2 in
(2.5-5 cm) tall. Many other species
and varieties.
Sempervivum (houseleek). Flowers
variously coloured; good plants for
pan culture in the alpine house
forming flat rosettes of fleshy
leaves; 3-8 in (8-20 cm) tall.
Thymus serpyllum. Flowers white,
pink or red; carpeting evergreen;
summer flowering; 1 in (2.5 cm)
tall.
Tulipa (tulip). Any of the small
species like *T. tarda*; yellow with
white petal edges; 4 in (10 cm) tall,
T. kaufmanniana; cream, red and
pink; 8 in (20 cm) tall and *T.
eichleri*; scarlet; 10 in (25 cm) tall.

Cold greenhouse

As in January interest and colour
will mainly be provided by small
pans of bulbs and alpines. Early
flowering hyacinths should also be
in bloom, especially the Roman and
'prepared' sorts from plunge beds.

As February wears on, early
tulips should be in bud and flower
before the end of the month; also
the first daffodils especially Paper
Whites, 'Soleil d'Or' and following

Crocuses, 'Paperwhite', narcissi and hyacinths ('Pink Pearl').

these 'Carlton', 'Cragford',
'February Gold' and many miniature narcissi.

Cool greenhouse

Check dahlia tubers stored from
the autumn, removing damaged or
rotted pieces before boxing up
sound plants in potting soil. These
will provide cuttings next month.
Keep them in the light to sprout
and on fine days lightly spray over
the tops with tepid water to
encourage the shoots to emerge.

Polyanthus in pots will now be
making a bright show but keep a
sharp lookout for greenfly and
spray as soon as these appear.

Start tuberous begonias and
gloxinias in boxes of moist peat at
the end of the month. Lightly
dampen them daily to encourage
sprouting and give them as warm a
place as possible. They can even be
sprouted on a radiator indoors but

will need potting singly next month
when top growth and roots are
active.

A small forsythia plant potted
in autumn and now brought into
the greenhouse can be forced for
early bloom. Similarly sprays cut
from outdoor flowering currants,
forsythia, lilac or horse chestnut
and stood in water on the greenhouse bench will flower much
earlier than usual. Camellias
growing in large pots under cover
should flower this month.

Fuchsias rested during the
winter may be given a good
soaking towards the end of the
month and started into growth
prior to repotting.

Prune back the side shoots to
about 1 in (2.5 cm) to encourage
new shoots. Lily bulbs arriving
from bulb merchants may be
potted if space is limited and kept
on the floor of the house until
growth appears.

Early potatoes can be laid out

in boxes, rose side uppermost and kept in a light place to sprout.

Take carnation cuttings and root them in pure sand; pot them in light soil as soon as rooted.

Root early flowering chrysanthemum cuttings towards the end of the month individually in peat pots and keep these in a box with a glass lid if you do not have a propagator.

Start sowing a few annuals for early blooms in the greenhouse, including calendulas, clarkias, nemesias and *Mentzelia lindleyi (Bartonia aurea)*.

Primula malacoides from June sowings will also start to flower this month.

Sow cauliflowers for planting out in April.

Sow sweet peas in Jiffy pots.

Sow onions in boxes if required for an early crop.

Sow tomato seed in clean pots of John Innes seed compost just covering them with sifted soil or sand. Keep in a temperature of 55°F (13°C) in a propagator, or on a window sill indoors. Water by the immersion method until the seedlings come through, using lukewarm water in very cold weather. Pot the seedlings singly when they are large enough to handle.

Keep watering to a minimum but give air on mild days.

Dahlias

Check old roots in store.

Chrysanthemums

Keep watching for pests and deal with them as necessary; slugs can be a nuisance in frames or in a greenhouse so put down slug pellets or water on a liquid slug killer if the slimy slug trails are seen or if the young shoots show signs of damage.

Continue taking cuttings of late chrysanthemums. These will not usually produce blooms before frosts.

Hardy border flowers

On fine dry days at the end of the month prick over the soil between plants, particularly in mixed borders where early doronicums and bulbs will soon be showing.

Bulbs

If imported lilies arrive from the bulb merchant pot these and keep them cool, either for planting outside next month or flowering them in containers. Keep stem-rooters low in the pots so that more soil can be added as they start to grow.

Check gladioli in store for signs of aphids and if necessary spray the corms with an insecticide.

Bring in the last of the forcing bulbs for indoor flowering.

Trees and shrubs

Provided the weather is suitable, various shrubs which normally carry their flowers on the young wood can now be pruned.

1. *Jasminum nudiflorum*. When the blooms are finished cut back the flowering stems almost to the old wood and occasionally remove a few of the older stems at the base.

Hardy jasmines are normally pruned after flowering.

2. *Buddleia davidii* and varieties. In the case of young bushes allow sufficient branches to develop to build up a sizeable foundation; on established shrubs take back the old flowering stems practically to the older wood.

3. *Hydrangea paniculata; Spiraea japonica* and hybrids, *S. douglasii, S. menziesii, S. salicifolia* and varieties; *Sorbaria arborea; Holodiscus discolor ariifolius; Tamarix pentandra, Hypericum moserianum* as well as varieties of *Cornus alba* like 'Elegantissima' and 'Sibirica' which are grown for their brightly coloured bark in winter should all be pruned hard back to within an inch or two of the old wood.

At the end of February (mid-March in the north) cut back all last year's stems of *Clematis jackmanii* and hybrids to 9-12 in (23-30 cm) of the ground. This will encourage strong new growths which will support the flowers in late summer.

Soil testing

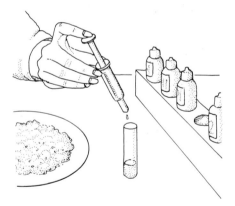

Checking the acid/alkaline balance.

Many shrubs, such as rhododendrons, will not grow in alkaline soil. Others will grow in most fertile soils, including those with a high chalk content. If you are uncertain of the conditions in your garden buy a simple soil-testing kit before deciding which shrubs and trees to plant. No skill is needed and instructions for the simple test are provided with the chemicals.

49

Flowers from seed

Name	Type	Height and spread	In heat 50-55°F (10-13°C)	Sow: Under cold glass	In the open	In flower	Comments
Acanthus	HP	24-36 in (61-91 cm); 24-36 in (61-91 cm)		March		June-Aug	Lilac white or purple flower. Sun or partial shade
Achillea	HP	3-4 ft (0.9-1.2 m); 15 in (38 cm)		March		June-Sept	White, yellow or pink flowers. Sun
Aconitum	HP	3-5 ft (0.9-1.5 m); 18 in (46 cm)		Mar-April		July-Sept	Blue. Sun
Ageratum	HHA	6-9 in (15-23 cm); 6-12 in (15-30 cm)	Mar-April			July-Oct	Blue, pink or white. Sun. Tubs, window boxes
Althea (Hollyhock)	HA HP HP	4-5 ft (1.2-1.5 m); 24 in (61 cm) 8-9 ft (2.4-2.7 m); 24 in (61 cm)	Feb-Mar		June-July	July-Aug	Single and double flowers; pink, red, yellow, white. Full sun
Alyssum	HHA HP	4-6 in (10-15 cm); 8-10 in (20-25 cm) 9-12 in (23-30 cm); 12-18 in (30-46 cm)	March	March	April-May	July-Oct April-June	White, pink, lavender, purple, sweet scented. Sun Golden or pale yellow. Sun
Amaranthus (Love lies bleeding)	HHA	3-4 ft (0.9-1.2 m); 18 in (46 cm)	Mar-April	April	April-May	July-Oct	Flowers red or green. Full sun
Anchusa (Annual)	HA	18 in (46 cm); 12 in (30 cm)		April	April	July-Aug	Blue. Full sun
(Perennial)	HP	4-5 ft (1.2-1.5 m); 24-36 in (61-91 cm)			April-May	June-July	Blue. Full sun
Antirrhinum	HHA	9 in (23 cm); 42 in (107 cm)	Feb-Mar			July-Oct	White, pink, red, yellow. Full sun. Good for cutting
Aquilegia	HP	18-24 in (46-61 cm); 12 in (30 cm)		March	May	May-June	Blue, red, cream, yellow flowers. Sun
Aster (Callistephus)	HHA	18 in (46 cm); 12 in (30 cm)	March	April	May	July-Oct	White, pink, red, yellow. Sun. Good for cutting.
Bellis perennis (Daisies)	HB	4 in (10 cm); 6 in (15 cm)		April	May-June	May-June	Red, pink, white. Sun
Candytuft (see Iberis)							
Calendula (Pot marigold)	HA	24 in (61 cm); 12 in (30 in)			Mar-May	June-Sept	Orange, apricot, yellow, cream; good for cutting. Sun, partial shade
Carnations (Annual)	HHA	18 in (46 cm); 12 in (30 cm)	Jan-Mar		Sept	July-Sept	Crimson, scarlet, pink, salmon, yellow, white. Good for cutting. Sun
Centaurea (Cornflower)	HA	18-36 in (46-91 cm); 12 in (30 cm)			Mar-May; Sept	June-Sept	Blue, white, pink, red. Good for cutting. Sun
Cheiranthus (Wallflower)	HP	18-24 in (46-61 cm); 12 in (30 cm)			May-June	April-May	Normally grown as a biennial. Yellow, orange, scarlet, ruby red, crimson. Sweetly scented. Good for cutting. Sun

HA = hardy annual; HHA = half hardy annual; HB = hardy border; HP = hardy perennial

Name	Type	Height and spread	In heat 50-55°F (10-13°C)	Sow: Under cold glass	In the open	In flower	Comments
Chrysanthemum (Annual)	HA	18-24 in (46-61 cm); 12 in (30 cm)			Mar-May	June-Sept	Single or double flowers. White, yellow, red, some with contrasting zones. Good for cutting. Sun, partial shade
Clarkia	HA	18-24 in (46-61 cm); 9 in (23 cm)			Mar-May	July-Sept	Salmon, scarlet, white, purple, pink. Sun. Good for cutting
Convolvulus	HA	6-12 in (15-30 cm); 15 in (38 cm)			Mar-May	June-Sept	Blue, pink, white, contrasting white or yellow centres. Sun or partial shade
Coreopsis (Calliopsis) (Annual)	HA	9-24 in (23-61 cm); 9 in (23 cm)			Mar-May	July-Sept	Flowers single or double. Yellow. Sun or partial shade
(Perennial)	HP	12-18 in (30-46 cm); 18 in (46 cm)			April	June-Aug	Flowers single or double. Yellow. Good for cutting. Sun
Delphinium (Annual see Larkspur)	HP	3-6 ft (0.9-1.8 m); 18-24 in (46-61 cm)	February	Mar-May		July-Aug	Flowers blue, white, purple, pink, yellow, red. Sun or partial shade.
Dianthus (Annual; see also carnations and Sweet Williams)	HHA	6-12 in (15-30 cm); 9-12 in (23-30 cm)	Jan-Mar	April	April	June-Aug	Flowers single or double, pink, rose, crimson, white; scented. Sun or partial shade
Digitalis (Foxglove)	HB	3-5 ft (0.9-1.5 m); 18 in (46 cm)		May	May-June	July-Aug	Flowers cream, pink, purple. Sun or partial shade
Dimorphotheca	HA	12-18 in (30-46 cm); 12 in (30 cm)		Mar-May	April-May	June-Sept	Flowers, white, yellow, orange, salmon-orange. Sun
Echium	HA	24-36 in (30-91 cm); 12-18 in (30-46 cm)			Mar-April	July-Aug	Pink, blue, mauve, purple. Sun or partial shade
Eryngium giganteum (Biennial)	HB	36-42 in (91-107 cm); 12 in (30 cm)			May-June	June-Sept	Silvery and metallic blue. Splendid for cutting, everlasting. Sun or partial shade
(Perennial)	HP	18-36 in (46-91 cm)			May-June	June-Sept	Blue, silvery. Good for cutting. Sun or partial shade
Eschscholzia	HA	12 in (30 cm); 12 in			Mar-April; Sept	June-Sept	Cream, carmine, red, orange, yellow. Sun. Good for cutting
Gaillardia (Annual)	HHA	12-18 in (30-46 cm); 12 in (30 cm)	March	April	April-May	June-Sept	Double flowers, yellow, red, cream, bicoloured. Sun or partial shade. Good for cutting
(Perennial)	HP	24-36 in (61-91 cm); 12 in (30 cm)		May-June	May-June	July-Aug	
Geum	HP	24-30 in (61-76 cm); 12-18 in (30-46 cm)		Feb-Mar June-Aug		June-Sept	Double and semi-double. Yellow, scarlet. Sun or partial shade.
Godetia	HA	12-18 in (30-46 cm); 9 in (23 cm)			Mar-May	July-Sept	Single or double, salmon, pink, red, white, mauve. Sun or partial shade. Good for cutting

Name	Type	Height and spread	In heat 50-55°F (10-13°C)	Sow: Under cold glass	In the open	In flower	Comments
Grasses (Ornamental)	HA	12-24 in (30-61 cm); 9-12 in (23-30 cm)			Mar-May	June-Sept	Good for cutting, also for drying for winter use. Sun or partial shade
Gypsophilia (Annual)	HA	18-24 in (46-61 cm); 9-12 in (23-30 cm)			Mar-May	July-Sept	White or pink. Sun. Good for cutting
(Perennial)	HP	36 in (91 cm)		May-June		June-Aug	White. Sun. Good for cutting
Helianthus	HA	2-6 ft (0.6-1.8 m)			Mar-April	July-Sept	Single or double. White, gold, bronze, crimson. Sun or partial shade
Helichrysum	HHA	12-30 in (30-76 cm); 12 in (30 cm)	April	April		July-Sept	Everlasting flowers. Good for cutting. red, orange, yellow, pink, white. Sun or partial shade
Helipterum	HHA	12-18 in (30-46 cm); 9 in (23 cm)	April	April	April	July-Sept	Everlasting. Good for cutting. Carmine, rose, white. Sun
Hesperis (Sweet rocket)	HB			April	May-June	July-Aug	Lilac, purple or white. Sweetly scented. Sun or partial shade
Iberis (Candytuft)	HA	12 in (30 cm); 9 in (23 cm)			Mar-May	July-Sept	Red, lilac, white, pink. Sweetly scented. Sun
Impatiens	HHA	9-12 in (23-30 cm); 12 in (30 cm)	Feb-Mar	April-May		July-Oct	Red, pink, white, bicolours. Sun or shade
Ipomoea	HHA	6-8 ft (1.8-2.4 m); 12 in (30 cm)	April			July-Oct	Blue, red, white. Climber; do not plant out before mid-June. Sun
Kniphofia (Red hot poker)	HP	3-6 ft (0.9-1.8 m); 30 in (76 cm)		May-June	May-June	July-Sept	Yellow, scarlet, white, bicoloured. Sun
Larkspur (*Delphinium ajacis*)	HA	12-36 in (30-91 cm); 15-18 in (38-46 cm)			Mar-April; Sept	June-Aug	Flowers, pink, lavender, white, carmine, blue. Sun
Lathyrus (see Sweet pea)							
Lavatera	HA	3-4 ft (0.9-1.2 m); 12 in (30 cm)			Mar-April	July-Sept	Pink flowers. Sun or partial shade
	HHA	24 in (61 cm); 12 in (30 cm)	April	April		July-Sept	White flowers. Sun or partial shade
Limnanthes	HA	6-8 in (15-20 cm); 6 in (15 cm)			Mar-April	July-Aug	Yellow and white flowers. Sun or partial shade
Linaria	HA	8-10 in (20-25 cm); 6 in (15 cm)			Mar-May	July-Sept	Red, yellow, white, purple, pink. Sun or partial shade. Trim after flowering to produce second crop
Linum (Annual)	HA	12 in (30 cm); 9 in (23 cm)			Mar-May	July-Aug	Red flowers. Sun or partial shade
(Perennial)	HP	12 in (30 cm)					
Lobelia	HHA	6-8 in (15-46 cm)	Feb-Mar			June-Oct	Blue, pink, white, wine red. Compact varieties for edging; trailing for hanging baskets. Sun or partial shade

Name	Type	Height and spread	In heat 50-55°F (10-13°C)	Sow: Under cold glass	In the open	In flower	Comments
Love lies bleeding (see Amaranthus)							
Lunaria (Honesty)	HB	30-36 in (76-91 cm); 12 in (30 cm)		May-June	May-June	April-May	White or purple, papery seed pods, fine for winter decorations. Sun or partial shade
Lupin (Annual)	HA	12 in (30 cm); 9-12 in (23-30 cm)			Mar-April	July-Sept	Pink, rose, blue, white, bicolours. Sun or partial shade
(Perennial)	HP	30-36 in (76-91 cm); 24 in (61 cm)		May-June	May-June	June-July	Pink, blue, red, yellow, bicolours. Sun or partial shade
Lythrum	HP	2-4 ft (0.6-1.2 m)			May-June	July-Aug	Pink to crimson flowers. Sun or partial shade
Marigold (see Tagetes; also Calendula)							
Matthiola (see Stocks)							
Mesembryanthemum	HHA	6 in (15 cm); 6-8 in (15-20 cm)		April	April-May	June-Aug	Pink, red, purple flowers. Sun
Nasturtium (Tropaeolum)	HHA	6 in (15 cm); 3-4 ft (0.9-1.2 m)			April-May	July-Sept	Red, yellow, rose, orange. Tall and dwarf varieties, single or semi-double flowers. Sun or partial shade
Nemophila	HA	9-12 in (23-30 cm); 9 in (23 cm)			Mar-May	July-Aug	Pale blue flowers. Sun or partial shade
Nepeta	HP	12-15 in (30-46 cm); 12 in (30 cm)		May-June		June-Sept	Lavender blue flowers. Sun or partial shade
Nicotiana	HHA	24-36 in (61-91 cm); 12 in (30 cm)	April-May			July-Oct	Flowers red, white or greenish yellow. Sweetly scented. Sun or partial shade
Nigella (Love in a mist)	HA	18-24 in (46-61 cm); 9 in (23 cm)			Mar-May	July-Sept	Blue, mauve, purple, rose, white. Good for cutting. Sun or partial shade
Pansy	HP	6-9 in (15-23 cm); 9 in (23 cm)	March	April-June	May-June	May-Oct	Blue, white, yellow, red, purple, lavender. Sun or partial shade.
Papaver (Poppy annual)	HA	30-36 in (76-91 cm); 6-9 in (15-23 cm)			April	June-Aug	Double and single forms. Pink, red, salmon white
(Poppy perennial)	HP	30-36 in (76-91 cm); 24 in (61 cm)		April-May	May-June	June-July	Orange, pink, red, white, single and double forms. Sun
Penstemon	HP	18 in (46 cm) high	Feb-Mar	May-June		July-Aug	Blue, pink, red, white. Sun or partial shade
Petunia	HHA	9-15 in (23-38 cm); 9-12 in (23-30 cm)	Mar-April	Mar-April		July-Oct	Pink, red, blue, white, red, salmon, yellow, also bicoloured; excellent for hanging baskets, tubs and other containers as well as bedding. Sun or partial shade
Phacelia	HA	9-12 in (23-30 cm); 6-9 in (15-23 cm)		Mar-April	Mar-May	June-Sept	Vivid blue; good for borders also as pot plants. Sun or partial shade

Name	Type	Height and spread	In heat 50-55°F (10-13°C)	Sow: Under cold glass	In the open	In flower	Comments
Phlox (Annual)	HHA	6-12 in (15-30 cm); 9-12 in (23-30 cm)	Mar-April	April		July-Sept	Red, pink, yellow, violet, white. Sun or partial shade
(Perennial)	HP	30-48 in (76-122 cm); 18 in (46 cm)		April-May	May-June	July-Sept	Lavender, violet, red, orange, pink, rose, white. Sun or partial shade
Poppy (see Papaver)							
Polyanthus (see Primula)							
Primula, including polyanthus and primrose	HP	9 in (23 cm); 3-4 ft (0.9-1.2 m)	Feb-Mar	April-May	May-Sept	April-Aug	Many types and colours. Most prefer moist, semi-shaded positions
Rudbeckia (Annual)	HHA	24-36 in (61-91 cm); 15 in (38 cm)	Feb-Mar	April		July-Oct	Large flowers, orange yellow or mahogany. Fine for cutting. Sun or partial shade
Salvia	HHA	12-15 in (30-38 cm); 12 in (30 cm)	Feb-Mar			July-Oct	Red, salmon, pink, purple, white. Sun or partial shade
Sidalcea	HP	36-42 in (91-107 cm); 18 in (46 cm)		April-May		June-Sept	Fine border plants. Pink, carmine. Sun or partial shade
Statice (Annual [Limoleum])	HHA	18-24 in (46-61 cm); 12 in (30 cm)	March	April		July-Sept	Blue, yellow, pink or white. Good garden plants; excellent everlasting cut flower. Sun or partial shade
(Perennial)	HP	24 in (61 cm); 18 in (46 cm)		April-May	April-May	June-Sept	Blue everlasting flowers. Good for cutting. Sun or partial shade
Stocks (Annual)	HA	12-15 in (30-38 cm); 9-12 in (23-30 cm)	Mar-April	April		July-Sept	Lavender, red, pink, white. Sweetly scented. Good for cutting. Sun or partial shade
(Biennial)	HB	18-24 in (46-61 cm); 12 in (30 cm)	Mar-April	April	July-Aug	June-Aug or May-June	As above. Late sowings will flower in spring
Sunflower (see Helianthus)							
Sweet peas	HA	2-8 ft (0.6-2.4 m); 4-6 in (10-15 cm)	March	Mar-April	Mar-April; Sept	May-June; June-Sept	Pink, red, crimson, blue, white. Splendid cut flowers. Sun or partial shade
Sweet William (*Dianthus barbatus*)	HB	18-24 in (46-61 cm); 12 in (30 cm)		April-May	May	June	Flowers, red, pink, white or 'auricula eyed' (ie, with a white centre). Sun
Tagetes (Marigold)	HA	6 in (15 cm); 24 in (61 cm)		April-May			Flowers, orange, yellow, dark red, or bicoloured. Double, semi-double or single. Sun
Verbena	HHA	6-15 in (15-38 cm); 9 in (23 cm)	Mar-April			July-Sept	Blue, pink, white, red. Good for bedding or cutting. Sun
Wallflower (see Cheiranthus)							
Zinnia	HHA	9-30 in (23-76 in); 12 in (30 cm)	Mar-April	April-May		July-Sept	Red, pink, yellow, green, white flowers. Dwarf varieties good for bedding, tall varieties for cutting. Sun

Nigella damascena (love in a mist).

Dimorphotheca aurantiaca.

Amaranathus caudatus (love lies bleeding).

Mesembryanthemum criniflorum.

Limnanthes douglasii

Aquilegia 'Long spurred' hybrids.

Rudbeckia 'Rustic Dwarfs'.

Eschscholzia californica.

Eryngium giganteum.

Sweet pea 'Frances Perry'.

A good mix of sweet williams.

Lavatera 'Sunset'.

Dwarf antirrhinums at Wisley.

Primula malacoides.

The annual border at Wisley with Californian poppies and other annuals.

Helichrysum monstrosum.

Large-flowered F, hybrid primroses.

Dwarf tagetes (marigolds).

MARCH

Fruit: Spray fruit trees. Prune Morello cherries; plant strawberries; start vines in a cold house; feed raspberries.

Vegetables: Sow cauliflowers, carrots, leeks and lettuces under glass; sow other vegetables in the open. Plant shallots, onion sets and potatoes; plant globe artichokes and asparagus; plant early summer cauliflowers, cabbages and lettuces.

Roses: Prune established and newly planted roses. Burn all prunings and spray the roses and the ground beneath with a suitable fungicide. Plant roses if possible this month.

Flowers from seed: Sow half hardy annuals in a greenhouse or frame; sow hardy annuals if the ground is workable.

Alpines: Plant alpines now in a rock garden or in containers. Watch for pests. Firm plants loosened by frosts. Sow seeds of alpines.

Cold greenhouse: Shade seedlings and cuttings from hot sun. Prepare border for tomatoes. Sow seeds of half hardy annuals; sow also vegetables.

Cool greenhouse: Root chrysanthemum and pelargonium cuttings. Pot lilies; repot ferns.

Dahlias: Start old plants into growth and take cuttings.

Chrysanthemums: Root cuttings of outdoor varieties.

Hardy border flowers: Lift and divide perennials if you want to increase the stock. Prepare ground well for new plantings.

Bulbs: Remove faded blooms; lift and divide snowdrops, crocuses and aconites. Keep weeds down; stake crown imperials; plant out bulbs grown in bowls after flowering. Plant gladioli and lilies.

Lawns: Rake and aerate the turf. Give lawn first cut. Apply fertilizers. Prepare site for new lawn; lay turf or sow lawn grass seed.

Trees and shrubs: Trim winter flowering heathers, also spartium.

Fruit

Morello cherries with thick congested growth can have some of the branches and shoots pruned this month.

Plant strawberry runners.

Start vines in unheated greenhouses; lower the rods and spray them each morning with tepid water. When growth starts give the borders a soaking, then mulch them with well rotted farmyard manure.

Give raspberry canes a dressing of sulphate of potash; ¾ oz to the sq yard (25 g to the sq metre).

Vegetables

If the weather is kind and the soil workable this is a busy month on the vegetable plots. But do not be in too great a hurry to sow or plant if the soil is cold and wet, or if the weather is unkind and if you live in a cold district. Seeds sown, or plants put in later, when the soil has begun to warm up will usually catch up with those sown or planted earlier and run less risk of rotting in the cold wet soil.

Sowing

Sow cauliflowers, carrots, leeks and lettuces in frames or under cloches.

Sow beetroot, broad beans, carrots, lettuces, onions, parsley, parsnips, peas, radishes, spinach and turnips in the open.

Sow Brussels sprouts, summer cabbages, calabrese, kales and leeks in a well prepared seed bed for planting out later.

The seed bed for these crops should be dug thoroughly and broken down to a fine tilth. If possible site it near a water supply as during the summer months seedlings waiting to be planted out may need watering twice a week in dry spells.

If not done in January, spray apple trees early this month.

Planting

Plant shallots and onion sets. The sets (tiny onion bulbs) are best planted so that they are just covered with soil. If even the tip is left showing birds pull them up, presumably to see if there is a worm underneath and you will have all the trouble of planting them again. Plant the sets in rows 8 in (20 cm) apart each way.

Plant rhubarb.

Plant seed potatoes in the south – better to wait until April in the north. Either take out a drill about 5 in (12 cm) deep with a hoe and set the tubers of early varieties in it 15 in (38 cm) apart, or plant each tuber with a trowel. Leave 18 in (45 cm) between the rows. Late varieties are planted 15 in (30 cm) apart in rows 30 in (60 cm) apart.

If plants of early summer cabbages and cauliflowers or lettuces have been raised under glass or bought locally, plant these out this month.

Asparagus and artichokes

If there is space available a small asparagus bed and a row of globe artichokes can be a very good investment.

Prepare the ground well for both asparagus and globe artichokes working in plenty of manure or compost. The asparagus should go on cropping for 15 years or more.

When buying asparagus plants seek out one-year-old crowns. There is far less mortality among these young crowns than when two- or three-year-old crowns are planted.

At one time it was always recommended to plant asparagus in raised beds. This is still a good idea on ground that may be wet at times but it is now normally planted on level ground. A good method is to plant the crowns about 8 in (20 cm) deep and 18 in (45 cm) apart. Another method is to plant three rows leaving a path 2-3 ft (60-100 cm) wide on either side.

The first cutting of asparagus should not be before two years after planting – ie, you plant this year and make the first cut the year after next.

The globe artichokes should be grown on a three-year succession plan – a row should be planted each year and after a row has produced its third crop it is discarded.

If artichoke plants grow too large they stop producing their large succulent flower heads. The number of shoots should be reduced to three each year – the offshoots removed can be used to make a new row.

The first year, the plants will produce three heads; the second and third year nine heads each. Set the plants about 2 ft 6 in (75 cm) apart in rows about the same distance apart.

Roses

The care of established roses begins with pruning this month in the south of England, and towards the end of the month in the cold north-east and in Scotland.

Pruning

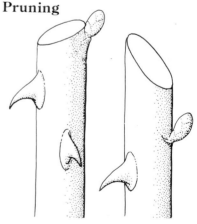

Pruning roses. The left-hand cut just above a bud, is correct; right, incorrect.

In March you have to prune the bush roses, the newly planted and established hybrid tea and floribunda roses and the established standard hybrid tea roses. The established shrub roses, and

Hybrid tea rose 'Alec's Red'.

Floribunda rose 'Matangi'.

Shrub rose 'Nevada'.

Rose 'Paul's Scarlet Climber'.

rambler roses which flower next year, on growths produced this year, are best pruned after flowering. New standards are normally pruned before they leave the nursery.

1. Newly planted hybrid tea roses. They come from the nursery free from spindly side shoots and need to be cut back quite severely to leave only about two or three buds or eyes – eyes are the slight swellings on the stem which arise at the point where a leaf joined the stem the year before and which will, in due course, produce a new growth.

Newly planted floribunda roses may be pruned rather less severely – back to say four buds or eyes.

If standard roses are delivered and have not been pruned, they should be cut back as above.

2. Established hybrid tea and floribunda roses may be pruned less severely. Firstly, hybrid tea roses. Cut away any dead shoots and thin spindly growths. Then cut back the stems and leave about a third to a half of the growth made last year, which may be to say 4 to 6 buds or eyes and always cut to an outward pointing bud or eye. Any stems that are crossing others or congesting the bush should, of course, be cut out.

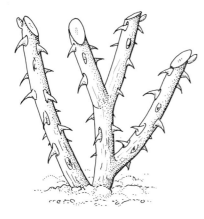

Pruning a newly planted hybrid tea rose. It should be cut back quite hard to leave only 2 to 3 eyes.

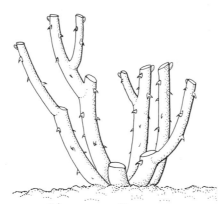

Pruning an established hybrid tea. This can be cut back less severely leaving about 4-6 buds or eyes.

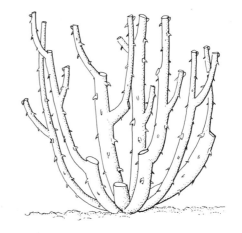

An established floribunda rose after pruning. Each cut should be made just before an outward pointing bud or eye.

Floribunda roses may be pruned less severely – cut the strong stems back to about half their length, always (as with the hybrid teas) to an outward pointing bud or eye.

3. Miniature roses are pruned in much the same way, removing unwanted twiggy shoots and cutting the main stems back by about half their length.

4. Established standard roses should have their main stems cut back to leave about half their length and of course any diseased or useless twiggy shoots should be removed.

5. Rambler roses are pruned after flowering (see p 155).

6. Climbing roses, however, are normally pruned in the spring. If the plant has made new growths that may be tied in to replace old stems, these may be cut out now. These climbers, however, are not usually very generous with their new growths. Tie them in as nearly a horizontal position as you can because this encourages them to produce side shoots which will bear the flowers. Left to grow vertically the stems will usually become bare below with only a few flowering stems on the top. When old stems reach this state cut them down to a couple of feet above ground. Short side shoots may be pruned to about half their length.

7. Shrub roses need very little pruning – one reason why they are becoming increasingly popular. If they are growing too big for their lodgings, they may be cut back or some of their oldest stems removed and of course any dead, frost damaged or old worn-out stems should be removed.

Diseases

This is also a good time to start the fight against the black spot disease which can be a killer. The spores persist throughout the winter on heaps of rose debris – fallen leaves and twigs. So after the pruning has been done and all the prunings carefully gathered up and burnt or thrown away you should go into action.

The roses and the ground should be given a really thorough spraying with a suitable fungicide such as those based on dithane, carbendazim and maneb, or thiophanate-methyl, bupirimate and triforine. All these fungicides are available in proprietary formulations and are very effective against black spot and mildew which are the two most common rose diseases.

Mildew is unsightly and a weakening disease but it is not a killer like black spot. But to have really healthy and vigorous roses you should try hard to keep these two diseases under control.

Manufacturers usually recommend spraying every 10-14 days but experience has shown that it is much better to spray at 10-day intervals. Too often the disease has appeared again after about 12 days. When the beds have been cleaned up they may be given a first dressing of a good proprietary general fertilizer. As with lawns, a second application a month later really does have a remarkable effect.

General tasks

Check ties holding climbing or rambler roses to their posts, wires, trellis, pergola, arch or whatever

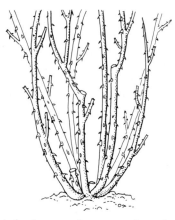

Most shrub roses do not need much pruning – only the removal of old stems from the centre.

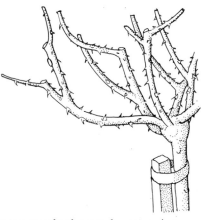

Prune standard roses by removing weak growths and cutting out older stems to keep the centre open.

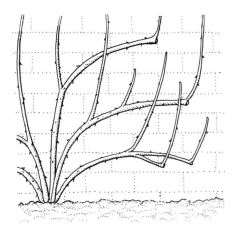

Climbing roses are pruned in the spring and should be tied in a horizontal position.

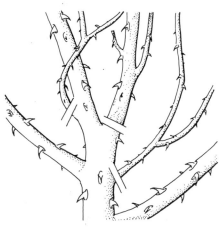

Pruning a bush rose. First remove any dead wood and then cut out spindly weak shoots.

support has been provided for them. If necessary renew ties.

There is still plenty of time to plant roses, either the 'bare root' plants ordered from a specialist rose nursery or those bought plastic-wrapped from garden centres or the high street.

Container-grown roses, like other shrubs, may be planted at any time provided you are prepared to water copiously in dry weather. This principle, of course, applies to all shrubs – the later you plant them the less time they have to make new roots before dry spells occur, and so the greater the need will be for regular and adequate watering.

Handy Hint: If roses are growing over bare ground – that is, they are not underplanted with other plants, the easiest way to prune them is to use a long-handled pruner. This consists of the ordinary secateur or pruner blades mounted on 14 in (36 cm) handles, with a moulded plastic grip.

You can snip away at the branches and let the prunings fall to the ground where eventually they may be raked up along with any of last year's fallen leaves.

The long-handled pruner is an excellent tool for anyone to use for any pruning job but is especially appreciated by those who have an impaired grip.

Flowers from seed

Many gardeners nowadays have given up raising flowers from seed and instead buy their seedlings of half hardly and tender annuals, (and of course vegetables) ready for planting out. This, of course saves time but is an expensive way of growing flowers that have been raised from seed.

One packet of hardy annuals such as candytuft, alyssum, calendula, godetia, clarkia and many more sown in the open will give a splendid return for maybe an

eighth of the price of a box of half hardy annuals.

Obviously, you will have to fork over the ground, break the surface soil down to a fine tilth, sow the seeds and in due course thin out the seedlings. But the beds or borders have to be prepared to receive seedlings of flowers bought from the garden centres anyway, so there is not much extra work involved in growing hardy annuals from seed.

Half hardy annuals may be sown in a cold greenhouse or a frame; or some varieties can be sown in the open in late May or June in the southern parts of the country. In the north this is a bit of a gamble.

Biennials such as myosotis (forgetmenots), foxgloves, wallflowers, sweet williams and Canterbury bells may be sown in May or June.

Many perennials such as phloxes, delphiniums, gaillardias, geums, oriental poppies, pansies, sidalceas, statice and many more may also be sown in May or June.

Sowing hardy annuals
If the soil is workable seeds of hardy annuals may be sown this month. Fork over the top soil removing any perennial weeds and large stones. Firm it by treading lightly and then rake it down to a fine tilth.

If the annuals are to be sown in irregular patches in beds or borders, or perhaps under roses or between shrubs, mark out the patch with a pointed stick and then draw very shallow drills across these patches about 9-12 in (23-30 cm) apart – slightly further apart for larger plants like larkspurs, lavateras and calendulas.

The drills may be made with a pointed label or the corner of a draw hoe and the seeds sown very thinly. The easiest way is to tip the seeds from the packet into the palm of your hand and take them between the thumb and forefinger of the other hand to drop carefully

in the little drills. This is a much safer way than trying to tip them out of the packet.

Sowing in drills is better than scattering seeds freely over the patches because you can easily recognize the annual seedlings and spot weed seedlings and pull these up before they rob the annuals of air, sunshine, food and water.

Sweet peas
The most popular annual flower is the sweet pea and while some modern sweet pea varieties have little scent there are many very fine sweet peas which are scented.

You can also buy the 'old fashioned' powerfully scented sweet peas as a mixture. These are smaller than the modern waved varieties and have fewer flowers on a stem; but some mixed in with the large flowered variety will ensure plenty of fragrance.

Recent introductions include several dwarf strains only 12-15 in (30-40 cm) high, some of which have good sized flowers on stems long enough for cutting; and also have scent.

Sweet peas may be grown up a wigwam of bamboo canes wrapped round with wire or plastic netting; or up pea sticks if these can be found. Alternatively, if prize blooms are wanted they may be grown as single-stemmed cordon plants each trained up a tall bamboo cane kept in place by special wire sweet pea rings or twists of plastic-covered wire.

When the plants have reached the top of the canes they may be taken down carefully (the stems laid back and forth horizontally just above the ground and tied to the canes which allows the leading shoot to grow up once more.

If sweet peas are fed with soluble fertilizer once a week, and well watered when necessary they will go on flowering well into the autumn but only provided dead flowers are assiduously removed. The more flowers you cut for the house the more you get.

Alpines

This is the time to plant alpines and in many cases to lift and divide plants such as campanulas, ajugas, gentians and polygonums, which have grown too large for their allotted space.

Keep up the war on slugs with slug pellets or powders.

Firm in any plants that may have been loosened by frosts.

Sow seeds of alpines such as aubrietas and *Alyssum saxatile* in a greenhouse.

Campanula garganica.

The dwarf Polygonum 'Lowndes Variety' is very free flowering and makes a fine display in the rock garden in autumn.

Cold greenhouse

As the weather warms up greater attention must be paid to ventilation and watering. Young seedlings and newly rooted cuttings will also need shading in hot sunshine, but continue to close the house down early in the afternoon to conserve warmth.

Alpines and bulbs in pots will continue to give pleasure, together with primulas and cyclamen corms started last autumn (see p 114) and late narcissi and tulips.

Sow seeds of half hardy annuals, asters, stocks, *Phlox drummondii,* ageratum, salvias and others for summer bedding outdoors.

Sow broad beans to fill gaps in outdoor sowings, celery, cucumbers, leeks, dwarf beans, tomatoes (both for growing in the cold greenhouse, and also outdoors).

Take and insert chrysanthemum cuttings.

Lilies can still be potted.

If tomatoes are to be grown in soil borders in the greenhouse the ground should be made ready in good time. Dig the soil deeply and work some well rotted compost between the layers. Allow to settle.

Cool greenhouse

Take dahlia, fuchsia and salvia cuttings.

If tuberous begonias and gloxinias have sprouted pot them singly in 3 in (8 cm) pots at the end of the month. Do not bury the crowns.

Take pelargonium cuttings, by using the young shoots cut across just under a node (joint). Root singly in small pots.

Divide and repot ferns in lime-free compost. Repot any house plants needing attention.

Repot asparagus ferns or divide some plants. Use good loamy compost.

Give calceolarias plenty of air; space them well out. Shade from hot sun and watch for greenfly.

Cinerarias should now be in full flower; keep them moist but not overwatered or the plants will collapse.

Sow *Solanum capsicastrum* (winter cherry) in a light compost.

Dahlias

Old dahlia plants kept in store may now be started into growth for planting out next month or to produce cuttings. Water the soil or peat covering the tubers but do not wet the crown too much – the crown is the point where the tubers join the old stem.

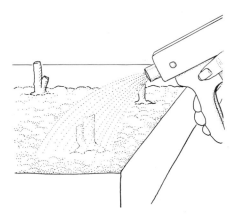

Old dahlia plants in store should be sprayed lightly once a day with tepid water to bring on new shoots.

Dahlia cuttings are inserted in rooting compost and covered with a plastic bag.

Iris danfordiae and the dwarf *Cyclamen coum* are excellent for the cold greenhouse.

Calceolaria and *Cineraria* are fine for the cool greenhouse.

at the end of May or in June. This saves the bother of potting them singly in pots in April.

Chrysanthemums

Time now to start propagating outdoor chrysanthemums. The cuttings should be about 2-2½ in (5-6 cm) and cut just below a leaf joint. Remove the lower leaves and insert the cuttings in pots or boxes of equal parts by volume of peat and coarse sand. Keep the cuttings in a temperature of around 50°F (10°C).

When the cuttings have rooted pot them singly in 2½-3 in (6-8 cm) pots. Alternatively the cuttings may be inserted into peat pots in which they may remain until they are planted out in May or June.

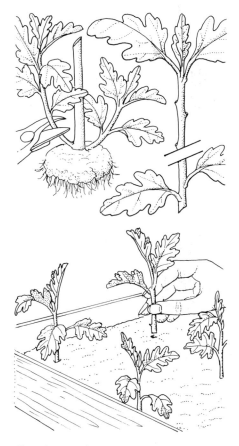

Cut chrysanthemum shoots just below a joint, removing the lower leaves. Insert in boxes or pots filled with a suitable rooting compost.

Spray the plants lightly once a day with tepid water to encourage new shoots which will make cuttings when they are about 3-4 in (7-10 cm) long. Cut them with a very sharp knife or razor blade about ¼ in (6 mm) from the base. More cuttings will grow from this point next month.

Trim off the lower leaves, cut the stem of the cutting cleanly just below a joint and insert it in John Innes No 1 potting compost or in a peat-based loamless seed and potting compost. Three or four cuttings may be inserted around the inner edge of a 3-4 in (8-10 cm) pot.

If possible place the cuttings in a box covered with a sheet of glass,

or cover the pot with a plastic bag and of course keep them in a warm place – a propagating case perhaps, on the bench of a heated greenhouse or on a window sill indoors.

Some growers dip the base of the cutting in a 'hormone' rooting powder but this is not really necessary.

An even easier way of propagating dahlias is to insert the cuttings in Jiffy 7's. These are neat little peat pellets encased in plastic net which swell up when wetted, into which you can sow seeds or root cuttings direct. If the cuttings are given several feeds with soluble fertilizer they may remain in the Jiffy 7's until they are planted out

Hardy border flowers

Herbaceous perennials (hardy border flowers) that die to the ground annually and then reappear the following year are a boon to busy gardeners. They do not have to be raised from seed each year, nor must they be taken under cover to preserve them over winter.

They also perform various garden functions, including the long established custom of grouping different kinds into a patchwork collection, set like a jigsaw puzzle in central islands on lawns; or more frequently in long beds backed by fences or hedges, the plants themselves graded according to their heights, colours and season. Such beds are known as herbaceous – or hardy – borders.

But herbaceous perennials can also be worked into mixed borders along with bulbs, and bedding plants as well as a few early or late flowering shrubs to extend the interest and flowering period. Some make good container plants, others can be introduced in open glades between shrubs while many provide fine flowers for cutting.

Some perennials persist longer than others, a few like the burning bush *Dictamnus albus* or paeonies can stay for years and years in the same bed, whereas others need dividing every three years or so or

Chrysanthemum coccineum
(Pyrethrum) 'Red Dwarf'.

the flowers deteriorate and the spread of shoots smothers their weaker neighbours. This is an excellent time of year to split over-large plants, as well as to transplant or introduce new perennials.

Planting

Plants with fibrous roots – like Michaelmas daisies, pyrethrums and heleniums – should be lifted in their entirety. Usually they can then be pulled apart or separated with a knife; but in very stubborn cases push two digging forks into

the clump, back to back, and lever the handles outwards. This will break the tangled root system so that segments can be separated. The procedure can be repeated if necessary.

Plants which resent too much root disturbance – like paeonies – can have small pieces cut away from the sides of the clump.

Because hardy perennials are intended to stay several years in the same place give them a good start by providing them with deeply dug, well manured and weed-free ground (see p 142).

Take out good planting holes, set the perennials in place spreading out their roots and return the soil, firming it with feet or hands – according to the size of the plant.

Watering is rarely necessary in March but it the ground or plants seem dry give the soil a good watering and later hoe the surface to remove footprints.

Single and isolated specimens rarely make much of a show so group your plants in threes, fives or sevens and label each grouping. Labels are a great help as to their whereabouts when the plants are dormant.

In the Granada television programme a pyrethrum *(Chrysanthemum coccineum)* and *Aster turbinellus*, a violet Michaelmas daisy, are planted this month, a reminder that March is the safest time of year to divide and plant a

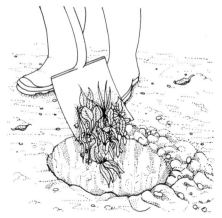

Tasks for March: forking over borders (left), chipping off weeds (centre) and burying them in a hole.

number of perennials including oriental poppies *(Papaver orientale)*, scabious *(Scabiosa caucasica)*, *Aster amellus* and varieties, catananches and hardy border chrysanthemums.

Bulbs

Many bulbous plants will now be in flower. Remove spent blooms to sustain a good show outdoors as long as possible. Snowdrops, winter aconites and crocuses can be carefully lifted, divided and immediately replanted – while still in leaf – to start new colonies. This is one of the safest periods of the year to transplant these small bulbs.

Weed and lightly prick over the soil between bedding tulips and other later blooming bulbs.

Stake crown imperials *(Fritillaria imperialis)* if this seems necessary.

Remove old forced hyacinths and narcissi from their bowls and plant them in a trench in an odd corner. Water and give them a soluble feed; then when they dry off lift the bulbs and either store them in a cool place until autumn, or plant them somewhere to provide cut flowers in a couple of years time.

When planting lily bulbs it is worth setting them on a handful of sharp sand placed in the bottom of the hole.

Plant gladiolus corms towards the middle of the month in the south, but a week or two later in

Snowdrops and these large-flowered 'Dutch' crocuses are the first harbingers of spring followed quickly by the miniature flowers of *Narcissus cyclamineus.*

Fritillaria imperialis (crown imperial).

67

the north. In damp heavy soil plant them 4 in (10 cm) deep, setting each corm on a bed of sand. In light soils plant 6 in (15 cm) deep.

For garden decoration grow each variety in a small colony with 5-6 in (13-15 cm) between corms, but if the blooms are intended for cut flowers it is preferable to plant them in rows, leaving 12 in (30 cm) between rows. This allows for quick and easy staking, with canes linked together with string. Gladioli should be planted at fortnightly intervals through next month in order to provide a succession of flowers.

In suitable weather lilies can now be planted outside.

Lawns

Provided the lawn is in a fit state – not waterlogged – this is the time to start its spring treatment. Rake out vigorously with a wire rake, the accumulation of dead grass and other rubbish – or what professional groundsmen call 'thatch'.

Aeration

Spiking to let air into the soil.

This lets in air to the grass roots, and enables rain to reach them – a thick spongy 'thatch' tends to soak up the water which then evaporates and does not get down to the roots.

Also, most lawns tend to be over-compacted especially if a motor mower is used or they are well trodden. Aerating the lawn at this time of year greatly improves the turf.

There are machines, of course, for piercing the turf. Some are hand operated; others, motorised, may often be hired from DIY firms. With these machines three or even four people with large areas to cover can scarify their lawns in a day and share the cost.

But on small areas aerating the lawn may be done with a garden fork, pushing it in to make holes about 4 in (10 cm) deep and 4 in apart. This allows air, water and fertilizer to get down to the roots quickly.

If the spring weather is kind grass will begin to grow now and will need its first cut. Check over the lawn to remove any stones, bits of dog's bones or other debris that may be a menace to the mower's blades.

Cutting
Set the blades of the mower high for this first cut. With cylinder mowers the height of cut is adjusted by raising or lowering the front roller – you lower the roller to cut closer and raise it for a lighter cut.

Rotary mowers usually have four wheels and these are normally raised or lowered by levers. The hover-type mowers which float on a cushion of air are adjusted for height of cut by inserting spacers or flat thick washers between the blade and the drive.

Once the lawn has had its spring grooming, or as much of it as you are able to carry out, it should be given a dressing of a good proprietary lawn fertilizer.

Fertilizers
These come in two forms – a straight general fertilizer mixture specially compounded for lawns; and 'weed and feed' mixtures, which consist of a fertilizer mixture to which has been added a selective lawn weedkiller.

These mixtures work well enough sometimes, but it is probably better to apply a straight lawn fertilizer in March, with a second application say a month later and then if there are weeds in the lawn deal with them in May.

The idea is to encourage both grass and weeds to grow vigorously so that when the time comes to apply the selective weedkiller the weeds will have a large leaf area which is better able to absorb the weedkiller.

You can apply fertilizers with a fertilizer spreader or very easily by hand. If you wish to be very accurate mark off the lawn into strips a yard wide with string. But if you can visualize easily a square yard this is not necessary.

Unless the fertilizer is very concentrated, it is usually possible to scatter it on evenly enough. Weigh out the amount recommended per square yard and see whether this is a handful or half a handful perhaps, and try to scatter it evenly. The fertilizer should be washed off the grass foliage gently with a hose, unless rain is imminent just in case it might scorch the grass. This can sometimes happen in freak weather conditions which are not unknown in Britain! Do aim to apply a second fertilizer dressing – it seems that the lawn really does respond remarkably to its second dose.

A new lawn
If a new lawn is to be made a start should be made on preparing the site now.

Dig it over and remove all roots of perennial weeds – or as many as you can. Let it settle and then rake it smooth.

Leave it for two or three weeks to allow annual weed seeds to germinate and then hoe them off. Tread the ground firmly in each direction and rake again to fill in any hollows and make the surface smooth and ready for turfing, or sowing seed. Rake in a dressing of fertilizer.

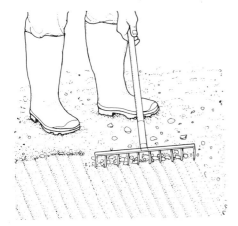

Preparing a site for a new lawn. After digging and levelling the site and removing perennial weeds, rake the surface smooth.

Firm the ground by treading in both directions – across and along the whole length of the site. Rake again.

When laying turf, 'stagger', or 'bond' the turves as with bricks when building a wall.

Turves should be laid in the same manner as bricks, staggering the joints. When they are all laid brush in some good fine soil with a birch broom to fill the joints. Keep the turf well watered in dry spells.

Do not sow grass seed until the soil has begun to warm up – usually about the end of April, later in the north. The warmer the soil, the quicker the seed will germinate.

For a fine lawn buy a lawn seed mixture without rye grass. For a lawn that is going to have a lot of wear sow a mixture containing rye grass or the new variety 'Hunter' – a tough but slow growing form of rye grass. Allow 1½ oz (42.5 g) of fine grass seed to the square yard – 2 oz (57 g) of a coarser mixture containing rye grass.

Handy Hint: Grass has a habit of growing in awkward places – under shrubs and hedges, around tree trunks or on banks. There are mechanized tools to cope with grass in these places – called strimmers, electric or petrol driven, with a short length of fishing line revolving at high speed that clips off the grass. If it should hit a tree trunk or the toe of your shoe it will do no harm.

Much cheaper are the long-handled lawn shears. These are similar to the long-handled lawn edging shears but the blades are at almost right angles to the handles so you can cut long grass round trees or in places where the mower won't go, without stooping or bending over.

Many lawns contain a percentage of 'bent' grasses – those which produce a wiry flower spike that springs up again after it has been flattened by a mower with a front roller. Of course if you have a rotary mower without a front roller, or a 'hover' type these will chop off the 'bents'.

If not, and the 'bents' annoy you, you can clip them off effortlessly with these long-handled lawn shears. They are not however of much use for trimming grass on banks.

Trees and shrubs

Those varieties of *Erica carnea* and *E.* x *darleyensis* which have finished blooming should be lightly pruned over to remove the old flowering stems. This will not only make them dwarfer and more compact but encourage new growths to develop.

Cut back straggling shoots on *Spartium junceum.*

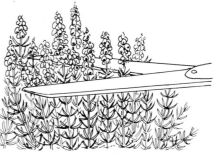

Trimming heathers. Do this lightly after the flowers have faded .

Handy Hint: Don't stay too long on one job. If you intend to cut the lawn, do a bit of digging or hoeing, stake some plants or trim a hedge; vary the work. Cut a bit of the lawn, then do a bit of digging or hoeing or hedge trimming. Don't press on with one job until your muscles ache. Don't wait to move on to another job until you are tired of the one you are doing and have probably exhausted various muscles.

Handy Hint: There are many one-wheeled barrows on the market and several two-wheeled barrows or trucks with a pram handle. The latter are so much easier to use, as the whole weight is carried on the wheels – with a one-wheeled barrow you are still half carrying the load.

Also if you have to walk with a stick and cannot manage a two-handled barrow the two-wheeled truck with a pram handle is a boon.

APRIL

Fruit: Finish planting strawberries. Prune soft fruit. Mulch fruit trees and bushes. Spray gooseberries.

Vegetables: Sow aubergines, sweet peppers and tomatoes under glass. Towards the end of the month sow other tender vegetables. Sow vegetables in a prepared bed in the open; sow celery. Sow French and runner beans under cloches. Plant summer cauliflowers, cabbages and lettuces. Protect potato shoots; protect crops from birds.

Roses: Underplant roses with attractive carpeting plants. Apply a residual weedkiller to rose beds and kill perennial weeds. Spray against pests and diseases; and apply a mulch.

Flowers from seed: Keep on sowing hardy annuals in the open when the soil is workable. Sow half hardy annuals in a frame, under cloches or in a cold greenhouse. Sow flowers for cutting; also ornamental grasses. Weed and thin seedlings.

Alpines: Hand weed, or hoe between rock garden plants. Water plants in sinks if necessary. Plant alpines and water in if soil is dry.

Cold greenhouse: Propagate plants by cuttings. Sow half hardy annuals; apply shading from hot sun and ventilate carefully. Sow alpine plants. Repot azaleas. Prepare soil in borders for tomatoes.

Cool greenhouse: Sow cucumbers, French and runner beans; also various flowers. Move bulbs after flowering to cold frame. Feed all growing plants.

Dahlias: Pot rooted cuttings and take more. Prepare planting site. Plant out old dahlia tubers or divide them if desired to increase stock.

Chrysanthemums: Harden off cuttings. Pinch out tip of plants towards the end of the month.

Hardy border flowers: Stake plants before they grow too tall. Deadhead daffodils. Plant summer flowering bulbs.

Lawns: True up or trim lawn edges. Fill hollows and level humps. Control worms. Repair bare patches. Apply fertilizer.

Trees and shrubs: Prune forsythias. Plant evergreens. Clip ivy on walls.

71

Fruit

Finish planting strawberry runners.

Prune gooseberries and red and white currants in areas where autumn pruning was postponed owing to possibility of bird damage.

Spread a thick mulch of rotted farmyard manure or compost over the roots of wall fruit trees and fruit bushes, including raspberries.

Spray gooseberries subject to powdery mildew, before the flowers open, with a suitable spray (see page 186). Repeat if necessary.

Vegetables

Vegetables like tomatoes which need to be sown under heated glass in March may be sown now in an unheated greenhouse or sun lounge. So too, late in the month, can French and runner beans, celery, cucumbers, marrows and sweet corn.

Sowings may still be made in the open ground this month of beetroot, onions, lettuces, peas, radishes, broad beans, summer spinach, turnips, carrots and parsley.

It is still not too late to sow leeks, Brussels sprouts, summer cabbages, calabrese and kales, sprouting broccoli, winter cabbages and savoys in a prepared seed bed.

Sow French and runner beans and cover with cloches in the south.

Celery

Celery is not the easiest of vegetables to grow well. Unless you have a heated greenhouse capable of maintaining a minimum temperature of 50°F (10°C) and a frame for hardening off the seedlings it is better to buy young plants for planting out in late May or June.

The self-blanching varieties are the easiest for the amateur to grow and may even be sown in the open ground in a well prepared seed bed in April. Set cloches in place early in the month to warm the soil, sow thinly and thin the seedlings.

Transplant the seedlings at the end of May or early in June. Ordinary celery may also be raised in this manner. Self-blanching varieties are not so hardy and will need to be harvested before the autumn frosts.

Plant these varieties in a block 9-11 in (23-28 cm) apart each way as this assists the self blanching. The ordinary or 'trench' celery may be planted either in a well manured trench 12 in (30 cm) deep and 18 in (45 cm) wide or on the flat in a single row 9 in (23 cm) apart.

The soil from the trench which has been placed on either side of it is used to earth the plants up gradually beginning about early August. To blanch the stems tie the plants together with string or raffia loosely. It is easier, however, to grow them on the flat and tie brown paper or black polythene in several stages round them as the sticks lengthen.

If you can buy young plants of summer cabbages, cauliflowers or lettuces these may be planted this month.

In milder districts potato shoots may appear above ground this month and if there is a frost warning should be protected by laying straw or even newspapers over them or drawing some soil with a hoe to just cover them.

Bird damage

In many gardens birds can be a great nuisance. They strip seedling lettuces, and decimate young pea plants; they pick off the buds of runner beans and of course when the fruits start to ripen they take far more than their fair share of strawberries, raspberries and later do much damage to apples and pears.

There are various ways of combating bird damage. Some gardeners acknowledge defeat and grow all their soft fruit, lettuces, peas and runner beans in a fruit cage. Now that there are fruit cages which can be easily erected and dismantled, made of plastic-covered aluminium tubing with strong nylon nets, it is possible to move the plot to be covered up or down the garden from one year to the next – always of course covering the soft fruit.

There are of course other

Modern cabbages make tight hearts without producing a lot of outer leaves.

methods of protecting plants from the birds. You can run black cotton up and down and across rows of peas or lettuces, on sticks say 6-10 in (15-25 cm) above the ground.

Or you can use chemical bird repellents such as Stayoff or Scoot, based on aluminium ammonium sulphate. This is quite harmless but is most distasteful to birds and if it is sprayed or watered on plants, the birds will usually leave them alone – provided there is alternative food around in the garden or in the neighbour's garden!

There are also various bird-scaring devices available but often the birds soon get used to them and take no notice.

Roses

While keen rose lovers frown on any underplanting with low growing plants as they claim they rob the roses of nourishment, experience has proved that roses can be underplanted happily.

Underplanting

Obviously you apply fertilizers more generously to underplanted roses – twice the amount, say, of soluble fertilizer – and of course roses, like most plants, respond well to foliar or leaf feeding. There are various leaf feeds available and these are sprayed on to wet both sides of the leaves and are additional to whatever fertilizer treatments are applied to the soil.

As soon as the bushes come into full leaf you can start applying a leaf feed and repeat it four or five times every 10-14 days.

Rose bushes are not attractive for six to seven months of the year and if they are in full view of your windows some plants growing under them cheer up the beds. In autumn you can plant small bulbs and other spring flowers.

In April you can plant dwarf campanulas such as *C. portensch-lagiana* and *C. garganica*, *Saxifraga umbrosa* (London Pride), *Polygonum*

vacciniifolium, *Iberis* 'Little Gem', or 'Snowflake', aubrietas, single and double white arabis, dwarf Michaelmas daisies, dwarf pinks and many other low growing perennial plants.

Hardy annuals may also be sown this month or early May – dwarf godetias, sweet alyssum, mignonette, night scented stock, California poppies, linarias and candytuft, for example. Dwarf nasturtiums may be sown in early May.

When danger of frost is past plant other low growing flowers – the half hardy petunias, really dwarf marigolds (tagetes) and nemesias for example.

Although it is not now the practice to underplant rose beds with named varieties of violas propagated from cuttings because of the danger of the 'pansy sickness' (an umbrella name for various virus diseases) many gardeners raise pansies from seed and these last very happily for a whole season. Sown in spring, they are planted in the summer and start flowering in autumn. Often they carry a few flowers all winter and really make a brave show from early spring right into late summer.

Weeds and pests

If you do not have plants growing under roses it is in some ways easier to keep them free from weeds. Once the ground has been cleaned by lightly forking over the topsoil, it may be watered with a residual weedkiller, such as Herbon Garden Herbicide, which will prevent the growth of annual weeds for up to 12 or 14 weeks.

If there are perennial weeds present, spot treat these with a total weedkiller such as Weedol or Tumbleweed. Take care, of course, not to let any of the chemicals come into contact with the foliage or green stems of your roses.

Aphis – greenfly – and caterpillars can appear this month so keep a sharp watch for them. Take

a look at your roses twice a week, and turn over a leaf here and there as there may be caterpillars underneath.

Spray with a suitable insecticide or with one of the 'cocktails' – a combined insecticide and fungicide such as 'Roseclear' or 'Hexyl', which will take care of various pests and diseases.

As soon as the soil begins to warm up – usually about the third week of April in the south, or in early May in the north – apply a mulch to the rose beds to conserve moisture, smother weeds and provide nourishment for the roses.

It is important to hoe off any weeds so that the mulch is applied to clean ground, also that the soil is thoroughly moist.

Flowers from seed

Continue to sow hardy annuals in the open ground – or if the weather and soil were not right in March make the first sowings when conditions permit. There is no need to worry if sowing has to be delayed even until late in April or early May. The seeds will germinate more quickly and the seedlings will grow faster as the soil warms up later in the month. Also slugs will have less time to find them.

It is important to weed and thin seedlings of annual flowers as soon as they are large enough to handle. It is surprising how much the seedlings suffer if their growth is checked by competition from weeds or indeed from each other.

Thinning seedlings is normally done in two stages. Firstly, pull out the surplus seedlings leaving those remaining at half the final desired distance apart – this is an insurance against slugs or other pests taking their toll. Secondly, a week or two later the seedlings should be given their second thinning to leave them at their final distance apart – this is usually indicated in the instructions on the packet.

Lagurus ovatus, ornamental grass.

If the soil is on the dry side it is wise to water the seedlings after thinning to settle them back if they have been loosened by the removal of their neighbours or weed seedlings.

Many half hardy annuals may be sown now in a frame, under cloches, or in a cold greenhouse.

Some hardy annuals are really splendid for cutting – such as sweet peas, larkspurs, cornflowers, love in a mist (nigella) and calendulas. So too are many of the half hardy annuals such as asters, annual rudbeckias, antirrhinums, stocks and zinnias which we may be planting out next month. If space is available it is worthwhile sowing or planting a few short rows of these annuals in an odd corner of the garden for cutting.

There are also various ornamental grasses which may be sown now and used in flower arrangements in summer and autumn, or dried to embellish winter arrangements.

Seedsmen offer a mixture of these ornamental grasses and several separate species and varieties such as *Briza maxima* (quaking grass), *Eragrostis elegans,*

Lagurus ovatus (hare's tail) and a form of pennisetum (fountain grass). All these are easy to grow and very useful for cutting.

Alpines

Remove by hand any weeds as soon as they are large enough to handle. Hoe gently any large areas and if the covering of stone chippings is disturbed add some more around the plants.

Slugs and snails are very active now if the weather is showery. Keep up the control by using slug pellets, powder or liquid slug killer.

Water plants in sinks or raised beds in dry spells if necessary.

This is a good time to plant alpines provided the soil is neither too wet nor too dry. All rock garden plants need to be planted very firmly. Press the soil down firmly with your hands and make sure the roots are well anchored. If they were pot grown as most bought plants now are, make sure the ball of soil is moist before you plant it. It is very difficult to wet a dry ball once it has been planted.

Water plants if necessary 30-40 hours after planting.

Cold greenhouse

This is a busy month with many annuals sown in March ready for pricking out. Propagation of hardy herbaceous plants, house plants and greenhouse plants like pelargoniums, coleus and fuchsias from soft cuttings may be done as well as sowing more annuals – like French marigolds, petunias, asters and alyssum. Herbs and primulas for next season may also be sown.

It is also a tricky time for cold and cool greenhouse management because of the greatly fluctuating temperature changes caused by April weather. Growing plants will require more water; air should be given whenever possible; tender young seedlings and newly rooted

cuttings, as well as primulas, cinerarias and other heat sensitive plants must be shielded from hot sun.

Raise alpine plants from seeds, sowing them in well crocked pans of light compost. Sow very thinly, barely cover the seeds with finely sifted compost or sand, then cover the pans with panes of glass topped by a sheet of newspaper.

Wipe the condensed moisture from the underside of the glass each morning and remove it entirely when the seedlings appear, but still protect these from strong sunlight. Later on they may be pricked off and potted singly and kept in a cold frame.

At the end of the month in the south of Britain tomatoes (raised from seed in March) may be planted in greenhouse borders or in large pots. They will need plenty of light.

Indian azaleas which have finished flowering indoors may now be brought into the cold greenhouse. Knock them out of their pots, trim off old blooms and repot them in slightly larger pots without breaking the soil balls. These must have ample drainage; the compost used for filling in is made up of peat (4 parts) and silver sand (1 part) (parts by bulk) or a proprietary loamless compost. Syringe the foliage morning and evening to encourage new shoots to sprout.

Unless there are benches either side of the house prepare soil borders where tomatoes, chrysanthemums or other crops may be grown. The soil should have been dug over in March or the previous autumn, so now only give it a topdressing of a general fertilizer and lightly work this in.

If bought tomato plants are used, go for stocky, short jointed, rich green leaved plants that have been hardened under cool (but not cold) conditions and plant them 18 in (45 cm) apart, in the south of the country. In the north it is best to leave planting until May.

It is important to stake each

plant right away and tie it to the cane as it grows. If planted late in the day, with the prospect of a cold night ahead, delay watering them until the following day.

Continue sowing annuals for planting outside next month or in early June. Use clean containers, filled with seed compost and very gently firmed. Sow thinly but evenly, just covering the seed with sifted compost or sand.

Spray over the surface with water lightly or – in the case of very small seeds – stand the containers in a bath of shallow water until the soil has drawn up enough to moisten the surface soil.

After placing containers on the greenhouse bench cover them with paper to prevent excessive drying out but remove it immediately germination takes place. Some gardeners use hessian for this purpose instead of paper and keep it nicely moist.

Cool greenhouse

Potting and pricking out seedlings will be the main tasks this month.

Sow cucumbers, coleus, stocks, French and runner beans; also primulas for next spring's flowering.

Remove bulbs which have finished flowering to a cold frame to ripen off.

Towards the end of the month start feeding plants in full growth.

Dahlias

Cuttings rooted last month should now be potted singly in 4 or 5 in (10 or 13 cm) pots. There is still plenty of time to take and root more cuttings.

Prepare the ground for dahlias now. They are not hungry plants but it is worth working in a double handful of bonemeal to the square yard/metre as you dig over the ground. Dahlias are not happy when planted right next to other

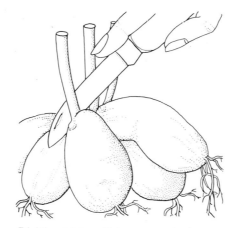

Dividing dahlias. Make sure each piece has one or two new shoots and at least one tuber.

plants. They are much happier on their own.

Towards the end of the month old dahlia tubers may be planted out, setting them down so that there is 6 in (15 cm) of soil above the tubers.

The old plants may be divided by cutting the old stem with a sharp knife, so that each piece has one or two new shoots and at least one tuber attached to it. Unlike potatoes, dahlia tubers will not produce new shoots. These have to come from the 'crown', the point where the tubers join the old stem.

Chrysanthemums

Cuttings of the early flowering varieties which were taken and inserted in March will be ready for hardening off now in a cold frame. If there are sharp frosts cover the frames with sacks or hessian.

Gradually accustom the plants to more air and towards the end of the month, in the south, the light at least may be left propped open all night. Watch for pests, especially slugs and aphids.

Most gardeners want to grow greenhouse chrysanthemums for cut flowers, either as sprays with several flowers on a stem, or disbudded to produce one large flower on say 6 to 8 stems on each plant.

To encourage the production of side growths the top of the plant may be pinched out later this month if the plants do not produce side shoots naturally. To obtain a large number of flowers pinch the tip out around the middle of this month and pinch or 'stop' the resulting side growths again in mid June.

For large flowers with outdoor or garden varieties those to bloom in the greenhouses are disbudded. The single Fiery Furnace is a greenhouse variety; the double garden is 'Gambit'.

Hardy border flowers

Garden varieties of wild plants often achieve their extra height or larger and heavier trusses of flowers at the expense of stamina. Moreover, when plants are grown in close proximity to others, as in hardy borders, the stems tend to elongate as the flowers stretch up to the light. The hollow stems of delphiniums and lupins also create problems. All these factors make certain plants vulnerable to strong winds, heavy rain and thunderstorms.

Staking

Unfortunately broken or bedraggled stems cannot grow straight again so to prevent them from sprawling in the first place susceptible plants have to be staked. April is a good time for this operation while the young growths are still quite small.

Plants which carry their inflorescences on tall spikes, like foxtail lilies (eremuri) and hollyhocks need individual stakes or canes to each stem, preferably painted green to make them inconspicuous. Tie the stems to the stakes firmly but loosely enough to allow for growth, using green twist, string or raffia.

The ideal support for most other plants, particularly those which make a lot of stems, are peasticks made from hazel twigs. Thrust these into the soil between and around the plants so that the young shoots can grow through and above them. By the time the flowers appear you should not be able to see any sign of the peasticks.

Unfortunately peasticks are hard to find these days but garden centres sell various types of metal stakes, usually in the form of thick galvanized hoops of various heights and sizes on two or more legs. Others have only one leg but the hoop can be opened at the top and latched onto a second support, so that given sufficient stakes you can support really large plants of peonies, delphiniums and such like.

Another idea is to combine netting with wire supports or wooden stakes, securing the two together so that the netting is stretched over the plant several inches up from its base. As the stems grow they will then work their way through the netting and receive adequate support.

Obviously the choice between these methods depends on price.

Staking hardy border flowers with peasticks. If you cannot get hold of these, then metal stakes make an excellent substitute.

Various types of wire supports for plants; rather expensive perhaps but they will last for many years and be cheap in the long run.

Old delphinium plants tend to produce far too many shoots. These should be thinned to leave about 5 to 8 of the strongest growths.

Bulbs

Narcissi will need constant deadheading this month in order to keep the garden tidy. Except where bulbs are left to naturalize do not let the flowers go on to develop seed-pods.

Once flowering is over give the bulbs a good watering and apply several soluble leaf feeds at fortnightly intervals. This will enable the foliage to manufacture and send down food to the new bulbs, thus ensuring flowers for next year.

Many summer flowering bulbs and tuberous plants can be put into the ground this month (see also p 106).

Divide schizostylis plants, giving them a moist sunny situation. They will bloom from September to November.

Lawns

Nothing smartens up a garden more than neat tidy lawn edges. If some have been a little worn down or the grass has grown down the edge and into a border (or on to a path), it may be necessary to cut back these edges using a spade or a 'half moon' lawn edging tool.

Cutting, repairing, trimming

Place a board along the edge and cut up to this. Try not to cut away more turf than is necessary to true up the edge, because over the years beds and borders will become larger and the turf area smaller.

After a few years of trueing up it sometimes happens that where turf borders a gravel path or drive, the regularly trueing up will result in an unsightly muddy patch between the gravel and the turf.

Either this has to be filled in with more gravel or the grass lifted and brought out again to come right up to the gravel. This is not difficult – the gap left when a section of turf is moved over is filled with fine soil; after it has settled and been firmed seed is sown.

Edging the lawn with long-handled shears each time it is cut also puts a finish on the garden. If it is done regularly and not in rainy weather or if you wish to have the garden especially spic and span for an occasion, you can usually leave the trimmings there to shrivel up.

But if the 'whiskers' have been allowed to grow too long it is best to gather them up. When using long-handled lawn edging shears, always lean over and lay the shears back towards you so that the handles are at an angle of about 45 degrees to the lawn. In this way you can trim the grass a good half inch or more into the lawn. Thus it will take several more days to grow again over the edge than it would if you merely stood upright and held the shears vertically.

Humps and hollows

The gardener's dream is of a smooth lawn an even lush green from end to end. This is not possible if there are humps and hollows on the lawn. The grass grows longer and greener in the hollows and tends to be 'scalped' by the mower or cut too closely and become pale coloured on the humps.

The humps can be levelled by making H-shaped slits across them

and lifting and turning back the turf each way from the crossbar of the H. Then sufficient soil is removed with a spade so that the turf when relaid is level with the rest of the lawn.

Hollows if they are not too deep may be filled in by sifting fine soil over them – just sufficient to cover the grass and brushing it into the roots, leaving some grass showing. The grass will soon grow through.

It may be necessary to repeat this operation several times. If the hollows are fairly deep it is probably easier and quicker to roll back the turf as described above for humps and fill in with enough soil to bring the turf level with the rest of the lawn. This smoothing up and levelling is really worthwhile and does make a great difference to the lawn.

It often happens, however, that after sifting on the soil to fill the hollows weeds will germinate. These will mostly be annual weeds which will disappear after a few mowings. If some perennial weeds appear among them such as dandelions or plantains these are easily dealt with by applying a selective weedkiller.

In April, worms are feeding near the surface of lawns and can make it very unsightly with their casts of soil. It is important not to

allow these casts to be trodden into the turf or flattened by the mower. Brush them off with a broom otherwise bare patches may occur and weed seeds or moss spores will usually germinate on them. There are various proprietary worm killers available which will destroy the worms below the surface.

Give the lawn its second dressing of fertilizer this month – or if you did not put one on in March apply the first one now and another in four weeks' time.

Trees and shrubs

Prune forsythias used as wall specimens or for hedges. Cut back flowering branches to younger un-flowered shoots and tie in as required.

Forsythia pruning.

Evergreen trees and shrubs, including conifers transplant well this month. Retain a ball of soil round the roots and spray over the foliage after planting to counteract moisture losses through transpiration.

Mulch the ground around with leafsoil, bracken or well rotted manure to conserve moisture and prevent drying by spring winds.

If for any reason the roots of evergreens become damaged reduce some of the leaves on the branches. For planting instructions, see p 145.

Clip ivy on walls.

Reducing a hump in a lawn. The first thing is to make an 'H'-shaped cut with a spade.

Roll back the turves, remove the necessary amount of soil and replace the turves.

MAY

Fruit: Thin grapes and gooseberry fruits. Prune vines; prune plums and cherries and other stone fruits. Remove flowers from newly planted fruit trees. Remove unwanted raspberry shoots; tie in old canes; spray if necessary. Keep weeds down and water in dry spells.

Vegetables: Sow sweet corn; sow outdoor cucumbers. Sow French and runner beans in the open; erect supports for runner beans. Sow marrows, or plant young plants. Plant brassicas, French and runner beans raised under glass. Plant tomatoes. Thin and weed seedlings. Earth up seedlings. Watch for pests.

Flowers from seed: Sow hardy and half hardy annuals; sow biennials. Plant half hardy and tender annuals late in the month.

Alpines: Sow seeds of alpines. Continue to plant new alpines and keep down the weeds. Trim aubrietas and alyssum after flowering. Water alpines in dry spells.

Cold and cool greenhouse: Ventilate and shade the house; damp down the floor on hot days. Prick off seedlings of tender plants. Plant tomatoes in a cold house in the north.
  Pot up begonias and gloxinias. Harden off hardy perennials and annuals in cold frame. Feed all pot plants. Rest cyclamen. Pot on chrysanthemums and place outside at the end of the month. Remove alpines that have finished flowering. Stake pelargoniums. Plant hanging baskets.

Dahlias: Plant young dahlias towards the end of the month in the south. Draw soil over shoots of old tubers planted in April if frost threatens.

Chrysanthemums: Plant outdoor chrysanthemums. Stand potted later flowering varieties outside. Spray as required against pests.

Hardy border flowers: Continue staking; thin shoots where required; lift and replant polyanthus.

Bulbs: Mulch lilies and spray against botrytis disease. Lift and heel in bulbs which have been used in spring bedding. Plant crinums.

Lawns: Apply selective weedkillers. Apply acid fertilizer if clover is present.

Trees and shrubs: Prune or trim shrubs as necessary. Plant bamboos.

Fruit

Reduce laterals on both indoor and outdoor vines to leave only one on each spur. Stop these in turn beyond the flower trusses as soon as they threaten to interfere or take light from other laterals.

At the end of the month give cold house grapes their first thinning.

To help newly planted fruit trees prevent first year fruiting by removing any flowers.

Remove stray raspberry shoots coming up between rows and mulch the ground around the new canes; tie in the latter.

Fix nets to protect strawberries.

Any necessary major pruning of plums, cherries and other stone fruits should be carried out between now and mid-August.

For large dessert fruits of gooseberries, thin some of the berries now.

Weed fruit bushes and trees regularly and water if required.

Vegetables

As seedlings show through the ground, thin and weed them as soon as they are large enough to handle. If the vegetable and weed seedlings compete with each other for air, light and water, and if the weeding and thinning is delayed even for a week or more the seedlings can suffer quite a serious setback from which they may not fully recover.

If you thin and weed seedlings when the soil is dry, run down the rows with a watering can fitted with a fine rose to water the seedlings and settle them back in the soil.

Plant Brussels sprouts, leeks, summer and winter cabbages and celery. To control cabbage root fly scatter a quarter of a teaspoonful of bromophos around each Brussels sprout and cabbage plant.

French and runner beans

Plant French and runner beans raised under glass or sow them in the open this month. Sow the French beans 4½ in (11 cm) apart and thin the seedlings to 9 in (23 cm) apart.

There are several ways of supporting runner beans; the traditional method is a long double row of bean poles laced together at the top with a horizontal pole. The poles are placed 6 in (15 cm) apart with the rows 24 in (60 cm) apart.

Then there is a 'maypole' method – one stout pole 6 ft (2 m) high with say 10 strings (not plastic covered wire), coming down from it to be anchored by 'hairpins' of bent wire about 24-36 in (61-91 cm) away from the pole.

One easy way to grow runner beans is to let them twine up four bamboo canes, or stakes tied together at the top into a pyramid.

The pole and strings should be put into place first and the bean plants set in position towards the end of the month in the south or in the first week of June in the north.

You can sow runner bean seeds at the base of these supports this month – better sow two seeds to each position as the germination of runner beans seeds is sometimes rather disappointing.

Yet another way of growing runner beans is by dwarfing them, ie, nipping out the climbing shoot as soon as it appears. The plants will not crop so heavily as those allowed to climb but they often set their pods better.

There is also a non-climbing runner bean 'Hammond's Dwarf'.

Most gardeners have experienced disappointments with runner beans failing to set pods. Sometimes this is due to birds stripping the buds, but they will also strip the flowers and it seems that they do more damage to red-flowered runner beans than to white-flowered varieties.

The old practice of syringing the flowers or spraying water from a hose is still worth doing. More important is to see that the plants have plenty of water at the roots in dry spells – up to 2 gallons per sq yard (7.5 litres per sq m) twice a week.

It seems that white-flowered runner beans tend to set better than the red-flowered varieties and various theories are advanced – one is that insects go more readily to the white than to the red flowers and better pollination results.

Dwarf or French beans it appears are self pollinated and the climbing varieties of French beans usually give an excellent crop.

A welcome recent develop-

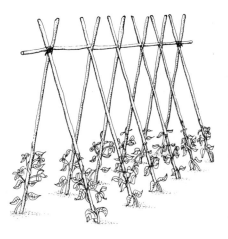

Runner beans grow well up a 'maypole' made with 10 strings, anchored with a hoop of wire and tied to the top of a pole.

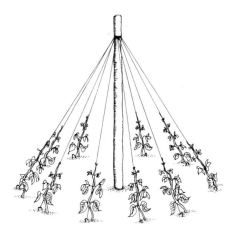

A barrage of bean poles – a very economical method of growing for small plot holders.

The popular pink-flowered Runner bean 'Sunset' may be relied on to produce heavy crops.

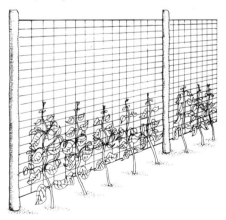

Wire or plastic net for staking peas or beans.

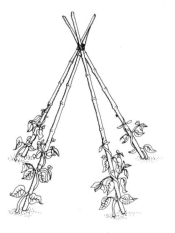

Wigwam supports for runner beans.

ment in runner beans has been the appearance of stringless varieties such as 'Fry', white flowered and 'Red Knight' red flowered.

General tasks

Towards the end of the month sow marrow seeds or plant out young marrow plants bought from a nursery or garden centre. Sow two or three seeds or plant young marrows at a distance of about 3 ft 3 in (1 m) apart.

Thin the seedlings to one per station. Many people plant marrows on top of a compost heap. This is not a good idea because perched up several feet above ground they will almost certainly dry out. It is far better to plant the marrows at the bottom of the heap and let them ramble up over it.

Start to earth up potatoes.

Stake peas, or provide netting support.

Black fly may infest broad beans this month – clustering thickly around the young top growth. Either pinch out the tops of the plants when four flower trusses have formed, or spray or dust the plants with a suitable insecticide.

In the south tomato plants may be planted outdoors at the end of the month or under cloches in more northerly districts.

Sweet corn may be sown in peat pots in a cold frame or greenhouse early in the month or in the open towards the end of the month and covered with cloches in the north.

Towards the end of the month sweet corn may be sown in the open in the south. Sow two or three seeds together leaving about 12-14 in (30-35 cm) between the groups and about 24-36 in (60-90 cm) between rows. To ensure good pollination and well filled cobs, sow or plant sweet corn in a block of short rows rather than in a long row.

Outdoor or ridge cucumbers may be sown in peat pots this month under cold glass.

A really colourful display of annual flowers at Wisley including ageratums, verbenas, tagetes and a form of *Chrysanthemum (matricaria) parthenium*.

Flowers from seed

Continue to sow hardy annuals. Several half hardy annuals such as nasturtiums, cosmeas and zinnias may be sown in the open ground now.

In the last week of the month half hardy or tender annuals, such as petunias, zinnias and marigolds may be planted out in the south half of the country. In the north and in Scotland planting should be delayed until the first or second week of June.

Wallflowers, myosotis (forget-menots), sweet williams, fox-gloves, and Canterbury bells may be sown this month in the open for lining out in a spare piece of ground when large enough in June or July.

Draw shallow drills as described for hardy annuals about 6 in (15 cm) apart in a well prepared seed bed. If possible have the seedbed and the plot intended for lining out as near a water supply as possible as it is virtually certain that both will need watering perhaps quite frequently during the summer.

If you have a greenhouse or cold frame you may prefer to sow these seeds very thinly in pots of seed sowing compost and prick off the seedlings when they are large enough to handle into boxes of potting compost. They may then be lined out when large enough.

A good way of raising seeds of biennials is to sow them very thinly either in drills 6 in (15 cm) apart, or scattered on a 2 in (5 cm) layer of fine soil in a cold frame or under cloches.

Remove the frame-light or lift off the cloches as soon as the seedlings are about 1 in (2.5 cm) or so high; shade them from strong sunshine and give plenty of ventilation until the glass covering is removed.

If you have an unsightly rubbish heap you want to hide, climbing nasturtiums on ornamental grounds trained up a low wire netting fence will make an excellent screen.

The ever popular *Gentiana acaulis*.

Iberis semperflorens, perennial candytuft.

Alpines

Continue to plant alpines and weed the rock garden or sinks. As soon as aubrietas and *Alyssum saxatile* have finished flowering trim them over to keep them neat and tidy. This close trim of aubrietas will encourage new young shoots which will make excellent cuttings to root in June or July.

Seeds of arabis, alyssum, *Aster alpinus, Erinus alpinus,* campanulas, helianthemums, iberis, primulas, edelweiss *(Leontopodium alpinum),* saxifrages, gentians and many other alpines may be sown this month.

As seeds of most of them are small it is best to sow them in pots, or seed trays and keep them under cover – in a frame, under a cloche or in a greenhouse to shelter them from rain until they have germinated.

General seed catalogues list a selection of the commoner rock plants but there are specialist firms that offer many of the choicer and rarer species and varieties.

Water alpines in dry spells if necessary.

Good form of Helianthemum

Cold greenhouse

In May damp down floors and benches regularly, particularly on hot sunny days; also provide plenty of ventilation, water regularly and shade young plants from hot sun.

Shading will present real problems now that the suns' rays are getting stronger. Blinds are useful for this purpose, failing which the glass should be painted outside with a shading material such as Coolglass.

At the beginning of the month prick out seedlings of plants to go outdoors when the risks of frost are past, for example petunias, French marigolds and alyssum.

Firm the compost in shallow boxes to leave a level surface, then hold each seedling carefully by its seed leaves if possible. Make a hole to receive it with a dibber – a short pointed stick – insert the seedling and firm it gently.

An ordinary seedbox takes about 50 young plants. Water with care and if the weather is warm lay a sheet of newspaper over the top to prevent scorching while the plantlets are rooting, but remove it when the sun goes down.

In the north of Britain tomatoes may now be planted in cold greenhouse borders.

Pot up started tubers of begonias and gloxinias.

Harden off hardy perennials and hardy annuals raised from seed or cuttings by putting them in a cold frame outdoors.

Feed pot plants normally kept in the greenhouse with a soluble fertilizer.

Begonias, geraniums, petunias, labelias and busy lizzies fill these tubs and baskets.

Rest cyclamen, including those which have flowered in the home by withholding water gradually, then laying the pots on their sides under the bench to dry off.

Pot on chrysanthemums in their flowering pots, and at the end of the month stand them outdoors on a hard or ash covered surface.

Forced bulbs which have finished flowering can be planted in the garden to provide future cut blooms.

Alpines which have been inside will now have finished flowering so put them in a cold frame early in the month. They can be divided and repotted if this seems necessary.

Regal and zonal pelargoniums will begin to flower and may require staking or tying, and also feeding.

Make up hanging baskets to suspend from greenhouse bars or for hanging outside in June.

Pinch out the growing tips of *Solanum capsicastrum* (sown in March) to make bushy plants.

Cool greenhouse

As above.

Dahlias

Many thousands of dahlia varieties have been bred since the first species were introduced to Europe nearly 200 years ago. New ones appear every year, old ones quietly disappear. Nowadays the giant decorative, giant cactus and semi-cactus varieties with flowers over 10 in (25 cm) across are mainly grown in public parks or by dedicated amateurs for the show bench.

For garden decoration and for cutting the most popular varieties are found in the following groups: small, medium and miniature decoratives; medium, small and miniature or semi-cactus varieties; small ball and miniature ball dahlias; and finally the pompon varieties with flowers up to about 2 in (5 cm) in diameter.

One small group in the small decorative section known as the 'water-lily' type because its slightly incurving florets somewhat resemble water lily flowers, has become very popular in recent years, particularly as cut flowers.

In the south of England the young dahlia plants may be planted towards the end of May. In the north it is best to wait until the first or even the second week of June to be sure that danger of frost is past. Indeed, even at Wisley (an area bedevilled by frost), dahlias are never planted until the end of the first week of June.

Place a good stout stake in position before planting the young dahlia.

If old dahlia tubers were planted in April the shoots may appear above ground early this

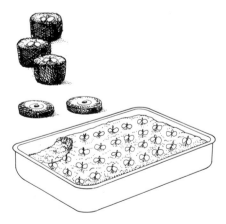

Seedlings may be pricked off in boxes of compost or into Jiffy 7's – compressed peat pellets which swell when wetted.

Protect dahlia shoots from frost by drawing soil over them or covering with sacks or newspapers.

month so if there is a threat of frost draw soil over the shoots or cover them with straw, an old sack or even two or three thicknesses of newspaper.

Chrysanthemums

If you are starting from scratch with chrysanthemums and have no greenhouse or frame, May is a good month to begin. Buy a few early varieties to grow outdoors. They may be planted out in the first week of the month in the milder parts of the country but in the north it is best to wait until the middle of the month.

Early flowering
Early flowering chrysanthemums may be grown for garden decoration in beds or borders or purely for cut flowers. For garden decoration they are grown as 'spray' flowers – which means all the buds are allowed to flower. Indeed if grown for cut flowers many people prefer spray blooms to the much larger disbudded blooms.

Also for garden decoration the hardy Korean varieties and pompon chrysanthemums are very popular. In borders for garden decoration the chrysanthemums may be planted about 18 in (45 cm) apart. For cut flowers they may be planted either in rows at the same distance apart and eventually supported with bamboo canes and strings.

Another and less time consuming way of growing chrysanthemums for cutting is to plant them in a square or rectangle and support them with welded 8 in (20 cm) square mesh wire.

Lay the wire panel on the ground and drive four stout stakes in, one at each corner of the wire panel sloping the stakes slightly outwards. The stakes need to be about 5 ft (1.5 m) long so that there is about 4 ft (1.2 m) above ground. Plant the chrysanthemums, one to every other square. Then, as

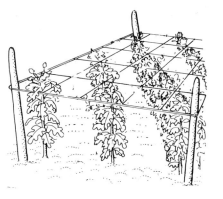

Planting chysanthemums under wire mesh. As they grow the panel is raised.

the plants grow, the wire panel can be pulled up the stakes to support the plants. As the stakes slope slightly outwards the mesh is held quite taut without any need to tie it to the stakes. It is important not to plant too deeply – the ball of roots should just be covered with soil, no more. Scatter plenty of slug pellets around the plants.

Late flowering
Plants of varieties to be brought in to flower in a greenhouse in late autumn may be potted now in 9 in (20 cm) pots in which they will flower. After a few days they may be stood outside until September when they should be brought back into the greenhouse.

For this final potting use John Innes potting compost No 3 or a peat-based, loamless compost. Insert three 5 ft (1.50 m) canes in each pot. In the north this final potting should be delayed until early June. Outdoors make a level standing ground in full sun for the plants. Cover the area with weathered clinker ash or even shingle.

To prevent the plants from being blown over by the wind fix a wire between two stout stakes along the row of pots and tie one of the canes in the pot to the wire.

Keep a sharp watch for greenfly from now on and be prepared to spray all chrysanthemum plants with a suitable insecticide every 7 to 10 days if necessary.

Hardy border flowers

Continue staking hardy perennials.

Thin down shoots of plants like Michaelmas daisies, phlox and delphiniums, removing thin shoots and weak growths and retaining only the sturdiest stems.

Polyanthus plants lifted from spring display beds should be replanted in moist shade. Many can be divided beforehand.

Bulbs

Established lilies growing in mixed borders or shrubberies should be given a generous mulch of leaf soil, not only to provide them with food but to keep the roots cool. This particularly applies to *Lilium regale, L. henryi, L. martagon* and their hybrids; but even newly planted stem rooters will appreciate a mulch.

Leaf spot or botrytis blight is a problem with many lilies. It causes brown spots on the leaves, which gradually enlarge and the flowers die. Stems, buds and flowers can all be attacked, but curiously not the bulbs.

The spores are wind borne, spreading to other plants during moist weather, but the disease can be controlled by giving the plants regular (fortnightly) sprays in rainy weather in early summer, using a copper fungicide.

Towards the end of this month spring bedding will be taken up and replaced with summer flowers. Any bulbs lifted should be heeled in and treated as described on p 97.

Crinums can now be planted in warm, sheltered, south or west facing borders. Set them 8 in (20 cm) deep. They may need winter protection – with leaves, bracken, glass or polythene sheeting. In the north they will probably be best planted in tubs which can be moved under cover for winter.

Handy Hint: When tulips have finished flowering in May we normally lift them and heel them in to dry off. The bulbs may be re-planted after the foliage has shrivelled away. The plants are laid in a shallow trench at an angle of about 30 degrees and covered with soil up to half their length.

Lay a piece of old wire or plastic netting on the bottom of the trench and place the tulips on this before covering them with soil. Then when the time comes to lift them in July or August, all you need is somebody to take the other end of the net and you lift up all the bulbs together so that none are left in the soil.

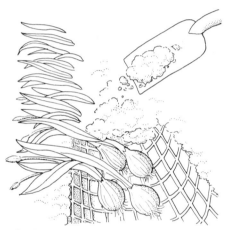

Spring bulbs laid on netting in a trench.

Lawns

By now weeds are growing in abundance – the more so if the lawn was given the dressings of fertilizer as recommended, in March and April. They may look ominous and unsightly now, but the larger the leaf area of the weeds, the more easily they will absorb a lethal dose of a selective lawn weedkiller and the quicker they will disappear.

Killing weeds
These weedkillers, watered on to the lawn, are absorbed by the weed leaves, and passed down to the roots. After a few days the weed

Crinum powellii, a lovely summer bulb.

leaves twist and curl, and very soon the weeds die. The grass is of course unharmed. Do not apply these weedkillers until the weather has really warmed up – mid to late May in the south, first or second week of June in the north – as they work much more quickly in warm weather. Ideally the night temperatures should not fall below 50°F (10°C).

There are many types of weed that infest our lawns. The commonest, of course, are daisies, plantains and dandelions and these

broadleaved weeds are the easiest to control. Less easy are the creeping weeds like yarrow, creeping buttercup, speedwell, mouse ear chickweed, pearlwort and yellow trefoil; these are more difficult to deal with.

There are weedkillers now that will kill virtually all lawn weeds, but to do so, the solution must thoroughly wet the weed foliage. It is well worth while raking creeping weeds up with a wire rake so that the greatest area of foliage is exposed to the chemical. With some stubborn weeds it may be necessary to give a second application.

The kinds of weeds that appear in a lawn may indicate whether the soil is acid or alkaline. Clover grows especially well in alkaline soils. Moss is generally a sign that the lawn is acid (but not always because there are dozens of kinds of moss).

The best grass, however, is produced on lawns that are slightly acid, so by applying an acid fertilizer such as sulphate of ammonia, one can bring an alkaline lawn into a mildly acid state and the clover will not reappear. Apply about ¼ oz per sq yard (7 g per sq m) of sulphate of ammonia every two weeks, well watered in for the next two months and repeat the applications in the autumn.

Moss is best dealt with by killing it with a proprietary moss killer. Leave it to disintegrate. There is no point in raking moss out of a lawn – you will only spread it because every tiny piece of moss left on the turf will grow and spread.

Normally most lawns have only isolated patches of weeds and these are treated by watering on a selective weedkiller from a watering can fitted with a fine rose or a 'sprinkle bar'.

These bars are obtainable in various widths to fit any watering can spout. If however there is a fair sprinkling of weeds all over the lawn it is worthwhile marking it off

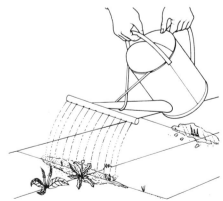
Apply weedkillers with a sprinkle bar.

in strips with string so that you do not water on the weedkiller twice over the same area.

Don't forget to wash out the can and rose thoroughly, several times, after use with warm water adding a good dash of detergent if you intend to use the can for other purposes.

Repairing

This is a good time of year to repair bare patches. The easiest way, if possible, is to lift a piece of turf from part of the garden where it will not be greatly missed and use this to repair the bare patch. Sow grass seed in the place where you lifted the turf.

The other quick method of repairing bare patches – if there is a local garden centre near – is to buy a few turves. It is of course much more expensive than sowing seed but if you want instant results it may be worth it. Alternatively prick up the bare patches with a fork, break the soil down fine and sow grass seed.

Plastic pegged over grass seed.

Water it well with a fine rosed can and then cover the patch with pieces of thin polythene sheeting pegged down with bent hoops of wire. This will keep the seed moist, hasten germination and prevent the birds from taking the seed or disturbing it by scratching about on the fine soil.

Another method of repairing

bare patches or indeed of making a new lawn quickly (which is much less costly than turfing the whole area) is to buy some turf, break it into pieces about the size of a small teacup and plant these about 3-4 in (8-10 cm) apart.

Then sow grass seed in the soil between the bits of turf. The whole area will knit together very quickly. The difference in cost of turfing or sowing a lawn is really considerable – turf can cost anything from 10 to 20 times the price of seed depending on the quality of the turf, and the supplier used.

Irrigation

Newly sown lawns may need watering if the weather turns dry just after the seed has germinated. Newly turfed lawns may also need regular watering in dry spells. Established lawns should, of course, be watered generously once a week in dry spells throughout the summer (also pp 19-20).

Trees and shrubs

Choisya ternata (Mexican orange blossom).

Cut out old wood from *Choisya ternata* and trim straggly bushes.

Plant bamboos.

To keep cytisus (brooms) compact prune them directly after flowering by taking these flowered shoots back to within ½ in (12 mm) of the old stems. Do not cut into this old wood or the plant may die.

Dahlia 'Nationwide'.

Dahlia 'Shy Princess'.

Dahlia 'Dana Jacklyn'.

Dahlia 'Ballade'.

Dahlia 'Senior Ball'.

Dahlia 'Yelno Velvena'.

Dahlia 'Shandy'.

Dahlia 'Cherida'.

Dahlia 'Quel Diable'.

Dahlia 'Hannah Gordon'.

Dahlia 'Hamari Saffron'.

Dahlia varieties

The following is a selection of varieties popular with the amateur garden:

'Alltami Classic'. Yellow; small ball; 4 ft (1.2 m).
'Ballade'. Orange and yellow; medium decorative; 4 ft 6 in (1.4 m).
'Burnside'. Lemon yellow; semi-cactus; 3 ft 6in (1 m).
'Cherida'. Bronze and lilac; miniature ball; 36 in (91 cm).
'Dana Jacklyn'. Mid-yellow; medium decorative; 5 ft (1.5 m).
'Dr Grainger'. Purple; pompon; 3 ft 6 in (1 m).
'Ebony Bay'. Ruby red; miniature decorative; 3 ft 6 in (1 m).
'Hamari Princess'. Yellow tipped lavender; large cactus; 5 ft 6 in (1.68 m).
'Hamari Saffron'. Yellow; medium semi-cactus; 4 ft 6 in (1.4 m).
'Hannah Gordon'. Coral pink; small decorative; 3 ft 6 in (1 m).
'Jan Lennon'. Pink and white; medium cactus; 4 ft 6 in (1.4 m).
'Lismore Peggy'. Lavender; pompon; 3 ft 6 in (1 m).
'Ludwig Helser'. Orange blends; medium cactus; 4 ft 6 in (1.4 m).
'Monk Marc'. Pink and white; small cactus; 36 in (91 cm).
'Moor Place'. Purple; pompon; 36 in (91 cm).
'Nationwide'. Bronze blends; small decorative; 4 ft (1.2 m).
'Pink Shirley Alliance'. Medium semi-cactus; 4 ft 6 in (1.4 m).
'Pink Symbol'. Pink; medium semi-cactus; 4 ft 6 in (1.4 m).
'Senior Ball'. White flushed lavender; small ball; 5 ft (1.5 m).
'Shandy'. Bronze; small semi-cactus; 3 ft 6 in (1 m).
'Shy Princess'. White; medium cactus; 5 ft (1.5 m).
'Willo's Violet'. Violet; pompon; 3 ft 6 in (1 m).
'Wootton Impact'. Bronze and yellow; medium semi-cactus; 4 ft 6 in (1.4 m).
'Yelno Velvena'. Deep red; water lily decorative; 3 ft 6 in (1 m).

JUNE

Fruit: Pick soft fruits regularly; protect strawberries with straw or mats; propagate some runners if required for a new bed. Remove unwanted runners. Thin pears, peaches and plums if bearing heavy crops. Summer prune soft fruits. Water in dry spells.

Vegetables: Sow various crops outdoors. Plant sweet corn, leeks, marrows, outdoor cucumbers and tomatoes. Stake and tie tomatoes; pinch out side shoots. Feed all vegetables. Gather and dry herbs. Cut off rhubarb flower stems. Watch for pests and spray if necessary. Protect crops against birds. Water all crops in dry spells.

Roses: Watch for signs of mildew and black spot or rust diseases and spray at the first sign of trouble. Remove suckers. Tie new growths of climbing and rambler roses. Remove dead heads.

Flowers from seed: Thin seedlings as required. Sow hardy perennial flowers. Plant some annuals in a reserve bed to fill gaps later.

Alpines: Keep trimming plants that need to be kept tidy; root cuttings; water alpines in containers.

Cold greenhouse: Plant out all hardy plants. Plunge Indian azaleas to the pot rim outdoors; feed pot plants; remove dead flowers and leaves. Dampen floors. Feed, tie and deshoot tomatoes.

Cool greenhouse: Sow seeds of primulas, cinerarias and calceolarias. Plant early chrysanthemums; stand pot grown varieties outdoors. Plant cucumbers. Pot on solanums.

Dahlias: Feed every two weeks; stop plants two or three weeks after planting. Thin shoots on old plants if necessary. Watch for pests. Water copiously in dry spells and mulch if possible.

Chrysanthemums: Water well in dry spells; feed every 7-10 days. Watch for pests. Stop outdoor varieties three weeks after planting.

Hardy border flowers: Remove dead flowers regularly; keep weeds down; water generously in dry spells, mulch and feed. Fill gaps with bedding plants.

Bulbs: Lift tulips after flowering and heel them in. Plant de Caen anemones.

Trees and shrubs: Remove dead flower heads of laburnums, rhododendrons and azaleas; trim dead flowers on heathers. Water recently planted trees and shrubs. Mulch where possible. Trim shrubs if required.

Fruit

Pick soft fruits regularly as these ripen. If left too long so that they start to rot this can affect succeeding fruits.

Protect strawberry fruits from soil splashes and slugs with a mulch of straw under the foliage. Alternatively use special strawberry mats (from garden centres) or black polythene.

Peg down a few runners for propagation purposes either in the soil nearby, or into pots of soil sunk into the ground. Remove superfluous runners.

Very heavy crops of apples, pears, peaches and plums should be thinned this month.

Summer prune red and white currants, also gooseberries; shorten all laterals back to 5 or 6 leaves but do not touch the leaders. Keep the centres of the bushes open so that the branches bear some resemblance to the ribs of an inverted parasol.

Cordons; prune in the same way and again leave the leaders until such times as these reach the required height. Then cut them back.

Water all fruits in dry weather.

Vegetables

Sow peas, French and runner beans, marrows, beetroot, maincrop carrots, lettuces, radishes, swedes, turnips, sweet corn, spinach and spinach beet in the open. On a prepared seed bed sow calabrese.

Plant sweet corn, leeks, marrows, outdoor cucumbers, and tomatoes. Stake tomatoes and as they grow tie them to their stakes, removing side shoots by pinching them out with the finger and thumb. Do not of course make the mistake of pinching out the flower trusses! Feed all vegetables once every 10-14 days with fertilizer.

Leeks like firm ground. Hoe off any surface weeds and then make holes about 6 in (15 cm) deep, 12 in (30 cm) apart, with a dibber. Trim the leek plants' roots a little and cut the leaves to leave about 6 in (15 cm). Just drop the leek plants into the hole, and fill it with water. This will wash enough soil from the sides of the hole to cover the roots and the leek plants will be able to grow for 6 in (15 cm) with blanched stems.

Protecting strawberries. Black polythene sheeting protects the fruit from mud and slugs.

Strawberry 'Cambridge Favourite', a good variety for growing under cloches.

A scattering of slug pellets.

When fruits start to colour tuck straw around the plants.

Protecting strawberries. As an alternative to straw or plastic sheeting you can use bitumenized paper mats.

Picking gooseberries for cooking or desserts. Running your hand beneath the fruits is the correct technique.

Success with outdoor tomatoes depends on regular feeding – once a week with a soluble fertilizer – and seeing that the plants never go short of water. After a dry spell and when the heavy rain comes, the rush of sap up the plant may cause the tomato fruits to split around the top.

Try to keep tomatoes well supplied with water at all times. One method is to sink a 5 in (10 cm) flower pot to the rim in the ground about 6 in (15 cm) away from the tomato at planting time. Then whenever watering is needed – twice a week perhaps in dry spells – you just fill the pot with water.

Herbs may be gathered and dried for winter use this month and next. The best stage is just before they begin to flower. Some people tie them in small bunches and hang them in an airy shed. But they dry better if spread thinly in a single layer on shallow trays such as tomato or fruit trays which can usually be had from the greengrocer. They may also be dried in an airing cupboard. As soon as they are dry and brittle enough, crumble them and store them in airtight jars.

Lift early potatoes.

With some varieties and in some seasons rhubarb plants may produce fat flower stems. These should be cut off as soon as they appear.

Pests

Pests can be troublesome this month. Black fly will continue to infest broad beans and may even infest runner beans.

In wet spells slugs and snails are on the move so it is worthwhile scattering around plenty of slug pellets or watering the ground with liquid metaldehyde slug killer around lettuces. If birds are a nuisance in the garden put wire or plastic netting over late sown peas or lettuces or spray them with a bird repellent such as 'Stayoff' until the birds lose interest in them.

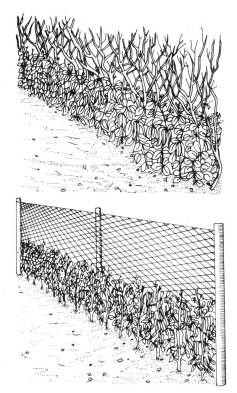

Supporting peas. When obtainable, hazel pea sticks are ideal. Push some small twiggy pieces in at the base to start the peas climbing. Peas may also be grown up plastic string mesh netting stretched between posts; or against wire netting.

Roses

This month the roses begin their summer show. The climbers are usually the first to flower. Often the thornless climber, 'Zephirine Drouhin', double, carmine, sweetly scented, is the first to bloom and incidentally, the first to show signs of mildew. So watch it every day or two and at the first sign of mildew spray with a suitable fungicide.

Spray all the roses in the garden to be on the safe side.

Suckers

Suckers begin to be a nuisance on rose bushes in June. Roses are propagated by budding the different varieties on wild rose stocks. So it often happens that vigorous shoots grow up from these wild stocks and have to be removed.

They are easily recognized; they come from below ground, are usually paler green than the rose variety and their leaflets are much smaller. It is no use just chopping these off at ground level – this is the equivalent of pruning them and each shoot will produce two or three more.

They must be cut off at the point where they leave the roots, below ground. Scrape away the soil and cut the suckers off with a sharp knife. If you have a lot of roses it would pay to buy a sucker cutter. This is a V-shaped blade on a rod about 15 in (38 cm) long with a wooden handle. You just push it down into the soil alongside the sucker on the side nearest the rose bush and chop it off below ground.

Some rose growers are now budding their roses on *Rosa laxa* and they claim that suckers are rarely a problem with this understock.

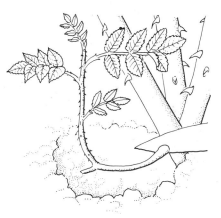

Sever suckers at their base.

New growths

Hopefully, about now, climbing and rambler roses will be producing new growths. The ramblers are much more free with their new stems which come up from ground level.

The climbing roses, however, are much less generous with their new growths. They may produce one or two from low down and generally a few new side growths higher up. They all need to be looked after carefully because they

Rose 'Zephirine Drouhin', thornless sweetly scented and one of the first to flower.

are very easily broken away at the base in heavy thunder showers or high winds; and new growths on these roses are most valuable for replacing worn out branches.

Keep an eye on the climbing varieties and as soon as a new growth has reached about 18-24 in (45-61 cm) in length tie it to the supporting trellis or wires. Or, if it is not long enough to reach them, push in a bamboo cane and tie it to this until it is able to be tied to its permanent support. As any gardener knows, it is heartbreaking to see a long new shoot broken away at the base.

Deadheading

From now on, to keep the garden looking smart, deadheading – the removal of faded flowers – must be done regularly several times a week and especially with roses.

Do not worry too much about climbing and rambler roses. Most of them are 'good diers' which means they drop their petals as the flowers fade. One exception is 'Albertine', that exceedingly

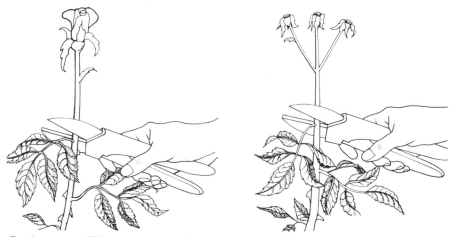

Cutting roses. When cutting for the house or removing dead roses cut just above a leaf with 5 leaflets, allowing another flower to grow.

vigorous climber and very popular, in spite of its habit of retaining the dead flowers, which look like balls of brown paper for several weeks.

When deadheading, or when cutting roses for flower arrangements, always cut to just above an outward pointing leaf with five large leaflets. This you will find, probably, about a third to halfway down the stem. Then, hopefully,

more flowers will be produced in the autumn.

Flowers from seed

Continue to thin seedlings of annuals sown earlier.

Many hardy perennial flowers may be raised from seed sown this month. The seed may be sown in the open as for biennials; but it is more satisfactory (if possible) to sow the seed very thinly in pots or boxes of seed sowing compost in a greenhouse or cold frame and prick them off into peat pots or boxes of John Innes or peat-based compost where they may remain until they are large enough to plant in their flowering positions.

It is worth while planting a few marigolds – varieties of tagetes – in an odd corner with the idea of transplanting them in August to take the place of annuals like clarkias, godetias or California poppies which have finished flowering. Plant them about 12 in (30 cm) apart each way.

Many perennial flowers breed remarkably true from seed – aquilegias, gaillardias, campanulas, oriental poppies, phloxes, red hot pokers (kniphofias), liatris, pyrethrums, monardas (bergamot) hollyhocks and many more. (It is not generally realized that in many garden centres the perennial herbaceous plants offered for sale have been raised from seed.)

Most of those mentioned above breed remarkably true from seed but there is often a certain amount of variation and some of the poorer forms will be discarded, the best of them being propagating by division or root cutting.

If you raise them from seed you may have dozens of plants from a packet of seed and if you have to discard a number of poor forms it is far more cost effective than buying unnamed herbaceous plants one at a time from the shops.

Many of these perennials flower in the year after sowing, so if you have a garden with empty beds and borders in a year or two you can have a fine show of herbaceous plants raised cheaply from seed.

Alpines

Continue to trim over any plants that are likely to become bare or

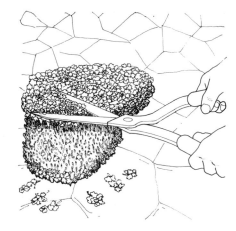

Trim aubrieta back to 6in (15cm) after flowering to stimulate growth of young shoots.

leggy, such as helianthemums and aubrietas. Also cut back any plants that may be growing too strongly and swamping their neighbours.

With many plants some of the growths cut back may be used as cuttings to increase the stock. Especially with shrubby rock plants like *Genista lydia* for example, the condition of the side shoots suitable for cuttings is all important. If they are too young and soft they will probably rot; if they are left too long and become hard they may never root or take many weeks or even months to do so.

Experiment by taking a few cuttings every week this month and next. You will soon find out at which stage of growth cuttings are most likely to root. Remove faded flowers and keep the weeds down – catch them when they are very small and on no account let any set seed.

Water alpines in containers on raised beds or in the rock garden if necessary – especially young plants planted this year.

Cold greenhouse

All hardy plants should be outdoors by now and bedding annuals planted.

Primula malacoides seed can be sown in the cool house to provide spring blooms next year.

Remove Indian azaleas from the greenhouse and plunge them up to the pot rims in moist peat in a semi-shaded part of the garden.

Feed pot plants and regularly remove dead flowers and leaves.

Dampen floors morning and afternoon.

Feed growing tomatoes after a couple of flower trusses have set fruit. If on a bright day you gently spray over the plants with a rose on the watering can, this helps the fruits to set. To be sure of a good set shut the house down about 8 or 9 am and splash water around on the path to create a humid atmosphere.

Tap the tomato supports – canes or strings – smartly to distribute the pollen and reopen the house an hour later. Tie up the main stems and pinch out any side shoots as soon as these are large enough to handle.

Colour in the greenhouse at this time of year will be available from many plants including coleus, ferns, pelargoniums, tuberous and fibrous begonias, abutilons, *Campanula isophylla*, *Plumbago*

Modern double tuberous begonia.

Colourful gloxinias are excellent pot plants.

capensis and gloxinias – also any indoor house plants which are taken into the greenhouse for a period of convalescence in summer.

Cool greenhouse

In the cool house further batches of *Primula malacoides* may be sown, also cinerarias and calceolarias. The calceolaria seed is very fine so must be thinly scattered on fine soil in a pan, then very lightly pressed down with the base of an empty flowerpot. Do not cover it with soil, but place glass or paper over the receptacle until the seeds germinate. Keep cool and in the shade.

Cineraria seed is also very small so is often mixed with a little fine sand to facilitate thin sowing. Cover with glass and paper and keep in the warmest part of the house to germinate.

Primula seed can be lightly covered with fine compost but otherwise treated as for calceolarias.

Chrysanthemums for pot cultivation should now go outdoors on ash beds or a firm surface. Stake and tie them to wires to prevent wind damage.

Early flowering chrysanthemums raised from cuttings may now be planted outside.

Plant cucumbers.

Pot on *Solanum capsicastrum* (sown March) and after a few days stand them outdoors on an ash base or plunge them in a cold frame. Syringe the flowers frequently to ensure good pollination and plenty of berries.

Dahlias

Feed dahlias every two weeks with a soluble fertilizer and two or three weeks after planting nip out the growing point of the plant. This will encourage the production of side shoots and make a nice bushy plant.

Old plants may produce several shoots. Reduce these to two or three and stop or pinch the growths as described above. When the growths are about 18 in (45 cm) high they will need to be tied to their stakes.

Greenfly may be troublesome from now on so if you see signs of this pest spray every 10-14 days.

See that the plants have plenty of water in dry spells – dahlias are thirsty plants and if you can, pro-

vide a mulch of peat, or compost to conserve moisture in the soil.

Chrysanthemums

Plants set out in May will need plenty of water once or twice a week in dry spells. They should also be fed with a recommended fertilizer every 7 to 10 days from the middle of June onwards until the blooms show colour.

Continue to keep a sharp watch for aphis or caterpillars, also for slugs and snails; spray as necessary for pests and either scatter slug bait around or water the ground with liquid slug killer.

To encourage the plants grown to produce flowers in the open pinch out the growing tip this month, certainly in the first three weeks. This will stimulate side growths from the leaf axils. It is usual to restrict the number of side shoots to five.

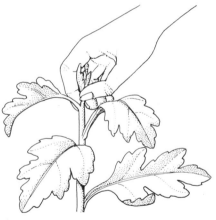

'Stopping' chrysanthemum plants.

Hardy border flowers

By now border flowers will be well forward and as the month progresses many of the early flowering kinds will soon pass their best. In order to keep the plants looking tidy and also maintain colour and continuity it is important to remove dead flowers regularly.

If the plants go on to make a lot of seed this not only exhausts plants like lupins unnecessarily but can result in unwanted seedlings. By all means allow seed to develop for propagation purposes but only for this purpose. As far as possible however, let the foliage die down naturally, as the leaves will continue to make and pass down food to the roots – helping them to produce a good display the following year.

For this reason very untidy diers like oriental poppies are best planted in mid-row positions in mixed borders, with late developers (such as *Eryngium giganteum* or sidalceas) growing in front.

Weeds will be another problem during the weeks to come and should be regularly removed – possibly by hand if the vegetation is very lush and congested. Plenty of water is also essential particularly when the weather turns dry; regular feeding is also essential.

Mulching and feeding

There are two useful methods of supplying nutrients to plants which have to remain in the ground for a long time. They can be mulched with some form of organic material spread on the ground around the roots; or they may be fed from time to time in the growing season with a soluble fertilizer – one can always be fed through the mulch.

Mulches keep the soil cool and moist and as they rot down release valuable plant foods which ultimately reach the roots. Well rotted farmyard manure, garden compost, mushroom compost, rotted leaves, spent hops or even moist peat with a little added bonemeal or general fertilizer all make suitable mulches and can be applied – according to convenience and the climate – between early May and late June.

Soluble fertilizer is sprayed over the foliage with a syringe or watering can and after absorption by the leaves is used by the plant for its own purposes. This leaf feeding is additional to the appli-

cations to the soil.

Gaps left by early bloomers can either be filled temporarily with bedding plants to prolong colour or growing perennials can be introduced from pots. Suggestions of suitable plants to maintain interest for several months are on p 116-117, together with their heights and colours.

Bulbs

Lift tulips in display beds and herbaceous borders when flowering is finished. Remove them carefully without damaging the bulbs and heel them in, in a shallow trench, as recommended for bulbs in bowls (see p 66-67), until they die down completely.

When this happens lift them again, remove dead material and other debris and pack them into shallow boxes. Store these in a well ventilated shed.

De Caen anemones can be planted at regular intervals through the summer to provide a continuous succession of flowers for cutting. Give them full sun and well drained soil, setting the tubers 2-3 in (5-8 cm) deep and 4-6 in (10-15 cm) apart. They can also be grown in rock garden pockets to flower when most other plants are over.

Trees and shrubs

Remove old flower heads from laburnums, azaleas and rhododendrons before these go on to make seed.

Shear over dead flower heads on spring blooming heathers.

Water newly planted trees and shrubs in dry weather and spray their foliage with plain water. Mulch rhododendrons, camellias and other evergreens with moist peat or rotted compost.

Buddleia alternifolia. Trim overcrowded shoots and take out some of the old flowered stems. If

As soon as the flowers of lilacs, rhododendrons and azaleas have faded they should be picked off, not cut with secateurs.

grown as a standard remove any shoots coming from the base or lower trunk.

Mock orange *(Philadelphus* species and varieties). Trim to shape after flowering is finished. Tall overgrown bushes can be cut hard back to strong growths lower down, which may cost a season's flower but will improve the look of the shrub for future years.

There are many modern varieties of the butterfly bush, *Buddleia davidii.*

Shade tolerant trees and shrubs

Name	Height	Colour	Season	Comments
Aucuba japonica	3-5 ft (0.9-1.5 m)	Scarlet or yellow berries	All year	Evergreen, variegated leaved sorts best. Two sexes needed to produce berries
Bamboo (*Arundinaria, Sasa* and *Phyllostachys*)	3-9 ft (0.9-2.7 m)	Mostly green	All year	Evergreen, strong grassy leaves
Camellia	S 6-12 ft (1.8-3.6 m)	Flowers pink, red, white, striped. Singles and doubles	Late winter/ spring	Dislikes lime. Evergreens. Moist soil necessary
x *Fatshedera lizei*	S 4-9 ft (1.2-2.7 m)	White in round heads	Autumn	Polished handshaped leaves, evergreen
Fatsia japonica	S 6-15 ft (1.8-4.6 m)	Cream, many small round heads	October	Evergreen, good maritime plant. Large polished leaves
Hedera Ivies	C Up to 100 ft (30 m)	Various shapes and colours – variegated and plain	All year	Self-clinging. Evergreen
Hypericum calycinum Rose of Sharon	S 12 in (30 cm)	Yellow flowers like pincushions	Summer	Ideal for banks and dry places. Dark green leaves, evergreen
Mahonia aquifolium Oregon grape	S 3-6 ft (0.9-1.8 m)	Small yellow flowers in terminal bunches	Early spring	Evergreen. Glossy leaves, sometimes reddish in winter
Osmanthus heterophyllus	S 6-10 ft (1.8-3 m)	White, jasmine like flowers, fragrant	April	Most soils. Evergreen
Prunus laurocerasus and cultivars, cherry laurel	T and S 15-20 ft (4.6-6 m)	White flowers in erect spikes	April	Glossy evergreen
P. lusitanica Portugal laurel	T	White, fragrant flowers	May	Will grow on chalk
Rubus odoratus	S 6-9 ft (1.8-2.7 m)	Purplish rose. Fragrant	June-Sept	Like a tall thornless raspberry. Deciduous
Ruscus aculeatus Butcher's broom	S 24-36 in (61-91 cm)	Red berries. Ornamental plant	Autumn	Green all winter, but tiny leaves. Deciduous. Spiny with red berries
Sarcococca hookerana Christmas box	S 3-6 ft (0.9-1.8 m)	Small white flowers	Late winter	Evergreen, black berries
Skimmia japonica and cultivars	S 3-6 ft (0.9-1.8 m)	Scarlet berries. White flowers Scented	Most of year/ summer	Plants of both sexes needed for fruits. Evergreen
Symphoricarpos rivularis Snowberry	S 5-10 ft (1.5-3 m)	Small pink flowers. White rounded fruits	Summer/winter	Deciduous
Vinca minor, V. major Periwinkle	S Prostrate	Blue, purple flowers, also doubles	Spring	Evergreen. Trailing habit

Hypericum calycinum, 'Rose of Sharon'.

Camellias, lime-hating.

Aucuba japonica 'Variegata'.

Symphoricarpos albus, snowberry.

Rubus odoratus.

Mahonia aquifolium.

Vinea minor, periwinkle.

99

JULY

Fruit: Gather fruits as they ripen. After the crop is over, remove and burn old leaves, straw and unwanted runners from strawberries. Tie new growths of loganberries and blackberries. Spray apples against codling moth. Thin berries on indoor vines; water well and spray foliage. Summer prune pear trees in the south.

Vegetables: Gather crops while they are young and tasty. Sow peas, turnips, spinach beet. In the north sow spring cabbages. Plant brassicas. Water regularly as required. Spray maincrop potatoes and tomatoes against blight. Continue to remove side shoots of tomatoes indoors and outside. Keep on top of the weeds, by hoeing while they are very small or by weedkillers. Continue to feed all crops every 10-14 days.

Roses: Keep down weeds; remove dead flowers and suckers and spray against pests and diseases.

Flowers from seed: Remove dead flowers regularly. Keep picking and deadheading sweet peas to encourage more flowers to be produced.

Alpines: Deadhead and weed rock plants; propagate if desired, by cuttings; watch for slugs. Water rock plants in dry spells and almost every day those in containers.

Cold greenhouse: Continue to feed, water and generally tend plants and give shade to those that need it. Propagate various plants by cuttings. Pot on pelargoniums, coleus, schizanthus or other plants as they need a larger pot. Nip out the growing tip of tomatoes and remove side shoots; feed and water regularly.

Cool greenhouse: Prick out seedlings of pot plants when they are large enough.

Dahlias: Continue watering and feeding dahlias and dealing with pests. Disbud some flowers for finer blooms and long stems for cutting.

Chrysanthemums: Continue to feed and water and control pests. Disbud if large flowers are required on outdoor varieties. In the north pot indoor varieties into their final pots and place outside. Stop side shoots as necessary.

Hardy border flowers: Lift and divide irises. Carry on deadheading and weeding.

Bulbs: Plant autumn flowering bulbs when available – usually late in the month. Order from specialist firms if not available locally. Root cuttings of shrubs. Clip hedges. Remove basal shoots of grafted shrubs if any.

Trees and shrubs: Pull, trim and root half-ripe cuttings. Clip privet and hedges. Remove basal shoots.

Fruit

Keep gathering soft fruits as they ripen.

When fruiting is over cut the old leaves from strawberry plants, remove the straw and any unwanted runners and burn the lot.

New canes on loganberries and blackberries should not be allowed to trail on the ground for fear of contracting diseases. Gather them together and tie them up to the supports above the fruiting canes. Spores from the latter cannot then wash down onto the new canes.

Apples will require spraying against codling moth; normally twice at an interval of three weeks.

Thin berries on indoor vines and spray over the foliage in hot weather to deter red spider. Keep the borders damp.

Summer prune pear trees in early July in the south of the country, two or three weeks later in the north. Cordons and espaliers especially demand attention. Mature bushes and pyramid trees are usually dealt with in winter.

Laterals coming from main branches of trained trees should now be cut back to 4 or 5 leaves to induce them to make fruit spurs. Laterals from spurs already present or branching from other laterals should be cut back to one leaf. Leave the leaders until the trees reach the desired height.

Raspberries produce many young growths and those not needed for next year's crop are removed – retain the strongest and cut out the weaker stems.

Summer pruning. On dwarf pyramids cut back the laterals (side shoots) to 5 leaves from the basal cluster. Do not cut the main leader.

Prune espaliers by reducing main stem side shoots to 3 leaves, and those shoots from spurs to one leaf beyond the basal cluster.

Red and green gooseberries, luscious raspberries and blackcurrants taste so much better picked straight from the garden.

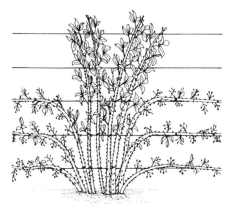

Tie new growths of loganberries and blackberries above the old stems. Then disease spores will not be washed down.

Cordon apple and pear trees are summer-pruned in a similar manner to that described for espalier trees (see p 102).

Pruning blackcurrants. In July August, after fruiting, cut back old canes to allow young shoots to harden off.

Marrow green bush.

Vegetables

This is the month when the vegetable plot begins to yield its harvest. It is a good general rule to start gathering crops when they are young. They taste better and are more nutritious than older produce.

Also with some crops like runner beans and marrows the more you pick the more you will get. If you leave beans or marrows to grow large, they will cease production in the knowledge that they have set enough seeds to ensure their continued survival.

If a runner or French bean becomes too large to be edible do not leave it on the plant, pick it and consign it to the compost heap. If marrows are picked when they are 4-6 in (10-15 cm) long as 'courgettes', one plant may produce up to two dozen marrows.

There is still time to sow an early variety of pea, such as 'Feltham First', 'Hurst Beagle' or 'Meteor'.

Sow turnips and spinach beet early in the month.

In the north towards the end of the month sow spring cabbage such as 'Offenham Compacta', 'Offenham Flower of Spring', 'Durham Early' or 'Wheeler's Imperial'.

Plant sprouting broccoli, Brussels sprouts, cabbages for autumn and winter, kales, leeks, late cauliflowers and cauliflowers such as 'St. George' for cutting in spring. If plants were not raised from seed it may be possible to buy them locally.

Tomatoes

Remove side shoots from tomatoes, indoors or in the open and as soon as four flower trusses appear on outdoor plants pinch out the top of the plant. This is because in most gardens in the southern half of England you can only expect four trusses to ripen on outdoor plants before the frosts arrive in September and October.

Some gardeners however allow five or six trusses to form and ripen the green fruits by placing them in a dish along with several tomatoes that are finishing their ripening

103

stage. Placed in a light, warm but not sunny position indoors, the green tomatoes ripen up very well – presumably because of the ethylene gas given off by the nearly ripened fruits.

Alternatively the plants may be lifted and hung up in a greenhouse or indoors in September or they may be cut down from their stakes, laid horizontally on the ground and covered with cloches. The green tomatoes should hopefully ripen.

Watering, spraying, weeding, feeding

July is obviously a month when there are long hot, dry periods. All fast growing crops like peas, beans, lettuces, root crops, leeks, marrows and sweet corn will therefore need regular and adequate watering.

Maincrop potatoes, and also outdoor tomatoes may need to be sprayed with a suitable fungicide against blight – *Phytophthora infestans,* which is common in wet summers.

At the first sign of the disease – dark blotches on the leaves of potatoes or on the stems and fruits of tomatoes – spray with zineb or maneb and repeat the spray at 14-day intervals maybe several times. Wash tomato fruits of course before eating.

Try to keep the weeds in control especially if you intend to go on holiday later. Keep hoeing or treating the weeds by watering on weedkillers like glyphosate or paraquat/diquat weedkillers which kill the weeds without affecting the soil.

Continue to apply soluble fertilizers every 10 to 14 days to all vegetable crops. Do not however give dwarf bush tomatoes a fertilizer such as nitrogen as this may encourage excessive foliage and not enough fruits.

Roses

General care consists of continuing

to keep down weeds, removing faded flowers and suckers and spraying against pests or diseases if necessary.

July is also a good month for tying new growths to their support for tidiness.

Flowers from seed

Deadheading – removing the faded flowers of annuals such as antirrhinums is essential, not only to keep the garden looking presentable but to encourage the continued production of flowers. When sweet alyssum, lobelias, linarias, and calendulas have finished their first flush of flowers, clip them over with shears and you will soon have a second flowering. In a good year – if the autumn is mild – you can often have even a third crop of flowers from alyssum and calendulas.

Keep picking sweet peas – the more times you pick the more flowers you will have. Allow only a few flowers to set seed and the plants will cease producing.

Alpines

Continue to remove dead flowers and cope with weeds. Also continue to propagate any plants you wish to increase by cuttings.

In dry weather water regularly. Alpines in sinks or raised beds will

need watering almost every day in hot dry spells; even those planted this year in a rock garden may need regular watering.

As always watch for slugs.

Cold greenhouse

Continue general treatment for pot plants as regards feeding, watering, syringing, removal of dead foliage and providing shading for those that require it.

Take cuttings of plants, including hydrangeas, various outdoor shrubs and perennials, rooting these in a sand/peat mixture in a propagator or stand the pots in a box with a glass or plastic top.

Pot on zonal pelargoniums raised from cuttings in April or May, also coleus and schizanthus. Make sure to leave sufficient room at the top of the pots for watering.

Nip out the tips of tomato plants that are carrying a good crop and regularly remove side shoots. Feed with a tomato fertilizer and water regularly.

Side shoots of tomatoes are removed when large enough.

Cool greenhouse

Prick out seedlings of primulas, calceolarias and cinerarias, keeping the little plants under cover for a few days, then remove them to a shady frame outdoors.

Dahlias

Keep watering and feeding dahlias, and watching for greenfly or black-fly; if these pests are present keep up the regular spraying with a suitable insecticide.

If you wish to have flowers on long stems for cutting disbud the flowering stems as soon as the buds are large enough to pick off. Each flower stem carries three buds, one at the top and two more immediately underneath it. Pinch out the two side buds which will result in a much finer flower from the top bud, and a long clean stem for cutting.

If you would rather have more flowers, but not perhaps so large, or on such long stems, pinch out the top bud leaving the two lower buds to flower, albeit on rather shorter stems.

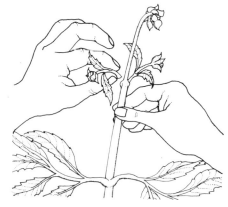

Disbudding dahlias correctly. Leave the terminal bud for fine flowers.

Chrysanthemums

Continue to feed and water the plants as recommended last month. Pests may be more troublesome now so inspect the plants twice a week and spray if necessary. See to staking and tying as the plants grow and if the square mesh wire system is used raise the panels as necessary.

By now outdoor chrysanthemums will have produced flower buds – several at the top of each

Garden *Chrysanthemum* 'Lemon Margaret'.

stem. Unless you want to have large blooms, let all the buds open and have 'spray' blooms. But for large blooms pinch out the side buds when their stem is about ¾ in

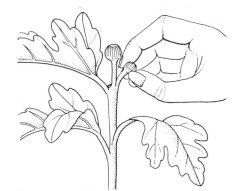

Removing side buds of chrysanthemums. Leave the top bud to develop.

(3 cm) long, leaving the topmost bud to develop.

In the north plants to be flowered in the greenhouse may now be put into their final pots (see also p 85) and stood outside. If the plants were stopped in April, the new side growths may be pinched out about mid July to produce more side shoots.

Hardy border flowers

This is an ideal time to lift and divide the May and June flowering *Iris germanica* hybrids, immediately after flowering and before new growth starts. Do this every

Iris germanica comes in a splendid range of colours. This is 'Party Dress'.

Bulbs

Towards the end of this month and in August seed merchants and garden centres will have quantities of autumn flowering bulbous plants available for immediate planting.

For example, colchicums, autumn flowering crocuses and sternbergias (which look something like garden crocuses and flower in October and November) should all be in the shops. It may be better however to order these bulbs from specialist bulb firms.

These bulbs are normally sent from about mid August and orders are accepted up to the end of September. Most of them require well drained soil and sunshine.

Summer flowering bulbs are often forgotten when the orders are made, yet many are useful for cutting, container cultivation and growing in mixed borders.

Tigridias are not unduly expensive and produce their gorgeous red, yellow or pink flowers heavily spotted with crimson from July through August. The flowers only last a day but each bulb produces several of them.

Most need planting in early spring, on rich but well drained soil; the less hardy kinds benefitting from sitting on 1 in (2.5 cm) of sand.

third year or the quality and quantity of flower will diminish.

Lift the rhizomes and cut them up into segments, each with a fan of leaves and several inches of attached rhizome. Dip the cut ends in powdered charcoal, shorten the leaves to 4-5 in (10-13 cm) and re-plant them – all facing the same way – in a position to receive maximum sunlight, and with the tops of their rhizomes just visible. Change the planting site if possible and give them moist soil.

Continue deadheading and weeding.

Trees and shrubs

Half ripe (heel) cuttings of rosemary, santolina, lavender and hebes can be pulled from the old stems, trimmed and rooted in cold frames of sandy soil, or in a sheltered half-shaded corner outdoors. For details see p 23.

Privet and hawthorn hedges can be clipped; also beech hedges. Any new foliage produced on the last will then persist all winter.

Remove basal shoots from grafted plants, for example ornamental hazels (corylus), sorbus, and ornamental cherries.

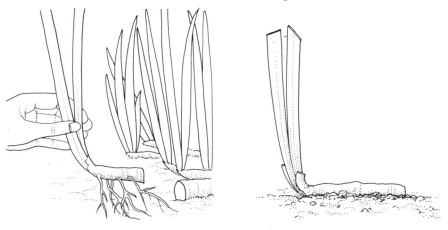

Bearded irises. Planting and increasing techniques.

Although each gorgeous flower only lasts a day *Tigridia* hybrids flower for many weeks in summer.

Summer flowering bulbs

Plant	Height	Colour	Season	Comments
Acidanthera murielae	24-36 in (61-90 cm)	White with purple centres	Aug-Sept	Plant 3 in (8 cm) deep in May. Store like gladioli. Very sweetly scented
Allium albopilosum	24 in (61 cm)	Lilac	June	All hardy in sheltered gardens and well drained soil
A. azureum	24 in (61 cm)	Blue	June-July	
A. moly	12 in (30 cm)	Yellow	June	
A. sphaerocephalum	24 in (61 cm)	Crimson	July	
Amaryllis belladonna	18 in (46 cm)	Deep rose	Late summer	Protect in winter. Best planted at the foot of a south wall
Anemone de Caen	12 in (30 cm)	Various	All summer	Plant in December to April, 2 in (5 cm) deep. Protect in winter
Brodiaea – various	18-24 in (46-61 cm)	Red or purple	Mid-summer	Reasonably hardy, best at the foot of a south wall
Camassia leichtlinii	18 in (46 cm)	Blue	June	Hardy
C.l. 'Plena'	24 in (61 cm)	Yellow, double	June	Hardy
Crinum powellii	3-4 ft (0.9-1.2 m)	Deep pink	August	Sheltered position
C.p. 'Album'	3-4 ft (0.9-1.2 m)	White	August	
Crocosmia masonorum and hybrids	36 in (90 cm)	Orange-red, yellow, deep red	July-Aug	Full sun, hardy
Cyclamen europaeum	4 in (10 cm)	Carmine	Late summer	Strongly scented
Eucomis bicolor	12-18 in (30-46 cm)	Green, lilac centre	July-Aug	Plant 5 in (13 cm) deep. Protect in winter
Galtonia candicans Summer hyacinth	2-4 ft (0.6-1.2 m)	White	July-Aug	Hardy
Gladioli	18-48 in (46-122 cm)	Various	Summer/autumn	Various kinds. None hardy
Ixia hybrids Corn Lily	15 in (38 cm)	Various	June-July	Plant 3 in (8 cm) deep. Lift or protect in winter
Liliums – many (See p 134)				
Nerine bowdenii Guernsey lily	12-15 in (30-38 cm)	Rich pink	Sept-Oct	Hardy in sheltered place
Ornithogalum arabicum	24 in (61 cm)	White	May-June	Hardy; fragrant
Roscoea cautleyoides	18 in (46 cm)	Pale yellow	June-July	Hardy
Sparaxis tricolor Hybrids Harlequin flower	12-24 in (30-61 cm)	Various	May	Light soil and sun. Lift or protect in winter
Tigridia Peacock flower	12-18 in (30-46 cm)	Various	July-Aug	Plant April. Store like gladioli

Allium moly.

Acidanthera bicolor 'Murielae'.

Galtonia candicans.

Allium sphaerocephalum.

Nerine bowdenii.

Large-flowered gladioli.

Amaryllis belladonna.

Ornithogalum umbellatum.

Allium albopilosum.

AUGUST

Fruit: Finish summer pruning pears and summer prune apples. When the crop has been picked cut out old raspberry canes and tie in new ones. When the peach crop has been picked, prune and tie in new shoots. Plant strawberries.

Vegetables: Harvest runner beans and conserve any surplus to daily needs. Lift onions. Sow spring cabbages in the south; also winter hardy lettuces. Plant winter cabbages, cauliflowers, kales, leeks and sprouting broccoli. Unless there is regular and adequate rainfall water all crops copiously.

Roses: Keep down weeds, deadhead and spray against pests and diseases if necessary.

Flowers from seed: Keep on deadheading. Cut everlasting flowers for drying. Transplant annuals from reserve bed to fill gaps elsewhere.

Alpines: Keep the plants tidy and keep weeds down. Make a frame, start building a rock garden or convert glazed sinks.

Cold greenhouse: Start cyclamen corms into growth; sow seed of cyclamen, cinerarias and calendulas. Root cuttings of pelargoniums and other bedding plants. Pot lachenalias and freesias.

Cool greenhouse: Sow schizanthus and stocks. Pot on cinerarias and primulas.

Dahlias: Feed, water, disbud, spray against pests particularly earwigs. Mark any plants showing signs of virus disease to be destroyed after flowering.

Chrysanthemums: Disbud, feed, water and spray outdoor varieties as necessary. Control earwigs.

Hardy border flowers: Cut back dead stems. Stake late flowering plants. Plan next year's borders – visit nurseries and gardens for ideas.

Bulbs: Plant lilies. Collect and 'sow' lily bulbils. Order bulbs for forcing and autumn planting.

Lawns: In the north and Scotland, sow grass seed for patching or a new lawn. Lay turf, although this may be done later.

Trees and shrubs: Prune wisterias. Trim holly hedges; deadhead hydrangeas and cut out weak shoots (if any).

Fruit

Finish summer pruning pears in the north of the country.

Trained apple trees should now be ready for summer pruning. Many methods are advocated including the complicated Lorette system or any modification of the same. Enthusiasts should consult an authoritative work such as *Pruning Apple Trees* by C. R. Thompson (Faber) or adopt the modified form described in the Royal Horticultural Society's *The Fruit Garden Displayed*. One simple method is to cut back all laterals to 5 or 6 leaves, following this up in due course with winter pruning.

When fruiting is finished cut out the old fruiting canes from raspberries. Train and tie new canes 3-4 in (8-10 cm) apart to supports. Keep eight canes per stool.

When all the fruits have been gathered from outdoor wall peaches cut out the old fruit bearing shoots and tie in replacement shoots.

Plant strawberries (which will crop next year) in humus-rich, well drained soil, adding a sprinkling of sulphate of potash ½ oz per sq yard (17 g per sq m) and bonemeal 3 oz per sq yard (100 g per sq m) just before inserting the plants. Set these 15-18 in (38-46 cm) apart, in rows 30 in (75 cm) apart. Water in if necessary. Recommended varieties are 'Grandee', 'Royal Sovereign' (but do obtain virus-free guaranteed stock), 'Cambridge Favourite' and 'Tamella' early; followed by 'Gorella', 'Merton Dawn' and 'Talisman' and for long fruiting (June to October) perpetual strawberries 'Gento', 'Rabunda' and 'Aromel'.

Handy Hint: Every year many short-sighted people suffer severe eye damage through bending over to admire or smell some plant, not noticing the canes, pea sticks or other supports that are holding it up.

Blackberries, loganberries and tayberries may be increased by tip layering. Peg a new shoot down and cover the stem with soil and it will root.

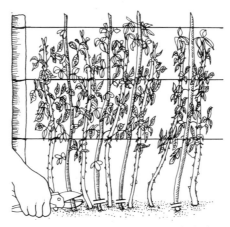

Cut out old raspberry canes and tie in new ones for next year's crop.

This tragedy can easily be avoided by tying some bits of coloured rag or ribbon on such sticks so that the short-sighted may see them and escape injury.

Vegetables

This can be a month when the weather (if it is kind) may make such a difference to the crops to be harvested later in the autumn, winter and next spring.

What the gardener hopes for is regular and adequate rainfall. If the rain does not arrive, then you should apply water especially to plants that still have a lot of growth to make – autumn, winter and spring brassicas such as Brussels sprouts, kales, cabbages, savoys, sprouting broccoli, leeks, salad crops and potatoes.

Strawberry 'Grandee'

Strawberry 'Royal Sovereign'.

Strawberry 'Cambridge Favourite'.

Harvesting now is in full swing. With runner beans, any surplus to daily requirements may be salted for winter use or put in the deep freeze.

Marrows and beans must be picked regularly.

Onions should be ready for lifting this month, set to dry in any airy place and then strung up in 'ropes' or in old nylon stockings.

Sow spring cabbages in the first half of the month in the south; also winter hardy lettuces such as 'Imperial Winter', 'Valdor' or the cos varieties 'Lobjoit's Green' or 'Winter Density'.

Although these are normally

Onion stems bend over naturally but it helps to do it by hand.

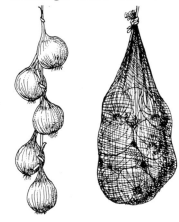

Onions tied and stored.

hardy enough to survive a British winter, it is always wise to have some form of cloche protection – glass or plastic – in reserve in case the winter turns really bitterly cold.

If not already done and plants are available, plant out winter cabbages and cauliflowers and kales; also leeks and sprouting broccoli.

Handy Hint: Mice can be a great nuisance in frames, under cloches where peas or beans have been sown, and in a greenhouse, shed or garage where produce has been stored. Set traps.

Mice often prefer other baits than cheese, such as a broad bean, a melon seed or even a piece of milk chocolate.

A good handy hint to speed up the ripening of onion bulbs is to bend over the tops.

Roses

Keep up the good work of keeping down weeds, spraying if necessary against pests and diseases and cutting off faded flowers regularly.

Flowers from seed

Annuals should be deadheaded regularly, once or twice a week. Everlasting flowers such as statice

and helichrysums should be cut just as they are fully open, tied in small bundles of not more than half a dozen stems and hung in a dry airy shed or garage to dry. Do not hang them in full light in a greenhouse because the colours may fade.

As soon as the flowers have dried pop them in a plastic bag to keep them free from dust, ready to be brought out later on for winter decorations.

If some marigolds (tagetes) were planted in an odd corner in May or June, with the idea of moving them to fill gaps left by annuals that have finished flowering, they may be transplanted this month.

Prepare the ground to receive them, taking out holes and filling them with water one evening. Water the marigolds as well. Then next day transplant them and water them in.

Alpines

Continue to tidy up, deadheading alpines and keeping the weeds down.

Take cuttings of pelargoniums, calceolarias, marguerites and other bedding plants.

Pot up lachenalias and freesias for early winter flowers.

If you so desire, make a frame, start building the rock garden or converting an old glazed sink into an imitation stone sink.

Cool greenhouse

Sow schizanthus and stocks and pot on cinerarias and primulas sown earlier in June and July.

Cyclamen corms which have been resting in their old pots under the greenhouse bench since April should now be repotted in loamless compost. Keep the tops of the corms at soil level, water and stand the pots on a bench.

Sow seed of cyclamen, cinerarias and calendulas.

Dahlias

The routine with dahlias in August is much the same as it was in July – feed, water, disbud, and spray if you wish to protect against pests and keep the plants tied to their stakes.

Earwigs can be troublesome now, eating pieces out of leaves and flowers. A dusting of derris powder or a spraying with a general insecticide, all round the base of the plants usually keeps them under control.

By now any plants affected by virus disease will be showing symptoms – mottling of the foliage – and should be marked for destruction when the plants are lifted in November.

Chrysanthemums

Keep on disbudding outdoor chrysanthemums, feeding and watering them and spraying against pests. Earwigs are often a nuisance as they run up the stems and chew the flowers. A smear of Vaseline on about 2 in (5 cm) of the stem below the flower bud usually discourages them.

Hardy border flowers

Continue cutting back dead stems and flowers and support late flowering perennials as required.

This is a good time to plan next year's borders and some useful plants to remember when ordering or replanting are included on pp 116-117. Some of these can be seen in flower in nurseries and gardens open to the public.

Bulbs

Plant madonna lilies *(Lilium candidum)*, leaving the tops of the bulbs just below soil level. Plant *L. testaceum* slightly deeper but with no more than 2 in (5 cm) of soil covering the bulbs.

Look for aphids and if spotted apply an insecticide.

Gather bulbils in the axils of the leaves from *Lilium tigrinum* and its hybrids.

These can be 'sown' in boxes of sandy soil and covered with ½ in (1 cm) of the same mix.

Order bulbs for forcing and autumn planting now from your local bulb merchant or high street store.

Lilium candidum, loved by cottage gardeners for centuries.

A wisteria festooning a wrought-iron moon gate — a lovely feature.

Lawns

In the north of England and in Scotland any seeding of new lawns, or sowing lawn grass seed on bare patches should be completed this month. Turfing may be done at any time of the year provided the ground is not frozen or covered with snow, but obviously the sooner it is done the better to give the grass roots a chance to establish themselves in their new lodgings.

Trees and shrubs

Trim back wisteria shoots made this year to about 12 in (30 cm).

Trim holly hedges; if these need severe cutting back this is best done in April.

Hydrangeas which have finished flowering can have the trusses removed back to the first plump bud. Remove weak spindly stems to ground level.

Handy Hint: It must always be remembered that a border at the foot of a wall may receive only a third of the rain that falls in the open part of a garden, so the gardener must be particularly generous when watering these borders.

Clematis, honeysuckles and other climbers planted against walls, particularly, need regular and copious watering and for them it is a good trick to sink a 4½ in (11.5 cm) or 5 in (12 cm) pot alongside the plant with the rim level with the surface.

When watering these newly planted plants just fill the pot with water; if it runs away quickly, fill it again and maybe a third time. In this way the water goes straight down to the roots and none is lost by evaporation.

The same trick of course is used for watering outdoor tomatoes. Some people bury a large handful of 6 in (15 cm) lengths of straw vertically in the ground next to the plants with the tips just showing and pour the water down through the straw. If you have plenty of straw this will save you buying flower pots! You could of course use a couple of plastic cups or beakers with the bottoms cut off if you have these.

Handy Hint: Secateurs, or pruners as some makers call them, vary considerably in shape and size, and you should go to a shop or garden centre which has a good selection where it is possible to try various makes.

For those with impaired grip – arthritis or rheumatism in the hands, perhaps – the two-handed pruners are especially useful. These consist of two ordinary secateur blades but mounted on 14 in (36 cm) handles with stout moulded plastic hand grips.

Anything can be pruned easily with this tool and it is very useful for pruning roses or other prickly shrubs.

Two other useful tools for pruning shrubs are the long-handled lopper and the pruning saw.

Hardy border flowers

Name	Height	Colour	Comments
Very early spring			
Helleborus orientalis Lenten rose	18 in (46 cm)	Green, cream, pink, red	Retains leaves all year. Shade loving
Bergenia hybrids Megasea	12-24 in (30-61 cm)	Pink, purple, magenta	Creeping habit. Tolerates dry soils
Brunnera macrophylla	12-18 in (30-46 cm)	Blue, forget-me-not-like	Tolerates shade
Doronicum plantagineum forms Leopard's bane	30 in (76 cm)	Yellow	Good for cutting
Epimedium perralderanum	12 in (30 cm)	Yellow	Evergreen, fine ground cover
Primula Polyanthus	12 in (30 cm)	All shades	Lift after flowering, shade for summer. Can raise from seed
Pulmonaria officinalis Lungwort and others	12 in (30 cm)	Pink turning blue. Others have red or blue pink flowers	Evergreen in mild conditions
Late spring			
Aquilegia hybrids Columbine	24-36 in (61-91 cm)	Yellow, pink, red, purple	Handsome foliage
Baptisia australes	4 ft (1.2 m)	Deep blue	Give full sun
Dicentra eximia and *D. formosa* hybrids	12-18 in (30-46 cm)	Pink, crimson, white	Leaves ground hugging
Eremurus hybrids Foxtail lilies	4-8 ft (1.2-2.4 cm)	Pink, cream, buff, yellow	Disappears after flowering. Leaves ground hugging
Euphorbia polychroma Spurge	18 in (46 cm)	Yellow	Clump forming
Heuchera sanguinea Coral bells	12 in (30 cm)	Scarlet	Good edging plant
Paeonia	2-4 ft (0.6-1.2 m)	Single, double and semi-double; various shades and combinations of white, pink and red	Chinese forms particularly good. Need staking
Papaver orientale	2-4 ft (0.6-1.2 m)	Scarlet, pink, white	Full sun, untidy diers, need staking
Pulsatilla vulgaris Pasque flower	12 in (30 cm)	Shades of mauve and purple occasionally white or pink	Full sun, well drained soil
Trollius x *cultorum* Globe flower	24-36 in (61-91 cm)	Yellow/orange	Moisture loving
Mid-season			
Aconitum x *bicolor* Monkshoods	3-4 ft (0.9-1.2 m)	Blue, blue and white	Hybrids of various species. Roots poisonous
Anthemis tinctoria	36 in (91 cm)	Yellow	Good for cutting

Name	Height	Colour	Comments
Aruncus dioicus Goat's beard	5-7 ft (1.5-2.1 m)	Cream	Impressive, fern-like leaves. Can be used singly
Campanula glomerata 'Superba'	12-24 in (30-61 cm)	Blue-purple massed in round tight heads	Front of border, dies away after flowering
C.lactiflora	4-5 ft (1.2-1.5 m)	Pink, blue in branching heads	Needs staking
Chrysanthemum coccineum vars Pyrethrum	24 in (61 cm)	Single and double. Pink, crimson, white	Good cut flowers. May need staking
Delphinium hybrids	3-8 ft (0.9-2.4 m)	Blues of all shades, white also pinks	Rich soil. Stakes needed
Erigeron speciosus	24 in (61 cm)	Mauve/purple	Flowers continuously
Geum 'Mrs. Bradshaw'	24 in (61 cm)	Brick red	Comes true from seed
Helenium autumnale Sneeze weed	3-5 ft (0.9-1.5 m)	Yellow, orange, mahogany	Divide frequently
Iris barbatus (I. germanica) Bearded iris	2-4 ft (0.6-1.2 m)	All colours and combinations	Likes lime
Iris sibirica	36 in (91 cm)	Mauve, white, purple, red	Likes moisture, leaves grassy
Lupinus polyphyllus hybrids Lupin	4 ft (1.2 m)	Combinations of blue, yellow, red, pink, white	Russell hybrids are best. Remove seed pods
Salvia nemorosa 'Superba'	24 in (61 cm)	Purple	Needs sun
Thalictrum delavayi (T. dipterocarpum). Meadow-rue	4-5 ft (1.2-1.5 m)	Lilac-blue; on feathery branching heads	Moist soil. Very elegant
Verbascum vernale Mullein	4-6 ft (1.2-1.8 m)	Yellow	Purple and pink forms exist

Late

Name	Height	Colour	Comments
Anemone elegans (A. japonica) Japanese anemone	4-5 ft (1.2-1.5 m)	Single and double pink, red, white	Shade tolerant
Aster novi-belgii Michaelmas daisy	3-6 ft (0.9-1.8 m)	Blue, violet, mauve	Many varieties. Need staking
Chrysanthemum rubellum	24 in (61 cm)	Pink, red, apricot	Divide and replant in spring to keep floriferous
Cimicifuga simplex Bugbane	4-5 ft (1.2-1.5 m)	White	Moist soil
Echinops ritro Globe thistle	4 ft (1.2 m)	Blue	Very sturdy plant. Full sun, any soil
Eupatorium purpureum	6-8 ft (1.8-2.4 m)	Purplish	Back of border plant
Heliopsis scabra 'Patula'	4 ft (1.2 m)	Yellow	Can be dried
Limonium latifolium Statice	12 in (30 cm)	Blue	Flowers can be dried
Phlox paniculata Phlox	3-4 ft (0.9-1.2 m)	Pink, red, white, purple, lilac	Must have moist soil
Rudbeckia nitida Coneflower	4 ft (1.2 m)	Yellow	
Sedum 'Autumn Joy'	24 in (61 cm)	Pink	Front of border. Fleshy leaves

Hardy border flowers

Helleborus orientalis.

Doronicums flower early in the spring.

Papaver orientale 'Picotee'.

Bergenia 'Abendglut'.

Euphorbia epithymoides.

Dicentra eximia.

Paeony 'Bowl of Beauty'.

Campanula glomerata.

Sedum spectabile 'Autumn Joy'.

Japanese anemone 'September charm'.

Echinops ritro.

Aruncus dioicus.

Russell Hybrid lupins.

Rudbeckia deamii.

119

SEPTEMBER

Fruit: Finish summer pruning apples and pears; prune blackcurrants, loganberries and blackberries. Gather apples when ripe.

Vegetables: Sow lettuces, spinach, onions, turnips and radishes. Plant spring cabbages and onion sets. Cut and burn potato haulms and lift potatoes. Lift onions and carrots.

Flowers from seed: Sow varieties of annuals to stand the winter.

Alpines: Remove fallen leaves from rock garden.

Cold and cool greenhouse: Bring in azaleas; pot bulbs for forcing later. Bring in tender plants from the garden; bring in plants of *Solanum capsicastrum*. Take late chrysanthemums into the house. Prune climbing plants to admit plenty of light. Remove tomato plants after crop has finished. Discard old or diseased plants.

Chrysanthemums: Take plants grown outside into the house now; spray against pests and diseases.

Bulbs: Plant bulbs in pots or bowls to flower at Christmas. Plant lily bulbs if available.

Lawns: Scarify and aerate the turf. Sow seed on bare patches. Repair worn edges. Apply moss killer if necessary. Apply autumn lawn fertilizer. Control worms if necessary.

Trees and shrubs: Root tree and shrub cuttings. Tie in climbers.

Fruit

Complete summer pruning of apples and pears.

Prune blackcurrants by taking out the old fruiting wood, either down to ground level or, if there are not many replacement shoots, back to where there is a new stem lower down the branch.

Remove fruiting canes from loganberries and blackberries when the crop has been gathered; spread out and tie new canes on the supports.

Gather apples when ripe. These are ready for picking when they part readily from the branches if gently cupped in the hand and lifted.

Pears may be protected from damage by birds and wasps by tying plastic bags over the fruits.

Vegetables

Lettuces, as recommended in August, may still be sown in the south in the open but in the north they should be sown under cloches. In the open, sow seed of a hardy spinach such as 'Norvak' or 'Sigmaleaf' for harvesting in the spring.

Another sowing of 'White Lisbon' onions for pulling as 'spring onions' may be made this month; and also of radishes and turnips such as 'Golden Ball' or

There are a surprising number of turnip varieties.

White Lisbon onions are the best for pulling as 'spring onions' for salads.

Radish 'French breakfast succulent' (left) and Cherry Belle.

'Green Globe'. The latter is a good variety to grow for turnip tops which are excellent 'spring greens' – these are very welcome in the lean spring months and should be grown more often.

Plant spring cabbages if not already done. Onion sets of the variety 'First Early' (specially suitable for autumn planting) may be planted this month.

If potato haulms (stems) have been affected by potato blight cut them off and burn them. A week or two later lift the potatoes. Choose a dry day for lifting the tubers; store in a frost-free place. If not already done lift and dry off onions (see p 113).

Maincrop carrots may be lifted this month, but the longer they are left in the ground the heavier will be the weight of the crop. Some of the crop may be left in the ground to dig later.

Twist off the leaves, set aside any cracked roots for use soon and pack the sound carrots in boxes with ½ in (1 cm) of sand between each layer of carrots and store in a shed or garage.

Roses

If rambler roses have finished flowering prune them by cutting out at ground level all the stems that have carried flowers and tie the new growths in to take their place.

There may not be enough new growths to replace the old ones so keep some of the best that have flowered and if they have produced many side shoots cut these back by about half their length.

Check ties on all climbing and rambler roses and renew any that look doubtful. Continue to remove suckers from bush roses.

If it is intended to plant new roses this autumn and the site is free, prepare it now so that the soil has time to settle before the bushes arrive in October or November.

Dig it over thoroughly, re-

moving roots of perennial weeds if any. If the soil is light or indeed very heavy it is wise to double dig the site – that is to break up the lower spit (the bottom of the trench) – with a fork. For method see p 17.

In light soil work into the bottom spit any organic manure you can find – well decayed farm or stable manure, hop manure (not spent hops) or well matured garden compost at the rate of a bucketful to the square yard.

Don't be mean with soil preparation for roses. If you do not feel able to double dig and manure the whole bed, at least take out a planting hole 2 ft (61 cm) across for each rose and enrich the lower spit with manure as described above.

Try to get this work done this month or early in October to give the soil several weeks to settle. Continue to remove dead flowers and if necessary spray against pests or diseases.

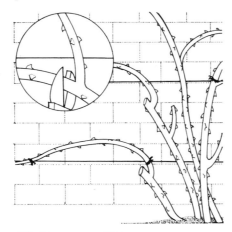

Climbing roses. Old stems are cut out and new stems, if available, are tied in horizontally.

Choosing roses

There are hundreds of varieties of roses to choose from today – one rose grower lists over 250. Of course the choice of roses in garden centres is very limited – they only stock, as with most other types of plants like shrubs and fruit trees, 'fast selling', popular lines.

If you only want a few nice

roses, you will find enough to choose from in the high street supermarket or the garden centres.

But, if you want to make a more considered selection write for catalogues from the leading rose growers who advertize in the press and gardening journals.

The following popular roses are generally available from specialist rose growers and a fair number of them are to be found in the better garden centres.

Shrub rose 'Rachel Bowes-Lyon', one of the new varieties cultivated at the Royal Horticultural Society's gardens at Wisley.

Hybrid tea roses

'Ace of Hearts'. Large crimson-scarlet flowers; upright bush. Slight fragrance.

'Alec's Red'. Cherry red; sturdy bush of medium height. Very fragrant.

'Alexander'. Orange vermilion; tall, upright grower.

'Alpine Sunset'. Creamy yellow flushed pink; medium sized plant producing large blooms. Very fragrant.

'Blessings'. Soft coral-pink; vigorous, bushy, branching grower of even height. Neat medium sized blooms. Exceptionally good for bedding.

'Blue Moon'. Silvery lilac; strong grower. Sweetly fragrant.

Hybrid tea rose 'Alexander'.

Hybrid tea rose 'Blue Moon'.

Hybrid tea rose 'Just Joey'.

'Double Delight'. Creamy pink heavily edged with rosy red; medium height, elegant bloom. Sweetly scented.

'Ernest H. Morse'. Brilliant red; vigorous, upright; withstands rain. Sweetly fragrant.

'Evening Star'. White; strong foliage, very free flowering.

'Fragrant Cloud'. Scarlet to red; strong growing. Outstanding fragrance.

'Grandpa Dickson'. Yellow; upright plant with attractive foliage.

'Just Joey'. Coppery orange, veined red; vigorous, upright growth, very free flowering.

'King's Ransome'. Rich pure yellow; very free flowering, vigorous; highly disease resistant.

'L'Oreal Trophy'. Orange, shaded salmon orange; free flowering, disease resistant. Lightly scented.

'Lovers' Meeting'. Dark bronze, green foliage, flowers tangerine-orange.

'Pascali'. White, cream centre; upright growth, medium size blooms of good substance and

shape; withstands rain better than most white varieties.

'Peace'. Yellow, edged cerise; vigorous, tall, branching plant.

'Piccadilly'. Scarlet and yellow; vigorous, upright and bushy grower of medium height; very resistant to wet weather but not at its best in hot sun.

'Pink Favourite'. Rose pink; upright spreading habit; resistant to disease.

'Precious Platinum'. Bright crimson; strong, upright habit.

'Rose Gaujard'. Pale pink and

124

Hybrid tea rose 'Rose Gaujard'.

Hybrid tea rose 'Tynwald'.

Hybrid tea rose 'Troika'.

silver; vigorous, tall branching growth, excellent for bedding; very resistant to weather.

'Silver Jubilee'. Pink, peach blend; upright, bushy habit producing an abundance of flowers on shortish stems.

'Simba'. Mid green foliage, bright yellow, well shaped flowers; vigorous.

'Troika'. Apricot orange; strong, upright grower with large leathery foliage. Fragrant.

'Tynwald'. Large cream blooms, shaded slightly deeper in the centre; medium height; dark disease-resistant foliage.

'Wendy Cussons'. Cerise flushed scarlet; strong; branching habit with dark green leathery foliage. Fragrant.

'Whisky Mac'. Gold; vigorous, bushy, compact. Fragrant.

Floribunda or cluster flowered roses

'Allgold'. Buttercup yellow, semi-double; vigorous compact growth. Slightly fragrant.

'Anna Ford'. Orange red; short, low and spreading; good for patios or containers.

'Anne Cocker'. Light vermilion; upright vigorous growth; lasts exceptionally well when cut.

'Anne Harkness'. Light orange; above average height, tough, healthy; large flower heads.

'Arthur Bell'. Bright yellow; tall, vigorous, upright growth; very resistant to wet weather and disease. Fragrant.

'Bonfire Night'. Orange scarlet; bushy, upright, compact growth.

'Burma Star'. Yellow with orange

125

Floribunda rose 'Bonfire Night'.

Floribunda rose 'Korresia'.

Floribunda rose 'Lili Marlene'.

Floribunda rose 'St Boniface'.

Floribunda rose 'Masquerade'.

Floribunda rose 'Escapade'.

Floribunda rose 'Congratulations'.

flush. Fragrant.

'Congratulations'. Soft pink; strong, upright, shapely; dark green foliage.

'Dame of Sark'. Gold flushed scarlet; vigorous upright growth.

'Deep Secret'. Deep velvet crimson flowers; very healthy. Very fragrant.

'Escapade'. Lilac rose; vigorous bushy growth. Fragrant.

'Eye Paint'. Magenta-rose with a white eye; medium height, bushy, semi-double flowers. Fragrant.

'Glenfiddich'. Golden amber; strong upright growth with large foliage.

'Iceberg'. White; vigorous branching growth of shrub proportions. Ideal for a massing in beds or at back of borders.

'Korresia'. Bright yellow; moderately vigorous, compact growth with medium green foliage. Fragrant.

'Lili Marlene'. Scarlet red; compact growth of medium height; may require protection against mildew.

'Living Fire'. Orange scarlet; vigorous upright growth. Slightly fragrant.

'Margaret Merril'. White; vigorous bushy habit with dark green foliage. Very fragrant.

'Masquerade'. Large semi-double flowers opening yellow, changing to pink and crimson; vigorous, tall.

'Matangi'. Vermilion red; moderately vigorous upright growth with dark green glossy foliage; tinted copper when young.

'Memento'. Salmon vermilion; moderately vigorous growth producing neat double flowers, good for bedding and cutting.

'Pink Parfait'. Pink; vigorous, tall branching growth producing an abundance of neat double flowers. Slightly fragrant.

'Queen Elizabeth'. Pink; very tall upright habit with the double flowers produced on long almost thornless stems; must be pruned quite hard to keep to a manageable height.

'Rob Roy'. Crimson; vigorous

upright growth.
'Saint Boniface'. Bright vermilion; low growing, perfectly shaped blooms.
'Southampton'. Orange apricot; upright, vigorous, a good variety for hedging and cutting.
'Topsi'. Scarlet; vigorous, dwarf bushy growth.
'Wembley Stadium'. Large heads of brilliant red flowers; medium height, bushy, thick foliage.
'Yesterday'. Lilac pink; moderately vigorous growth with trusses of small double flowers that open flat to display golden stamens.

Miniature roses
The following are all about 12 in (30 cm) high:
'Angela Rippon' (Ocaru). Salmon.
'Anna Ford'. Orange red; low, spreading growth, bushy, good for containers.
'Baby Faurax'. Violet.
'Baby Masquerade'. Yellow, flushed pink and red.
'Dresden Doll'. Shell pink, yellow stamens.
'Golden Angel'. Yellow.
'Green Diamond'. Greenish shade.
'Judy Fischer'. Rose pink.
'Little Flirt'. Orange vermilion.
'Pour Toi'. Cream.
'Starina'. Bright orange red.
'Stars N' Stripes'. Red and white striping.

Repeat flowering climbers
'Compassion'. Salmon orange double; strong grower up to 16 ft (5 m). Very pronounced fragrance.
'Danse Du Feu'. Orange scarlet semi-double; moderately strong climbing growth up to 8 ft (2.5 m); ideal for use on walls or fences.
'Golden Showers'. Yellow double; may be trained on pillar or wall up to 8 ft (2.5 m) or grown freely as a hedge.
'Handel'. Cream flushed rose pink double; strong growth up to 16 ft (5 m); suitable for wall, pillar or fence.
'New Dawn'. Pale pink double; a moderately vigorous climber up to 6 ft (2 m); good for pillar or fence or may be grown freely without

Floribunda rose 'Anna Ford'.

Climbing rose 'Handel'.

Hybrid tea rose 'Double delight'.

Shrub rose 'Fred Loads'.

supports as a shrub.
'Pink Perpetue'. Moderately vigorous growth up to 8 ft (2.5 m) with deep pink double flowers repeated continuously.
'Zephirine Drouhin'. Carmine, double; thornless, up to 8 ft (2.5 m). Fragrant.

Rambler roses
'Alberic Barbier'. Yellow buds ageing to white; very vigorous, semi-evergreen. Fragrant.
'Albertine'. Salmon opening to coppery pink; very vigorous. Very

fragrant.
'Dorothy Perkins'. Rose pink; very vigorous, old favourite; may need protection from mildew.
'Francois Juranville'. Deep pink; rampant. Fragrant.
'Kiftsgate'. White, single flowers; very vigorous; may scramble up tree to 20 ft (6 m).
'Paul's Scarlet'. Bright scarlet crimson, semi-double; recurrent flowering, vigorous.

Shrub roses
'Blanc Double de Coubert'. Pure

white, double; free flowering, vigorous. Very fragrant.

'Buff Beauty'. Large apricot yellow flowers; vigorous.

'Canary Bird'. Rich yellow, single, free and early flowering.

'Fred Loads'. Large single vermilion-orange; tall upright growth.

'Fruhlingsgold'. Light yellow, semi-double; vigorous. Fragrant.

'Nevada'. Creamy white, single; vigorous.

'Roseraie de l'Hay'. Purplish crimson, loosely double; fragrant.

Handy Hint: Suckers are a great nuisance in the garden – they arise from the roots of roses, lilacs and other plants and they must be severed at the point where they leave the roots. Chopping them off at ground level only serves as pruning and encourages several shoots instead of one. The soil may be scraped away and the sucker severed with a knife, but there is an easier way – which is to use a sucker cutter.

This has a V-shaped blade at the end of a metal rod about 12 in (30 cm) long with a comfortable wooden handle. You just push the blade into the ground alongside the sucker, between it and the parent bush and it chops it off at the point where it leaves the root.

Where there are many suckers, as perhaps around a plum tree or lilac bush, they may be destroyed by watering on a solution of paraquat/diquat (Weedol) which (not being a systemic weedkiller) will kill the suckers but will not affect the parent plant.

Do not attempt to kill suckers with a systemic weedkiller such as those used to kill weeds on lawns – this can have disastrous results.

Flowers from seed

Some annual flowers such as larkspurs and calendulas may be sown this month where they are to flower. They will bloom several weeks earlier than those sown in the spring. Sow them in patches.

Sow very thinly and do not do any thinning of the seedlings until the spring. Slugs and other predators, and also the weather may take their toll but hopefully there should be enough seedlings left to give an early show next summer.

Sweet peas may be sown in September in northern districts but are usually sown in early October in the south.

Alpines

As leaves begin to fall they may cover fragile alpine plants and do much damage. On a fairly large rock garden, if there are many leaves likely to fall in the next couple of months, it is worth spreading some old netting over the area. Lift it off every week or two if it has caught any appreciable quantity of leaves.

This will save a lot of time in the long run and the plants will benefit from not having been submerged by leaves.

Cold greenhouse

Late in the month in the south (mid-September in the north) bring Indian azaleas in from their plunge bed. They can stay in the cold greenhouse until early December (unless frost threatens) and then they may go indoors. Keep the roots moist at all times but not sodden – both drought and overwatering cause the leaves to drop.

Early flowering varieties of tulips and narcissi, potted now and treated in the same manner as the forcing kinds (see p 130) are useful to supply colour in the cold greenhouse in spring.

As no artificial heat will be provided these will naturally flower later than any which are taken indoors after leaving the plunge beds.

Take pot chrysanthemums into the house to flower.

Prune any roof climbers so that as much light as possible will be able to get through to other plants.

Remove tomatoes as cropping finishes.

Tender plants in the garden may be lifted and boxed or potted and brought under cover for the winter. In many cases the top growth may be greatly reduced which will allow more plants to be accommodated inside.

Throw out old, diseased or unwanted plants to make room for these newcomers.

Solanum capsicastrum plants which have been outside all summer will by now be well furnished with green berries. Bring them onto a bench and sprinkle a salt spoonful of magnesium sulphate (Epsom salts) over each pot.

Water this in but do not let the compost get too wet or alternatively too dry at the roots. Careful watering plus the Epsom salts will prevent leaf drop and the berries shrivelling while they ripen.

Solanum capsicastrum 'Red Giant'.

Cool greenhouse

As above.

Chrysanthemums

Once tomatoes have been cleared from the greenhouse this month (the amateur gardener's normal main summer crop) chrysanthemums which have been growing in pots outdoors may be brought inside. If they have been planted in the open ground they may be lifted carefully and potted in 9 or 10 in (23 or 25 cm) pots and staked.

Spray if necessary against pests and diseases – a combined insecticide and fungicide used according to the maker's instructions should take care of pests and mildews.

Garden spray *Chrysanthemum* 'Margaret'.

Bulbs

Few plants provide greater or more reliable returns for a small outlay than bulbs. The hardy kinds are easy to grow, increase steadily through the years and when naturalized in grass or wild gardens seem to thrive on neglect.

They also disappear after flowering – an advantage in mixed borders – have flowers of various sizes and shapes, some fragrant, in a wide range of colours and neat foliage. Some bulbs are also excellent for forcing, providing flowers for homes and offices in the depths of winter when other blooms are scarce. This is a good month to pot some for Christmas flowering.

Forcing
Success with forcing depends on good bulbs and for Christmas flowering only the best are good enough. Choose top-sized, solid, firm bulbs free from blemishes, bruises or signs of disease. Be ready to pay slightly more for these than for bulbs to flower a few months later.

Bulbs can be forced in a variety of ways, including using ordinary potting soil and loamless composts as well as specially prepared bulb fibre, which consists usually of peat or moss fibre with charcoal lumps and some fertilizer added.

Hyacinths are very hardy and can also be grown on walnut-sized pellets of wet newspaper loosely packed in a bowl; in brick rubble; lodged on pebbles with water underneath or set in hyacinth glasses containing water nearly up to their bases.

The bulbs should be planted closely together but not touching, usually just covered with compost except for hyacinths and daffodils which are often left with the noses exposed.

Clay or plastic 'pans' or half-pots are ideal for small bulbs.

Next set them outdoors, on a hard surface if possible and cover the containers with 6 in (15 cm) of light soil, sand or weathered ashes. If the pots must be stood on the garden dig a trench around them and heap 6 in (15 cm) of the excavated soil over the top.

Bowls can be protected by wrapping them in newspaper, which will get wet after rain, enabling the bulb shoots to push their way through.

Containers without drainage holes should have a sheet of plastic or some other form of covering laid over the plunge bed in very wet weather, to prevent water collecting inside them.

Bulbs can also be forced indoors. Wrap the pots and bowls in black polythene and keep them in a cold place such as a cellar or attic, a cupboard or fireless room.

After eight or nine weeks in the dark the containers should be full of roots with their shoots coming from each bulb. They can then be removed from the plunge bed to the light, preferably on a cool window sill. When the leaves are well up and the flower buds ready to open they can be taken into the living rooms to flower.

Three stages of temperature should be kept to if possible: 40° F (4° C) for root growth; 50° F (10° C) for foliage and 60° F (15° C) plus for flowers.

Early bunch-flowered narcissi such as 'Cragford' and the 'Paperwhites' do splendidly when lodged on pebbles in a bowl. Never let the bulbs sit in the water however, or they will rot and keep them away from fires and hot radiators. Temperatures around 50-55° F (10-13° C) are ideal.

Forcing tulips should be planted before the middle of September for Christmas flowering and again plunged outdoors. It helps root development if the brown skins on the bulbs are peeled off before planting. Grow them in potting compost.

Some bulbs resent forcing particularly when this is associated with warmth. Snowdrops and dwarf irises for example, produce long leaves which obscure the flowers unless kept cool at all times. However, they do particularly well when grown in pots in unheated greenhouses.

Crocuses too should be kept away from all forms of heating, as well as most rock garden bulbs like anemones, chionodoxas, aconites and muscari until the flowers are just about ready to open.

Planting

From mid-September onwards lily bulbs start arriving from bulb merchants. Try to get them all planted, preferably in dryish weather, between now and the end of November. The overlapping fleshy scales must never be allowed to dry out, so if planting has to be delayed keep them in a box and covered with damp – but not wet – peat or leafsoil. (Incidentally home produced bulbs with plump scales and fresh roots attached are infinitely preferable to imported, rootless, drying bulbs.)

If new bulbs arrive after November, treat as suggested in December. Although many lilies

Planting bulbs. If bulbs are planted in fancy glazed bowls, to be plunged in the garden, protect the bowl by wrapping it in newspaper all round.

can be planted outside in spring, it is not the best time and certain kinds, like *Lilium canadense* sometimes resent it.

As for lilies already growing in the garden, if these are doing well it is best to leave them alone. Should transplanting seem advisable however, or you wish to increase the stock move them when the bulbs are dormant; ie, as soon as possible after the stems have withered.

In the case of *Lilium candidum* however, the resting period is extremely short, for new leaves appear from the base within a month of the flowers falling. Plant these as recommended on p 115.

Lilies may be beautiful but they are also demanding. They must be planted in good soil and kept moist at the roots; and they must be well fed and protected from slugs and botrytis disease. Some need shallow planting because all their roots come from the bases of the bulbs; others make roots above as well as below the bulbs. These are known as stem-rooters and must be deeply planted, usually between 6-8 in (15-20 cm) but sometimes as much as 12 in (30 cm). It is obviously an

Hyacinth 'Myosotis', very happy in an earthenware 'strawberry pot'.

advantage to know when they are stem-rooters and most catalogues give this information.

However some growers advocate shallow planting – with not more than 4 in (10 cm) of soil over the bulbs – even for stem-rooters. Then when the growths appear through the ground in late May or early June they should be top-dressed with moist leafsoil.

Lilies must always be damp at the roots, which usually means planting the bulbs a little deeper in light soils than you do in heavy soils – except for *Lilium candidum*.

Preparation

To give them a good start prepare the planting area by removing the topsoil and work in with it plenty of old leafsoil, plus a little coarse sand or grit if the resultant mix is inclined to be wet and sticky.

You can also add fertilizer if the soil is poor, for example hoof and horn meal (2 oz per sq yard [57 g per sq m]) plus ½ oz (14 g) of sulphate of potash and 4 oz (113 g) of bonemeal per sq yard/metre. Failing leafsoil, very well rotted farmyard manure or compost can be substituted, although leafsoil – especially when obtained from oak or beech trees – is the best soil medium for lilies.

At the planting pockets take out the next layer of soil, discard some and fork over the subsoil. Now put in the bulbs and if the ground is very heavy place a few stones beneath each to draw away surplus water and then cover each bulb with coarse sand. This helps to deter slugs.

Finally fill the holes with the compost/topsoil mixture and insert a bamboo cane with the lily name attached behind each bulb. This cane will not only mark the site of a hidden bulb – essential in mixed borders – but serve as a stake if required.

In succeeding seasons a top-dressing or mulch of leafsoil will greatly benefit the growing plants and keep the roots moist.

Lawns

If you are not too tired of gardening and there are not too many other pressing jobs to do, this is the month when you can really give the lawn a worthwhile facelift which will make it strong and hardy for the spring.

Facelift

First give it the scarifying treatment – raking out all the dead grass and other debris. Even lawn mowers with a box or plastic catcher to collect the clippings do not pick up all the mowings and quite a lot will have fallen on the lawn during the summer.

If you use a rotary mower that does not pick up the clippings, obviously there will be all that much more decaying grass which should be raked out. This is hard work so it is advisable to do a bit at a time and then move on to some other job.

If the lawn has been trodden down over the summer, give it an aerating treatment (see p 68) and if worms are a nuisance, as they often are at this time of year, deal with them too.

There may well be bare patches which need to be repaired.

Seed may still be safely sown this month or next, or the worn patches may be replaced by turf.

Scarifying a lawn.

Sometimes there are thin patches on the lawn – in other words there is some grass but it needs thickening up. With these areas just loosen the surface with a fork and sow seed; or sow the seed and just cover it with fine soil or sand.

It also often happens during the summer that parts of the lawn edges become worn away. These are easily repaired.

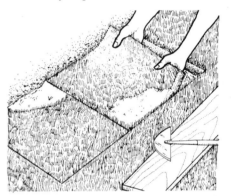

Repairing worn edges of a lawn by lifting and reversing a square of turf to form a new edge; sow seed in the bare patch.

Cut a section back into strong turf, lift it carefully with a spade, and turn it round so that sound turf now fits neatly up to the lawn edge. Then prick up the soil in the bare part, work it down fine and sow some grass seed – 1½ oz per sq yard (42 g per sq m). Cover the patches with pieces of thin plastic.

If moss is still present on the lawn kill it now with a proprietary moss killer. Moss can grow at a surprising rate during the low-light winter conditions (when grass is dormant) and cover several times an area by the spring.

Feeding and caring

Most important of all autumn lawn treatments is the application of a lawn fertilizer specially formulated for applying at this time of year. Experience has shown that a good autumn lawn fertilizer does more good than one, or even two dressings in the spring.

Worms are often more trouble-

Buddleia alternifolia.

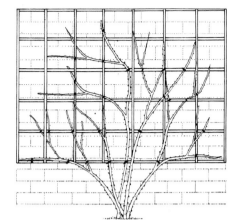

A rose trained to cover a pergola.

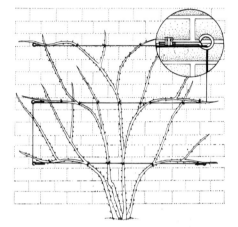

Inset shows a straining bolt.

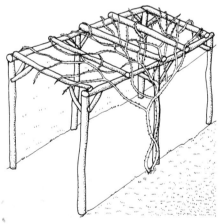

Trellis makes a sturdy support.

some feeding near the surface of lawns in the autumn than they are in the spring. If there are not too many of them you can sweep off their worm casts before they are trodden into the turf or rolled flat by the mower.

If there is a heavy infestation the worms should be killed by watering on a proprietary worm killer. Conversely a few worms in the lawn do a useful job for the gardener by tunnelling about in the turf and aerating it.

It is important to remember that time spent caring for lawns now will pay handsome dividends next year.

Handy Hint: If you often have bare patches to repair on a lawn caused by dogs urinating or general wear and tear, it is worthwhile sowing a square yard or two in an odd part of the garden with grass seed.

Then next year, from about June onwards, there will be a reserve of turf to use for repairing the bare patches. Sow the reserve patch where you can easily mow it until it is required for lawn repairs.

Trees and shrubs

Take cuttings of ceanothus and buddleia and root in a cold frame. Privet, willow, flowering currant, rose species and other shrubs will often root outdoors in a sheltered bed.

Tie in trailing shoots on climbers.

Supports for climbers
If you are planning to plant climbers, including roses, this autumn it is a good idea to fix the supports while the weather is still pleasant for working. Wooden trellis is unobtrusive but must be

secured with spacers an inch or two away from the wall. Fix wires with vine eyes (for straining) at 16-20 in. intervals. A pergola makes an attractive garden feature when clad with climbing roses or other flowering shrubs.

133

Lilies for special purposes

Lily	Colour	Height	Comments
Easy lilies			
L. hansonii	Yellow spotted brown	36 in (91 cm)	Turk's cap shape, stem rooting
L. henryi Henry lily	Orange-yellow recurved	5-6 ft (1.5-1.8 m)	Stem rooting, partial shade
L. martagon and hybrids	Light to deep purple; white	3-4 ft (0.9-1.2 m)	Shade tolerant
L. regale Regal lily	Sulphur-white	3-4 ft (0.9-1.2 m)	Very fragrant, good for cutting. Stem rooting
'Olympic hybrids'	Pinks	4-5 ft (1.2-1.5 m)	Trumpet flowers
'Asiatic hybrids'	Oranges, reds, rose pink, plum, yellow, white	24-36 in (61-91 cm)	Stem-rooting
For mixed borders			
L. regale and hybrids	Cream, gold	3-4 ft (0.9-1.2 m)	Stem rooting
L. speciosum rubrum	White red spots and blotches	5 ft (1.5 m)	Recurved, very fragrant, good cut flower
L. regale and hybrids	Sulphur white and cream	3-4 ft (0.9-1.2 m)	Long lived, easily propagated
Water garden			
L. canadense	Orange-yellow, bell shaped	36 in (91 cm)	Partial shade
L. pardalinum Panther lily	Orange spotted, crimson	4-5 ft (1.2-1.5 m)	Lime tolerant; partial shade
For shade			
L. henryi	Orange-yellow	5-6 ft (1.5-1.8 m)	Stem rooting
L. martagon and hybrids 'Blackhouse hybrids'	Light to deep purple	3-4 ft (0.9-1.2 m)	Very long lived
L. regale	Sulphur white	3-4 ft (0.9-1.2 m)	Stem rooting
L. tigrinum splendens Tiger lily	Fiery-red, spotted	4-5 ft (1.2-1.5 m)	Plant 7-9 in (18-23 cm) deep
For sun			
L. candidum Madonna lily	Glistening white	4-5 ft (1.2-1.5 m)	Lime tolerant. Shallow planting
L. x testaceum Nankeen lily	Apricot	4 ft (1.2 m)	Lime tolerant
For containers			
'Brandy Wine'	Apricot-yellow	36 in (91 cm)	Stem rooting
'Connecticut King'	Lemon-gold	36 in (91 cm)	Stem rooting
'Destiny'	Lemon-yellow	36 in (91 cm)	Stem rooting
'Enchantment'	Bright orange-red	36 in (91 cm)	Stem rooting
L. regale	Creamy white	3-4 ft (0.9-1.2 m)	Stem rooting
'Pink Pearl'	Shades of pink	4-5 ft (1.2-1.5 m)	Scented
'Royal Gold'	Rich gold	4-5 ft (1.2-1.5 m)	Stem rooting
For naturalizing			
American hybrids	Yellows, oranges to reds	36 in (91 cm)	Stem rooting
L. hansonii	Yellow with brown spots	36 in (91 cm)	Stem rooting
L. henryi	Orange-yellow	5-6 ft (1.5-1.8 m)	Stem rooting
L. martagon	Purple, recurved	3-4 ft (0.9-1.2 m)	Shade tolerant
L. pardalinum Panther lily	Orange spotted, crimson	4-5 ft (1.2-1.5 m)	Lime tolerant
L. regale Regal lily	Creamy	3-4 ft (0.9-1.2 m)	Stem rooting
L. speciosum	White and crimson very large	4-5 ft (1.2-1.5 m)	Plant 10-12 in (25-30 cm) deep. Stem rooter. Sun or partial shade. Fragrant
L. x testaceum	Apricot-yellow	4 ft (1.2 m)	Lime tolerant
L. pyrenaicum	Greenish-yellow with black spots	2-4 ft (0.6-1.2 m)	Flowers pendulous, unpleasantly scented

Lilium 'Enchantment'.

OCTOBER

Fruit: Prepare ground for new fruit plantings. Start winter pruning of apples and pears. Pick apples and pears when they are ready and store in a frost-free place. Prune blackcurrants and other bush fruits. Spray with a winter wash after pruning. Deal with old neglected trees.

Vegetables: Plant onion sets and in the south spring cabbages. Thin lettuce seedlings. Lift potatoes and carrots for storing. Tie onions in 'ropes'. Clear away all spent crops. Dig ground cleared of crops.

Roses: Cut back long new growths on bush roses. Heel in roses from the nursery if the ground is not ready to receive them.

Flowers from seed: Sow sweet peas and cover with cloches. Plant out biennials raised from seed while the ground is still warm. Plant young perennials raised from seed if large enough. Control mice.

Alpines: Plant small bulbs in pots or pans to move indoors or into the cold greenhouse later. All small bulbs should be planted outdoors in the rock garden or containers this month. Watch for slugs and snails; renew layer of chippings if necessary.

Cold greenhouse: Bring in shrubs in containers that may need protection from cold and wet. Bring in chrysanthemums. Remove shading from glass. Rest fuchsias. Pot roots of mint.

Cool greenhouse: Pot on flowering plants. Plant bulbs to flower in the New Year.

Chrysanthemums: Lift outdoor chrysanthemums and bring under cover. Give late flowering varieties plenty of air and a little heat.

Hardy border flowers: Dig and manure sites for new borders.

Bulbs: Plant bulbs in bowls. Plant small bulbs outdoors or in pots or pans – also daffodils.

Trees and shrubs: Plant trees and shrubs. Prepare the sites well. Insert stakes in the holes before planting.

Fruit

Even the smallest garden has room for a few soft fruit bushes and usually one or two small trained fruit trees. If you plan starting a new fruit garden, the ground should be dug and manured this month.

Planning and preparation

Work in plenty of well rotted farmyard manure if possible, or, failing this, garden compost or mushroom compost and allow the ground time to settle before planting next month. If the soil is very heavy it may be advantageous to leave the ground rough to allow the weather to break up the clay clods and then plant in spring.

When planning a mini-orchard, give the plants as open a situation as possible.

Fruit is usually grown well away from the house, often at the end of the garden. In suburban areas there is frequently a fence divider and this can, with advantage, be used for growing climbing cane fruits – like loganberries, blackberries and wineberries.

Some tree fruits, like morello cherries will also succeed in such situations. At the end of the plot it should be possible to segregate the orchard – and vegetable garden if desired – with a fruit hedge or a line of trained cordon or espalier apple or pear trees.

Naturally, if you take food out of the soil you must give some back, so it is highly important to plant fruit bushes and trees in fertile ground, properly prepared beforehand by cleaning, deep digging and manuring. In later years the fertility can be kept up by regular mulching – particularly in the case of soft fruits.

The chief causes of poor fruit and indifferent cropping are:

1. Over planting. Too many trees and bushes for the area involved.

2. Growing poor or outmoded varieties.

3. Worn-out bushes, particularly of soft fruits. The latter need renewing every 10 to 15 years at most; strawberries every third season.

4. Lack of regular attention in the way of pruning, mulching and pest control.

An apple fruit hedge.

Planting

Although there are exceptions, for example in the case of strawberries and container plants from a garden centre, most fruit trees and bushes are best transplanted during the dormant season – and in early autumn for preference.

October is an ideal time to plan and plant fruit gardens so that the trees and bushes have the opportunity to settle in before the worst of the weather arrives.

An open, well drained site in good loamy soil is the ideal. Although not mandatory and remembering that there is sun and shade in every garden, it is wise to plan fruit tree placements according to the plant's requirements.

Peaches and apricots for example must have a warm place, preferably a south-facing wall. Pears, plums and apples will do equally well against east or west-facing walls or fences while, if you are stuck with a north-facing wall use it for a morello cherry, or perhaps a few trained (fan or cordon) red currants or gooseberries.

Raspberries and blackcurrants however need a fair amount of sun, so keep these to the centre of the plot, and strawberries need full sun so give them an open position – unless you choose to rotate them with vegetables in the kitchen garden area.

It is good policy to have a firm path around the centre plot, since this will enable you to work both sides dry shod during such operations as spraying, weeding, pruning and picking. A fruit cage is essential in a bird-infested garden; without it you will have very few strawberries, raspberries, currants or gooseberries. The alternative is to spread nets over the bushes when the fruits are ripening.

When planting a fruit tree take out holes seemingly larger and deeper than will be required, place a layer of well rotted manure over the base, covering this with several inches of light soil.

Morello, or sour cherry.

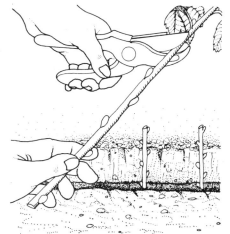

Hardwood cuttings. With black currants leave the buds in place. Insert in shallow trench with some sand at the bottom.

Set the tree inside with its roots well spread – cutting out any damaged parts. Mix together moist peat and bonemeal (about two handfuls of the latter to 2 gallons [9 litres] of peat) and work this quantity over and between the roots. Fill the hole gradually with garden soil, shaking the tree from time to time so that the soil settles round the roots; tread it firmly at each stage.

Continue in this fashion until the hole is full and the soil slightly higher than that of the surrounding ground – it levels itself out as it settles. The grafted part of the tree should be above ground level or the tree planted up to its old planting mark. This is easily discernible as it will be a different colour from the above-ground part. All trees should be staked at the time of planting. Planting distances vary according to the type of tree (see p 152).

Planting distances in the case of soft fruit will vary slightly according to the nature of the soil; closer planting being more permissible in light soils than on heavy ground. General recommendations, based on the Royal Horticultural Society's *Fruit Garden Displayed* are as follows:

Blackcurrants: 6 ft (1.8 m) apart

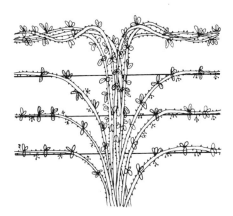

Training hybrid blackberries. This can be done up a post, or on wires (above) stretched between posts or against a wall.

and in between rows.
Red and white currants: 5 ft (1.5 m) except cordons which should be 15 in (38 cm) apart.
Gooseberries: 5 ft (1.5 m) in and between rows; cordons 1 ft (30 cm).
Raspberries, loganberries and other **hybrid berries:** 6 ft (1.8 m) apart; 15-18 in (38-46 cm) in the rows.
For recommended varieties see p 164.

Pruning

Winter pruning of apples and pears can begin this month and continue

With cuttings of white and red currants, also gooseberries which are normally grown on a short 'leg', remove the lowest four or five buds.

in suitable weather while the trees remain dormant. Early pruning is nevertheless advisable, partly because it gets much uncomfortably colder outdoors as the weeks slip by, but mainly because trees should be sprayed with a winter wash once pruning is completed.

Neglected old trees probably demand major surgery. Clear the centre of the tree to let in light and air, cutting back obstructive branches to the main trunk if possible. Next remove inward growing, damaged, crossing or weak branches and paint all large wounds over 1 in (3 cm) across with a wood preservative.

Next deal with the laterals (side growths), bearing in mind the need to strike a balance between the shoot growth and root growth. Very vigorous varieties like 'Bramley's Seedling' usually need less severe cutting than a weak grower like 'Cox's Orange Pippin,' for cutting stimulates growth and can inhibit fruit bearing in the first instance.

But on the other hand it encourages the formation of fruit buds in the case of 'Cox' since the roots are encouraged because more leafy shoots are produced. In the main there are two methods of treatment:

1. Some laterals can be cut back to about 6 in (15 cm) of the old wood; the rest can be left uncut (in very vigorous varieties), which slows down extension growth, while stimulating some of the leaf buds near the branch to convert to fruit buds. Another year the shoot may then be taken back to these and form a fruit spur. This method is also adopted for tip bearers.

2. Weak growers should have most of the laterals cut back to form 2-3 in (5-8 cm) spurs. This will stimulate replacement wood shoots from the top buds and in most cases a fruit bud will form behind each stub. Trained fruit trees will also be shortened back at this time to a few buds.

Sound fruits of apples and pears ready for gathering should now be picked and stored in a cool frost-free place.

Finish pruning blackcurrants. Except in areas subject to much damage from bullfinches and other birds taking the dormant buds, this is a good time to prune red and white currants and gooseberries.

Start by removing damaged, diseased and very old branches, also any which interfere with others or block the centres of light and air. This is most important in the case of currants, which should

have well spread branches arranged like the spokes of an umbrella.

Cut back all the laterals on these to within two buds of their base and reduce the leaders by half – always to an outward pointing bud if upright, inward if drooping. Occasionally a whole branch may need replacing with new growths from the base.

Cordons: Cut back leaders when the bushes have reached the desired height and take laterals back to ½ in (1 cm).

Gooseberries: Remove weak growths and any others which block the light or seem likely to make picking difficult. Shorten back laterals to around 3 in (7.5 cm); the leaders by half. Treat cordons as for red currants.

Complete planting of strawberry runners.

Take hardwood cuttings of black, red and white currants and gooseberries. For methods see p 23. The lower buds of bushes intended to be grown on a leg (short trunk) should be picked out before planting, leaving only the top 3 or 4. Bush gooseberries can be left as they are; in which case old branches will be regularly removed and replaced by young basal shoots.

Vegetables

There is still time to plant onion sets and spring cabbages in the south.

Thin seedlings of lettuces sown in August or September. If desired the seedlings may be lifted carefully and transplanted under cloches. Lift potatoes, maincrop beetroots and carrots for storing.

Tie onion bulbs in ropes and hang in a dry frost-free place. Clear away to the compost heap all spent crops – runner and French beans, old cabbage or cauliflower stumps – as there is no point in leaving them to use up plant food or as fodder for pests or diseases to live

in or multiply. Burn woody material like the stems of cabbages.

As soon as the ground is cleared of crops start to dig it over working in manure where this is appropriate and leave the ground rough for the winter. Heavy clay soils are best dealt with in this way in the autumn so that winter frost may break up the surface and make it easy to work in the spring.

Roses

By now roses are just about finished for the year. The strong growing varieties of hybrid tea or floribunda roses may have made long growths 3-4 ft (0.9-1.2 m) high. These tall plants may be rocked about in autumn gales, so it is wise to cut their strong shoots back to about half their length.

If new rose bushes arrive and the ground is not yet ready for planting unwrap the bundle and heel the bushes in separately in a shallow trench; cover the roots with soil and firm it well.

They will be safe like this for weeks if necessary. If it is not possible to heel the bushes in – the ground may be too wet, frozen or covered with snow – unwrap the bundle and stand the roses in a frost-free place. Keep the roots moist.

Flowers from seed

Sweet peas sown now in the open and covered with glass or plastic cloches will flower a good month earlier than those sown in the spring. Alternatively, you can sow the seeds in pots or boxes, and keep them in a cold frame or under a cloche or two for planting out in March – again aiming for early flowers say in June.

Mice may be a problem with sweet peas sown in the open ground and it is worthwhile scattering some holly leaves or such like to deter them – the older and

A good mix of wallflowers.

pricklier the better – in the drill among the seeds.

Biennials – wallflowers, myosotis, foxgloves, sweet williams, Canterbury bells – and also perennials raised from seed should be planted out early this month while the soil is still fairly warm. They will then make some new roots before the winter sets in.

If you intend to plant tulips or other spring flowering bulbs among your wallflowers or other spring bedding plants, plant the bedding plants first and then plant the bulbs. This may seem rather obvious advice, but many a gardener has done it the other way round and chopped precious bulbs in half with a trowel when planting the wallflowers!

If young plants of herbaceous perennials are large enough they may be planted out this month, but small plants would be better kept in a cold frame or under glass or plastic cloches until the spring.

Alpines

Slugs and snails are on the move again if the ground is wet. If the layer of stone chippings on the rock garden or on stone sinks has been disturbed during the summer when weeding had to be done, top it up now. Slugs do not like stone chippings as they are too rough to slither over.

Small bulbs may be planted now in pots or pans for growing in a frame to be moved later on into a cold greenhouse – or even indoors.

All small bulbs such as crocuses, miniature narcissi, snowdrops, triteleas, winter aconites, tulips such as *Tulipa kaufmanniana, T. praestans, T. pulchella, T. linifolia* and many more, should be planted in October as they need to have a long growing period to do well.

Cold greenhouse

Bring under cover those plants in tubs and containers which are likely to suffer in cold wet weather, for example camellias, agapanthus, and bay trees (in the north). The agapanthus can be allowed to get practically bone-dry, but the others will need enough watering to keep the soil always moist.

Finish bringing chrysanthemums indoors to flower.

Remove shading from glass to allow the maximum amount of light to penetrate in winter.

Rest fuchsia plants by gradually withholding water so that the leaves fall.

Pot roots of mint and bring into the house to provide early shoots in the spring.

Cool greenhouse

Pot on cinerarias, calceolarias and schizanthus from late sowings.

Continue planting bulbs for spring decoration.

Chrysanthemums

Outdoor chrysanthemums finish flowering this month. The hardy Korean varieties may be left in the ground. Many of the other outdoor varieties will usually overwinter in the open in the warmer southern parts of the country although they may be killed in exceptionally severe weather in the winter.

To be on the safe side cut the plants down, lift them carefully, wash the roots free of soil and place them in boxes in a cold frame, or even in a heated greenhouse. Just cover the roots with a soilless, peat-based compost.

Late flowering varieties in the greenhouse need plenty of ventilation and a good circulation of air. A little heat will ensure this.

Hardy border flowers

Before the ground gets too cold dig over the site intended for new border flowers. Choose an open sunny site if you plan a herbaceous or mixed border, although those

141

areas intended for shade lovers need to be similarly prepared.

Remove weeds and deeply dig the soil, working in generous quantities of well rotted farmyard manure or garden compost. Leave the ground to settle until planting takes place in spring (see p 66).

Dividing clumps of hardy herbaceous plants. Clumps may be pushed apart by two forks back to back (top) and smaller plants can be separated into strong new pieces by a knife.

Bulbs

Carry on with planting the bulbs in bowls for forcing, particularly hyacinths, tulips and narcissi. By staggering these plantings at fortnightly intervals it will be possible to have flowers for the house from the New Year through until March. For techniques see p 130.

Planting small bulbs

This is also a good time to plant the smaller bulbs outdoors. Never leave these out of the ground longer than is necessary for they soon deteriorate when exposed, especially winter aconites (*Eranthis hyemalis*) and bluebells which, when allowed to get really dry will probably fail to come up in spring.

Small bulbs have many uses. They can be potted in well crocked pans to bring colour and interest to cold greenhouses early in the year; or they can be planted round tree trunks or established in rock garden pockets to provide flowers before there are many alpines in character.

Small bulbs also look attractive in sink gardens or in containers standing at vantage points on patios and in town gardens. Some kinds, like grape hyacinths (muscari) and triteleias can also be used for edging flower beds, particularly rose beds which are not very interesting to look at when the bushes are dormant.

Nevertheless small bulbs never look better than when naturalized in grass or shrubberies or in wild garden settings. Once established they tend to spread to large colonies, coming up year after year and making broad carpets of colour.

One of the first to appear is the engaging winter aconite (*Eranthis hyemalis*); its golden buttercup-like flowers are on short stalks, each backed with a Toby ruff-like collar of green leaves.

Next come the snowdrops, (both singles and doubles are good colonizers), followed by colourful mixtures of crocuses which, selected with care will provide flowers from January until the end of March – and again in early autumn (September and October) if late flowering kinds like *Crocus nudiflorus* and *C. speciosus* are planted.

Bulbs and their locations

White, blue, pink and even yellow anemones are available and especially useful in open landscapes, for they flower and die before the trees produce their canopies of leaves and so do not mind shade in summer. *Anemone blanda* and *A. appennina*, both blue flowered but with varieties in other shades, are particularly attractive and if kept free of perennial weeds will soon make carpets of colour under deciduous trees.

Narcissi

Dwarf narcissi demand more open positions and look best growing in grass. A damp meadow-like area is the ideal, the grass cut annually at the end of June which gives the bulb foliage an opportunity to die down naturally. There are various

Eranthis hyemalis.

Anemone ranunculoides

142

kinds like the March/April flowering hoop petticoat, *Narcissus bulbocodium* which has its petal-like perianth segments reduced to mere strips so that the central trumpet stands out prominently.

In the aptly named *N. cyclamineus* the petal segments curve backwards like the flowers of a cyclamen, or as they were once described, 'like the ears of a kicking horse'. Growing only 4-8 in (10-20 cm) high it flowers in February and March – before the bulbocodiums – but must have a damp situation to thrive.

Taller and larger flowered hybrids derived from *N. cyclamineus* include the 12 in (30 cm) 'February Gold' as well as 'Peeping Tom', 'Snipe' and 'Charity May'. All are available from bulb merchants.

N. asturiensis, also known as *N. minimus,* is the smallest daffodil, a miniature but perfect trumpet variety only 2-4 in (5-10 cm) high. It flowers very early, February outdoors in a good season or even in January in a cold greenhouse but needs dryer conditions than the others and spreads less rapidly.

Nevertheless it is an attractive species for raised beds in rock gardens or can be grown in sinks and other containers if left undisturbed and protected from excessive wet when dormant.

The so-called Tenby daffodil *N. pseudo-narcissus* which occurs wild in large quantities in the Pyrenees, and a form of which has naturalized itself in the Lake District, is useful to plant on grassy banks or grow in rough grass bordering driveways. The sturdy little flowers appear in March and are usually under 12 in (30 cm) high.

The graceful *N. triandrus* and its varieties are best grown in a cold frame or unheated greenhouse, where the little flowers are not only protected from the worst of the weather but where the bulbs can survive competition from other plants.

Narcissus cyclamineus.

Narcissus bulbocodium.

Narcissus asturiensis.

The flowers borne in loose umbels on 6-12 in (15-30 cm) stems in March and April may be white, cream, yellow; or bicolours of several shades. Popular varieties include *N. triandrus albus,* which is white and commonly called 'Angel's tears'; 'April Tears' (corn yellow) and 'Silver Chimes' – white and pale yellow.

Planting narcissi and hyacinths

Most bulb growers offer assorted narcissi – dwarf as well as tall varieties – at cheap rates for naturalizing. The best way to deal with these is to scatter them on the grass or soil and plant each bulb where it falls. This is also a good method with bluebells, snowdrops and crocuses.

It is easy enough to plant them in open ground; but more difficult in grass, in which case choose a time when the turf is soft and wet after rain. It may be possible to make a nick in the turf with a spade – at various angles – to insert small bulbs but the ideal method is to lift the turf first, especially when dealing with large bulbs.

Fork over the soil beneath, adding a little fertilizer and plant the bulbs in the usual manner. Then replace the turf. Since the grass should not be cut after flowering until the leaves have ripened or turned yellow, you may prefer to keep small colonies in specific areas.

The larger narcissi and hyacinths should also be planted this month, leaving the tulips until next month to lessen their chances of contracting disease.

Hyacinths with their stiff erect habit are usually grown in formal beds or planted in containers, including window boxes. They are also inclined to be expensive so gardeners tend to keep them within view from the house.

Unfortunately hyacinths are never as persistent as narcissi and never produce such a dramatic display after their first season. This is largely due to the British climate and soil conditions, plus the special care and feeding given them by, say, Dutch growers. Nevertheless it is worth keeping the old bulbs if they can be properly dried off and replanted in a sunny sheltered position and grown on for cut flowers. Even bulbs from forcing bowls can be laid in somewhere to ripen and given a good watering and some soluble fertilizer to help the process.

Small groups of hyacinths can also be planted in mixed borders or between herbaceous perennials. Their early flowers are very welcome in spring. Narcissi can also be used in this way, but look most effective when the varieties are kept distinct. After flowering they can be lifted and replaced with later blooming plants.

In order to obtain the best results from narcissi they must be correctly planted. Too often they are not set deeply enough in the ground and then become dry at a critical stage of their growth, receiving a check which induces blindness (flower failure) the following year.

Plant them soon after they arrive from the grower in situations where they can remain undisturbed. There should be 6 in (15 cm) of soil over the top of each bulb in light well drained soil, or 5 in (13 cm) if the ground is heavy. Plant them 9 in (23 cm) apart. Another safeguard against 'blindness' is to give the leaves a foliar feed and good watering when the flowering is over.

Experiments at the Royal Horticultural Society's garden at Wisley in Surrey have revealed that narcissi are more tolerant of having their leaves cut before dying than was once believed. Even so wait for four to six weeks after the flowers have finished before mowing down the foliage of large flowered narcissi, and let the leaves of the dwarf kinds and other small bulbs die down completely first.

Other bulbous flowers for naturalizing include deep blue chionodoxas, the dog's tooth

violets *(Erythronium dens canis)* and others, snake's head fritillaries *(Fritillaria meleagris)* with drooping bells of white or chequered purple and white flowers in April, ornithogalums, snowflakes *(Leucojum* species) both spring and summer flowering, autumn colchicums and various crocuses like *C. nudiflorus* and *C. sativus,* the saffron crocus.

Choosing bulbs

Very attractive results can also be achieved by mixing small bulbs, possibly setting them in defined areas to start with but then allowing the self set seedlings to integrate with the others.

When choosing varieties personal preference obviously plays a big part. Some people like white

Narcissus 'Carbineer'.

Narcissus 'Ice Follies'.

daffodils; others yellow or bi-colours; there are doubles as well as singles and varieties with short trumpets as well as medium or long ones; there are seasonal differences and also bunch flowered kinds.

Catalogue pictures are a help as well as visits to prominent daffodil shows such as the one held each year at the RHS hall in Westminster. Finally, many growers also offer collections (five or ten varieties of their own choosing) at a cheaper rate, plus of course various mixtures for naturalization.

Lawns

Remove leaves from the lawn as they fall, either with a spring-tined rake or a wheeled sweeper. If left, they form a soggy mass on the surface which will harm the grass and may encourage moss. Rotted, they make excellent compost.

Raking up leaves and other debris.

Trees and shrubs

Trees and shrubs may be likened to the bones of a garden – the dependable arboreal structures which give it strength and character. There are many reasons for their importance apart from the obvious one of providing flowers, foliage and in some cases fruits at different seasons. October is a

144

good month to start choosing which trees and shrubs would be suitable for your garden.

Planning

The tree's permanence for example can be exploited to define boundaries, or to enclose private areas of the garden such as sitting out areas or swimming pools. Trees provide shade and shelter for many living creatures; they mask ugly features on or beyond one's own property and they filter strong winds, thereby protecting other plants.

Trees come in various shapes and sizes. They can be large, medium or small; evergreen or deciduous; of spreading habit, upright (pyramidal) or weeping. Once planted however trees usually stay many years in the same place, so the decision of what to grow and where needs careful consideration.

A solitary tree on a lawn for example should be symmetrical with a balanced all round effect. Its size will depend on the area of the garden and its ultimate function. Is it planted to provide shade – or are flowers or fine foliage the prime consideration?

In very small gardens large trees can become a nuisance to neighbours as well as the owner, so pyramidal kinds like the upright cherry *Prunus* 'Amanogawa' or *Robinia pseudoacacia* 'Pyramidalis' may be more appropriate especially near boundary fences.

A small weeping tree like the silver birch *Betula alba* 'Youngii' does not take up much room and looks attractive all the year round, especially when planted in an island position. There are also small weeping cherries, for example *Prunus subhirtella* 'Pendula Rosea' and *P.* 'Kiku-shidare Sakura', a good double form.

Some conifers make fine boundary screens especially *Chamaecyparis lawsoniana* 'Green Hedger' and *Cupressocyparis x*

leylandii, and there are also silver, golden or bluish-leaved conifers of various sizes which can be used in various places to provide winter colour.

It is not advisable to plant poplars or indeed any British native trees close to the house. Apart from providing dense canopies of leaves most of them produce roots which extend outwards as far as their height. Since a fully grown tree – like an oak for example in full leaf – can take up a ton of water a day, both soil and house foundations can then come under extreme pressure.

Shrubs are less of a problem, being more readily kept in bounds and easier to remove if necessary. Along with trees they can be selected for foliage effect, beauty of flower, autumnal tints, fragrance, fine fruits or even winter blooms.

Planting

Deciduous trees and shrubs can be planted whenever the weather is suitable in the dormant season between now and March. Evergreens can be planted in October but early spring is a better time, when the sap is rising and new growth starting. These of course must be transferred with a large ball of soil attached to their roots (see p 77).

Exceptions to these planting rules only occur in the case of container specimens. These, carefully divested of their wrappings, can be planted at any season, including summer, except when frost or snow is on the ground.

Because they have to stay many years in the same place it is important to see that trees and shrubs go into good soil. Very wet sites must be drained or else avoided, since when their roots get down to standing water – maybe after some years – it can cause rotting so that, the trees may die suddenly and mysteriously, sometimes in full leaf.

The other alternative is to

plant trees which will tolerate a lot of moisture – like willows, alders or the bog cypress, *Taxodium distichum.*

Having settled situations take out planting holes which look considerably larger than seems necessary for the tree roots. Remove the top spit (spade-depth) of soil and put it to one side, then take out another and fork over the base.

Place several inches of well rotted farmyard manure or garden compost over the base of the hole and cover this with some of the soil last excavated. Mix together equal parts by bulk of moist peat and topsoil plus two handfuls of bonemeal for every tree and use this mixture for filling in.

Prior to this the roots should be well spread out in the planting hole – any broken roots being trimmed with a slanting cut underneath. As the soil is returned tread it down from time to time so that the roots are really firm and leave the ground slightly higher than the surrounds.

It will level out as the soil settles. However should the ground be exceptionally dry leave a saucer-like depression all round the tree, bolstering up the edges with soil – which can be used for filling in later. Water into the depression and this will go straight down to the roots.

Two other points need to be remembered. Firstly, standard trees usually need staking, but put in supports before or at the same time as you plant the tree; not afterwards or you may stab the roots. To protect the bark wrap a piece of hessian or a strip of inner tube from a car or cycle round the trunk before tying it to the stake.

Secondly, avoid overplanting in the first flush of making a new garden. Too many gardeners do this and then either have to remove some plants after a time or risk spoiling their shape through overcrowding. It is also an expensive mistake to make.

Trees and shrubs with autumnal tints

Name	Height	Colour	Comments
Acer palmatum cultivars Japanese maple	S 10-15 ft (3-4.6 m)	Orange/red	Shelter from cold winds desirable
A. rubrum and forms Red maple	T 20-25 ft (6-7.6 m)	Green turning scarlet	Does not colour so well on chalk
Ampelopsis – all	C 25-30 ft (7.6-9 m)	Reds and yellows	Climbs by means of tendrils
Berberis – many	S 1-10 ft (30 cm-3 m)	Red and orange	Grows on any good soil
Betula – various	T 18-20 ft (5.4-6 m)	Mainly golden	Some with attractive silver bark
Celastrus orbiculatus	C Up to 30 ft (9 m)	Round leaves turn yellow	Very vigorous
Ceratostigma willmottianum	S 36 in (91 cm)	Foliage red tinted	Rich blue flowers late summer. Well drained soil
Crataegus – many	T 10-40 ft (3-12 m)	Shades of red	Also have ornamental fruits
Enkianthus – all	S 6-10 ft (1.8-3 m)	Yellow to various shades of red	White flowers like heather in May
Fothergilla major	S 6-10 ft (1.8-3 m)	Brilliant red	White fragrant flowers before leaves
Hamamelis – all	S 6-10 ft (1.8-3 m)	Red and yellow	Winter flowering
Liquidambar styraciflua	T 20-25 ft (6-7.6 m)	Brilliant red, yellow gold and green – all on same tree	Needs moist, drained soil. Not suitable for chalky soils. Maple-like leaves

Rhus typhina.

Vitis coignetiae.

Name	Height	Colour	Comments
Nyssa sylvatica	T 15-20 ft (4.6-6 m)	Red; yellow and orange	Moist soil
Parrotia persica	T 10-20 ft (3-6 m)	Crimson and gold	Bark flakes like the plane tree. Leaves look like beech foliage
Parthenocissus quinquefolia Virginia creeper	C 25-30 ft (7.6-9 m)	Orange and scarlet	Leaves with 5 leaflets
P. triscuspidata Boston ivy	C	Crimson and scarlet	Leaves 3-lobed
Rhododendron (Azalea) *luteum*	6-12 ft (1.8-3.6 m)	Orange, crimson and purple	Fragrant yellow flowers in spring
R. (Azalea) *reticulatum*	15-20 ft (4.6-6 m)	Purple	Flowers purple
Rhus typhina Stags-horn sumach	12-15 ft (3.6-4.6 m)	Red, scarlet, orange	Crimson fruits retained into winter
Ulmus procera Elm	T 18-30 ft (5.4-9 m)	Golden	Subject to Dutch elm disease
Vaccinium – most of the deciduous species	S 3-6 ft (0.9-1.8 m)	Scarlet, bronze or purple	Needs acid, boggy soil and some shade
Viburnum opulus Guelder rose	S 10-15 ft (3-4.6 m)	Red and yellow	Maple-like leaves
Vitis – all especially *V. coignetiae* Glory vine	C Up to 100 ft (30 m)	Crimson and scarlet	Very large leaves; one of the best

Nyssa sylvatica

147

Bulbs for naturalizing

Bulb	Height	Colour	Time to plant	Depth	Flowering
Anemone blanda	6 in (15 cm)	Deep blue	October	2 in (5 cm)	Feb-April
A. appennina	6 in (15 cm)	Blue, white, pink	October	2 in (5 cm)	March-April
A. nemorosa	6-8 in (15-20 cm)	White, pink, blue	October	2 in (5 cm)	March-April
A. ranunculoides	6-8 in (15-20 cm)	Yellow	October	2 in (5 cm)	March-April
Chionodoxa luciliae Glory of the snow	6 in (15 cm)	Brilliant blue and white	October	2-3 in (5-8 cm)	Late March-April
Colchicum autumnale Naked boys	6 in (15 cm)	Mauve, white also doubles	July-Aug	4-5 in (10-13 cm)	September
C. speciosum and hybrids	12 in (30 cm)	Lilac, white, crimson, also doubles	July-Aug	4 in (10 cm)	Sept-Oct
Crocus (Winter flowering) (Spring flowering) (Autumn flowering)	4 in (10 cm) 4 in (10 cm) 4 in (10 cm)	Various All shades Mostly mauve	October October July-Aug	3-4 in (8-10 cm) 3-4 in (8-10 cm) 3-4 in (8-10 cm)	Dec-Feb Feb-March Aug-Nov
Cyclamen neapolitanum	1-2 in (2-5 cm)	White, pink	July	4 in (10 cm)	September
Eranthis hyemalis Winter aconite	2-4 in (5-10 cm)	Yellow	September	3 in (8 cm)	Feb-March
Erythronium dens-canis Dog's tooth violet	6-8 in (15-20 cm)	Lilac-rose	October	3 in (8 cm)	March-April
E. revolutum Trout lily	8-10 in (20-25 cm)	Creamy-white	October	3 in (8 cm)	April-May
Fritillaria meleagris Snake's head fritillary	12 in (30 cm)	White or chequered purple	Sept-Oct	4-5 in (10-13 cm)	April
Galanthus nivalis and varieties of snowdrop	6-10 in (15-25 cm)	White, single and double	Late summer or immediately after flowering	3 in (8 cm)	Feb-March
G.n. reginae-olgae	4-5 in (10-13 cm)	White	After flowering	3 in (8 cm)	October
Leucojum aestivum Summer snowflake	24 in (61 cm)	White tipped green	Sept-Oct	2-3 in (5-8 cm)	April-May
L. vernum Spring snowflake	8 in (20 cm)	White	October	2 in (5 cm)	Feb-March
Muscari armeniacum Grape hyacinth varieties	6-8 in (15-20 cm)	Blue, honey scented	October	3 in (8 cm)	April-May
Narcissus bulbocodium Hoop petticoat daffodil	6 in (15 cm)	Yellow	Sept-Oct	2-3 in (5-8 cm)	February
N. asturiensis	3 in (8 cm)	Yellow	Sept-Oct	2-3 in (5-8 cm)	Jan-Feb
N. cyclamineus	6 in (15 cm)	Yellow	Sept-Oct	2-3 in (5-8 cm)	Feb-March
N. pseudo-narcissus Lent lily, Tenby daffodil	6 in (15 cm)	Yellow	Sept-Oct	2-3 in (5-8 cm)	March-April
Ornithogalum species Star of Bethlehem	5-12 in (13-30 cm)	White	Sept-Oct	3 in (8 cm)	March-April
Scilla hispanica Spanish bluebell	12 in (30 cm)	Blue, pink	Sept-Oct	4 in (10 cm)	April-May

Colchicum speciosum 'Album'.

Crocus zonatus.

Colchicum autumnale.

Scilla sibirica.

Anemone blanda, mixed varieties.

Ornithogalum umbellatum.

Muscari armeniacum.

Leucojum aestivum.

Chionodoxa luciliae.

149

NOVEMBER

Fruit: Plant fruit trees and bushes.

Vegetables: Clear away spent crops. Remove yellowing leaves from brassicas. Sow peas and broad beans. Lift and store beetroots, carrots, and turnips. Draw soil up to the stems of brassicas; or in windy gardens 'heel the plants over'. Break leaves over cauliflower curds. Lift and box up mint plants to take indoors.

Roses: Finish pruning climbing and rambler roses. Plant new roses.

Alpines: Cover plants susceptible to wet conditions with glass or plastic. Tidy up rock plants. Plant bulbs. Watch for signs of slugs.

Cold and cool greenhouse: Ventilate whenever possible. Cut down chrysanthemums after flowering. Clean the greenhouse both inside and outside.

Dahlias: Lift dahlias after they have been blackened by frosts and bring under cover.

Chrysanthemums: Check plants overwintering in a frame or greenhouse. Cut down pot grown plants. Watch for pests.

Hardy border flowers: Cut down stems of herbaceous plants. Tie leaves of kniphofias together. Cover doubtfully hardy plants with leaves or bracken. Tidy up the borders.

Bulbs: Finish planting outdoor bulbs.

Trees and shrubs: Prepare ground for planting hedges, trees or shrubs. Deal with shrubs that arrive from the nursery if the site is not ready for planting.

Fruit

Continue planting apple trees. Recommended distances apart will depend on the stocks on which they are grafted (strong or weak growing) and their intended shape and habit. Nowadays, most people with small to medium gardens favour small trees on short trunks, such as dwarf pyramids, bushes, cordons and espaliers.

Cordons – which only have a single stem – should be planted at an angle of 45 degrees, sloping the tops if possible towards the north. Posts with horizontal wires 18 in (46 cm) apart are necessary to support cordons, and also espaliers in their early stages.

Plant cordons 2-3 ft (61-91 cm) apart in a straight line; closer together on light soils than on heavy soils. Espaliers on dwarfing stock are normally planted 10 ft (3.2 m) apart; dwarf pyramids 4-5 ft (1.2-1.5 m) and bushes 12 ft (3.5 m) or a little more for very vigorous varieties like 'Bramley's Seedling'.

Although some apples are self-pollinating, most must be pollinated by another variety flowering at the same time, for example 'Cox's Orange Pippin' with 'James Grieve'; or 'Worcester' and 'Egremont Russet' with 'Lord Lam-

Heeling in fruit plants. A method of keeping plants fresh in a temporary siting until you want to replant in a permanent setting.

bourne'. The ornamental crab *Malus* 'John Downie' is a good pollinator for most apples. 'Bramley's Seedling', on the other hand, is an unreliable pollinator. Recommended Dessert Varieties include the following:

Dessert varieties
Early blooming
'Lord Lambourne' (ready October)
'Egremont Russet' (October-December)

Mid-season flowers
'Discovery' (August-September)
'James Grieve' (September-October)
'Sunset' (October-December)
'Cox's Orange Pippin' (November-January)
'Sturmer Pippin' (January-April)
'Greensleeves' (September-November)
'Spartan' (October-January)
'Worcester' (September-October)

Late flowering
'Ashmead's Kernel' (December-March)
'Laxton's Superb' (November-January)

Cooking varieties
Early blooming
'Revd. W. Wilks' (Late August-November)

Mid-season flowers
'Bramley's Seedling' (November-March)
'Grenadier' (August-September)
'Lanes' Prince Albert' (October-February)

Late flowering
'Howgate Wonder' (November-February)

Recommended pear varieties
Most pears are self-sterile or unreliable when grown as solitary specimens. If your neighbours have trees this may prove helpful; otherwise choose more than one variety, or grow a family tree with three varieties (selected to ensure

Apple 'Egremont Russet'.

Apple 'Discovery'.

Apple 'James Grieve'.

Apple 'Sunset'.

Apple 'Ashmead's Kernel'.

Pear 'Gorham'.

Apple 'Cox's Orange Pippin'.

Apple 'Bramley's Seedling'.

Pear 'Doyenné du Comice'.

Apple 'Spartan'.

Apple, Lane's 'Prince Albert'.

Pear 'Louise Bonne of Jersey'.

Plum 'Victoria'.

Damson 'Shropshire Prune'.

Tayberry.

Pollinators for pears, plums and gages

Recommended pear varieties

Variety	Suitable pollinators	Season
'Baurré Hardy'	'Doyenné du Comice' 'Conference'	October Pick just before ripe
'Conference'	Self-pollinated 'Williams' Bon Chrétien'	October-November
'Doyenné du Comice'	'Beurré Hardy'	November-December
'Gorham'	'Doyenné du Comice'	Mid-late September
'Josephine de Malines'	'Conference' 'Louise Bonne of Jersey'	October
'Louise Bonne of Jersey'	'Josephine de Malines'	October
'Williams' Bon Chrétien'	'Conference'	September

Recommended plums and gages

Variety	Suitable pollinators	Season
'Cambridge Gage'	Most kinds	August-September
'Czar' (Culinary)	Self-fertile	August
'Early Laxton'	'Czar', 'Victoria'	Mid-July
'Kirke's Blue'	Most kinds	August-September
'Marjorie's Seedling' (Culinary)	Self-fertile	October
'Oullins Golden Gage'	Self-fertile	August
'Victoria Gage'	Self-fertile	September

Autumn raspberry 'Zeva'.

Raspberry 'Malling Delight'.

pollination) on the same tree. If only one sort can be grown plant 'Conference' which is not only self-fertile but makes a good pollinator for others.

Raspberries may also be planted this month. Set these in straight lines about 18 in (46 cm) apart; cut the canes down to 9-12 in (23-30 cm). Raspberries need supporting so fix straining wires to end posts to which they may be tied as the canes develop. Normally three wires are sufficient; at 2 ft (61 cm), 3 ft 6 in (1 m) and 5 ft (1.5 m) from the ground.

Make these supports strong as they have to take a lot of weight when the plants are in full growth. Good soil is essential for raspberries so work organic matter into the ground during the initial digging.
Recommended varieties include:

Summer fruiting
'Malling Promise', 'Glen Clova' – early.
'Malling Delight', 'Malling Jewel' – mid season.
'Malling Admiral', 'Norfolk Giant', 'Leo' – late.

Tayberry; Medana Strain, a cross between a blackberry and a raspberry, large fruits, July-August; prune and treat as for loganberries.

Autumn fruiting
'September', 'Zeva', 'Fallgold' (yellow fruited).

Vegetables

This is a dreary month on the vegetable plot, but every hour spent clearing up, disposing of material that will rot down on the compost heap, or burning woody debris will save time later on.

There may still be snow and frost after the turn of the year. So if you can have the clearing up and digging behind you there will be less of a backlog of work to clear up in the spring when there is so much to be done anyway.

Remove yellowing leaves on Brussels sprouts and other brassicas and put them on the compost heap.

In sheltered gardens sow a row of an early pea such as 'Feltham First' or 'Meteor' and a broad bean such as 'Aquadulce Claudia' and cover them with cloches.

In mild districts it is worth taking a gamble and sowing these vegetables in the open. But in colder districts provide cloche cover.

Beetroots, carrots and turnips if not lifted earlier may be lifted now to put into store.

In exposed gardens draw soil up to the stems of kales, Brussels sprouts and sprouting broccoli to prevent them from being blown over in gales. In some gardens, it may be necessary to stake large plants.

Some gardeners in very windy gardens go to the trouble of heeling over these tall brassicas. Some soil is taken out on the side of the plant away from the wind, the plant is then pushed over at an angle and the soil removed is packed round the stem on the windy side.

If autumn cauliflowers are now producing nice white heads, break a couple of leaves over them to protect them from frost.

Lift some roots of mint and plant them in a large pot or a box; place them in a frame, greenhouse or in a room indoors to provide welcome mint shoots early next year.

Roses

Finish pruning rambler roses and if time permits prune climbing roses and tie in the new growths securely so that they are not damaged by winter gales.

Planting
Roses may be planted at any time between now and the end of April provided the ground is in good condition. Naturally the later they are planted the more assiduously they will need watering in dry spells in the spring and summer.

Roses normally arrive from the grower having been cut back quite hard but not given a final pruning which is done in the spring (see pp 60-61). Before planting, cut off any damaged roots or cut back a little any stems that have been lacerated.

If the ground has been prepared, dig out a hole large enough to accommodate the roots well spread out. Never try to cram the roots into too small a hole.

Except on very heavy ground use plenty of a mixture of moist peat and bonemeal when planting roses – or indeed any other shrubs or trees. This helps the new roots which the roses must form to develop and the bonemeal gives available nourishment slowly for months. A double handful of bonemeal to a 2 gallon (9 litre) bucket of peat is a good mix.

Always try to find sterilized bonemeal because there is the danger that imported unsterilized bonemeal may be infected with anthrax, a nasty and often fatal disease. So, as a precaution always use gloves when handling bonemeal.

Cover the bottom of the hole with an inch or two of this mixture and as you fill the hole in with soil work in a few handfuls of the mixture with it.

Shake the bush up and down gently as you fill in the hole to settle the soil round the roots and firm it with your foot once or twice as the filling proceeds. The hole must be deep enough to allow the 'union' – the point at which the rose variety was budded on to the understock – to be 1 in (2.5 cm) below the surface when the hole has been filled in.

Naturally it is wise when planting standard roses to insert the stake to support the rose before placing the rose in the hole. Driving the stake in after planting may damage the roots. Always tie a standard rose firmly to its stake.

Roses should not be planted in ground where roses have already been grown during the past five years or so. The new roses will almost certainly not grow well. If you are determined to grow roses in ground where roses grew before however, remove the top soil and replace it with fresh soil from another part of the garden.

Alpines

Cover plants that are susceptible to unduly wet conditions with a sheet of glass or a cloche.

Clean up the plants, removing decayed leaves or dead flowers and be diligent in removing any leaves that may have fallen from nearby trees. If bulbs were not planted in October there is still time to put them in.

Attend to alpines in pots or pans; in frames; under cloches; or in a cold greenhouse. Water as necessary and watch for signs of slug damage.

Cold greenhouse

Damp foggy weather must be anticipated this month, and if there is too much moisture lying about leaves and even whole plants can rot.

Accordingly go sparingly with watering, letting the pots become reasonably dry before adding more. A great deal can be told about a plants' moisture requirements by lifting it and gauging the weight. If it is very heavy it is probably too wet.

Floors will no longer need damping down but open the ventilators whenever conditions allow. Movement of air is the best safeguard against mildew and leaf rotting.

Cut down chrysanthemums which have finished flowering; box up the roots and keep these on the floor of the house.

This month and next when the weather prohibits work outdoors is a good opportunity to clean the greenhouse. Woodwork and inside glass should be washed; also dirty pots which should then be stacked in a shed.

Handy Hint: Many people find difficulty in keeping house plants alive and happy. Nine times out of ten it is because they have been overwatered. As a general rule you should allow pot plants to almost dry out between waterings but there is a much easier and almost foolproof way of giving them the water they need. Stand each pot plant in a saucer – plastic saucers in various sizes are available and they are quite cheap.

Every morning pour water into the saucer. Look at it at lunch time and if the plant has drawn up all the water give it rather more next day. If there is still water in the saucer tip it out and don't put quite so much in the next day. Very soon you get to know how much to put in the saucer.

Obviously as the plants grow bigger they will need more water; also of course they need more water on hot days and when they are growing strongly than when they are resting in the winter months. More plants are killed through overwatering than by being kept too dry.

Cool greenhouse

As above.

Dahlias

As soon as frost has blackened the dahlias – and it is wise to wait until this has happened – cut the plants down to about 12 in (30 cm) above ground. Lift the plants carefully with a fork, and try not to damage the tubers if possible.

Wash the soil off the tubers and cut off any that have been damaged. Stand the roots upside down for a couple of weeks in a frost-proof place so that the water in the stem may run down.

Then place the roots in a box or tray and just cover the tubers with soil or peat. Do not cover the crown. This is very liable to rot if kept wet and it is from this point that the new shoots will arise next spring.

Keep the roots in a frost-free place – an unheated shed or garage or even the loft of a house cannot be guaranteed to be frost-proof in a very cold spell. If frost does not lift for three days and nights it can even penetrate into a brick-built shed or garage.

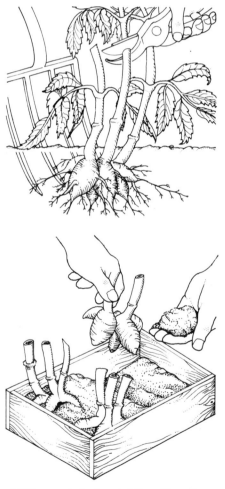

Lifting and storing dahlias. Do not damage the tubers while lifting, and store carefully in a box in a place with some warmth

156

Chrysanthemums when lifted are cut down to about 12 in (30 cm) and the roots washed free of soil.

Chrysanthemum plants, washed free of soil are placed in trays and the roots covered with peat or sandy soil for the winter.

Chrysanthemums

Check early flowering chrysanthemum plants overwintering in a cold frame or greenhouse. Keep the roots just moist – no more – and watch for pests. They will not do much damage now, or in the next month or two but there is no point in letting them multiply.

Grown pot plants as they finish flowering may be cut down to about 12 in (30 cm) and either kept in their pots or shaken out and replanted in boxes of fresh soil – John Innes No 1 compost.

Hardy border flowers

By now most border plants will either have died down and disappeared or will be reduced to an untidy forest of brown stems. They should be tidied up for winter which in the south and warmer parts of Britain means cutting back the stems with secateurs, practically to soil level.

In very cold exposed areas they can either be left to protect the crowns or partially cut back and then reduced to ground level in spring.

Evergreen perennials like pinks, border carnations, hellebores and bearded irises should not be touched, but kniphofias (red hot pokers) are susceptible to winter wet, especially if this gets into the hearts of the plants and freezes.

To avoid disaster gather the leaves together over the crowns and knot or tie them together. Dry leaves or bracken laid over doubtfully hardy plants like eremuri, agapanthus and some alstroemerias will also help to safeguard the roots.

Finally, lightly fork the ground between plants, remove old stakes, take out weeds, reinstate labels and leave all tidy.

Bulbs

The great urgency this month is to complete the outdoor planting of narcissi and hyacinths (see also p 144) and then deal with the tulips. It is wise to postpone dealing with tulips until November because then there is less risk of them contracting the devastating disease called 'tulip fire'.

As a further precaution do not plant tulips where decayed and infected bulb material from previous years was left to rot in the ground. It is also important not to dig diseased compost or other organic material into the ground where tulips are to go.

Plant the bulbs in full sun if possible, setting them 3-4 in (7.6-10 cm) deep and 6-7 in (15-18 cm) apart.

When choosing types and varieties it is important to note that those with short sturdy stems are most likely to survive in windy situations; doubles dislike excessive rain but make good container plants; the parrot types with large floppy flowers are vulnerable to both wind and heavy rain; but the graceful waisted lily-flowered types, the Darwins and May flowering types are excellent for most situations, particularly in formal, mixed or herbaceous borders.

Trees and shrubs

Prepare the ground for new hedges by clearing the site of perennial weeds and digging the ground two spits deep if possible. Work rotted farmyard manure or compost between layers and allow the soil a week or two to settle before planting.

Various plants are suitable for hedging purposes, both evergreen and deciduous. Some, like beech, privet, chamaecyparis and yew make dense compact barriers; others have a deterrent value, for example *Berberis stenophylla*, holly and certain roses; while loose flowering hedges of lavender, cistus, forsythia and such heathers as *Erica mediterranea* are sometimes used to enclose features within a garden.

Smallish plants are preferable to large ones for hedging purposes as they settle in more quickly; 1½-2 ft (38-61 cm) are popular sizes. Planting distances vary according to the nature and normal spread of the plants and are usually quoted in the grower's catalogue. Double rows of hedging – with the plants staggered – provide a quicker, denser hedge than a single row.

Climbers can also be planted in

157

December, adopting the same technique as for trees and shrubs (see p 145). Evergreen climbers, along with clematis varieties, jasmines, honeysuckles and ornamental vines, are usually sold in containers and need to be turned out of these without breaking the soil ball.

Any that arrive from the grower with dry roots should be stood in a bucket of tepid water for half an hour, then left to drain before removal from the container. Plant them carefully, staking if necessary but leave the old stems of clematis intact as winter protection. They can be cut back if required in spring.

Handy Hint: There are many winter precautions worth taking, such as the following:

1. Have a heap of sand, sifted ashes or a bag of salt handy to put on paths or steps when covered with frost, ice or trodden snow. Some local authorities provide salt free or for a small charge. Specially dangerous are paths or steps of York stone and brick.

2. Have handy also a long pole or a long handled broom to knock snow off hedges, trees or shrubs. Do it as soon as the snow has stopped falling as there may be another fall an hour or two later.

Honeysuckle, *Lonicera periclymenum* 'Belgica.'

3. Protect any tender shrubs and any newly planted shrubs with plastic sheeting wrapped round three or four bamboo canes. Leave the top open except during periods of severe frost.

Planting a tree. The hole is taken out and the supporting stake is inserted first.

A hole is dug leaving enough to take the roots of a tree when they are spread out flat.

Clematis 'Nelly Moser'.

Forsythia spectabilis as a hedge.

Low hedge of lavender.

The tree is planted against the stake and the hole is filled with a mixture of soil, peat and bonemeal.

As the hole is filled with soil, peat and bonemeal it is firmed by treading once or twice as the filling proceeds.

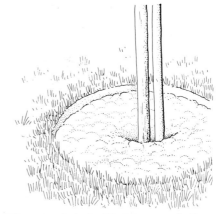

When the hole is filled leave a shallow depression around the tree to allow for easy watering.

159

Tulip varieties

Types of tulip	Approximate height	Colours	Season
Early single	10-15 in (25-38 cm)	Apricot, orange, scarlet, pink	Mid-April
Early double	11-14 in (28-35 cm)	Orange, white, red, gold	Late April
Paeony-flowered	16-20 in (41-51 cm)	Rounded flowers of large size. Gold, white, red, pink	April-May
Mid-season	16-24 in (41-61 cm)	Very robust, selfs and bicolours	April-May
Darwins	24 in (61 cm)	Well shaped, many good selfs. Fine for bedding	April-May
Lily-flowered	18-24 in (46-61 cm)	Long waisted flowers selfs and bicolours; all shades	Early May
Multi-flowered	18-24 in (46-61 cm)	Several on a stem; yellow, scarlet	Early May
May flowering	18-28 in (46-71 cm)	Good self colours, red, pink, white, mauve, orange	Early May
Parrot	20-24 in (51-61 cm)	Large, fringed, variously marked	Mid-May
Rembrandt	24 in (61 cm)	Interlaced in various shades	Mid-May
Viridiflora	9-12 in (23-30 cm)	Much green in the flowers	Mid-May

Mid-season tulip 'Dawnglow'.

Single early tulip 'Pink Beauty'.

Lily-flowered tulip 'Maytime'.

Double early tulip 'Peach Blossom'.

Tulip 'Valentine'.

Tulip 'West Point'.

Varieties for exposed positions

Tulip	Type	Colour
'Apricot Beauty'	Early single	Apricot rose
'China Pink'	Lily-flowered	Rose-pink
'Dr. Plesman'	Early single	Scarlet
'Golden Melody'	Mid-season	Yellow-gold
'High Society'	Mid-season	Orange-yellow
'Maytime'	Lily-flowered	Purplish, white edged
'Peach Blossom'	Early double	Deep rose
'Tambour Maitre'	Mid-season	Glowing red
'Valentine'	Mid-season	Purple, white edged
'Westpoint'	Lily-flowered	Lemon yellow

Tulips, besides being lovely spring garden flowers are excellent for cutting. Usually the taller varieties are the best for this purpose and they may be cut just as soon as the buds are showing colour. The Viridiflora varieties, each with a flashing of green are very popular with flower arrangers.

To extend the life of tulips pierce through the stalks just beneath the buds with a pin just after they have been gathered. This stops them from flopping.

Flopping flowers or buds which will not open can also be brought round by shortening the stems and putting them in warm water.

Rembrandt tulips.

Parrot tulip 'Esther Ringuelo'.

Tulipa viridiflora 'Spring Green'.

161

DECEMBER

Fruit: Deal with fruit bushes. Heel in fruit bushes if they arrive and the ground is not ready to receive them or is frozen or covered with snow.

Vegetables: Clear spent crops. Dig vacant ground. Check roots in store and remove any that are rotting.

Roses: If not done cut back long new growths on bush roses. Rake up and burn all fallen leaves and petals. Check ties on climbers and ramblers.

Alpines: Check alpines in frames once a week. Water if necessary and watch for slugs.

Cold greenhouse: Pot lily bulbs. Bring bulbs in from plunge bed.

Cool greenhouse: Keep plants on the dry side now. Care for pot plants, being particularly careful not to overwater. With greenhouse chrysanthemums water sparingly; remove dead leaves.

Chrysanthemums: Water old plants sparingly and watch for pests.

Bulbs: Pot late delivered lily bulbs and plunge in peat, or soil outdoors or in a cold frame if the ground is cold. Bring in bulbs from the plunge bed as and when ready.

Trees and shrubs: Prune or lop as necessary. Fork over ground between shrubs. Apply mulches. Plant trees, shrubs or hedges.

Fruit

Soft fruits may still be planted if the weather and state of the ground permit. New trees and bushes arriving from growers during periods of snow or severe frost should be unpacked, given a drink if the roots are dry and 'heeled in' in a hole or trench in the garden (only in good weather); or be kept in a shed or garage with plenty of soil or moist peat round the roots. As soon as the weather improves they should be planted.

Recommended varieties of soft fruits include:

Blackcurrants: 'Boskoop Giant', 'Mendip Cross', 'Laxton's Giant' – early;
'Seabrook's Black', 'Ben Lomond' and 'Blackdown' – mid season;
'Jet', 'Baldwin' and 'Westwick Choice' – late.

Red currants: 'Jonkheer van Tets', 'Laxton's No. 1' – early;
'Red Lake' – mid-season;
'Rondom' – late.

White currants: 'White Dutch' and 'White Versailles' – mid-season.

Blackcurrant 'Boskoop Giant'.

Gooseberry 'Lancer'.

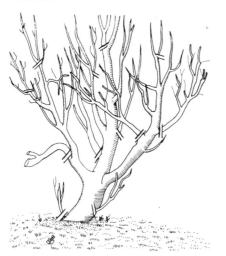

Except in severe weather, fruit trees may be pruned at any time up to February. Deal with a neglected tree, such as this one, by removing some of the centre branches, and those that cross or are excessively tall. Remove dead or deseased wood.

Gooseberries: 'Careless' and 'Green Gem' (green fruits); 'Whitesmith' (white fruits); 'Leveller' (yellow fruits) and 'Whinham's Industry' (red fruits) – all mid-season.

Blackberries: 'Bedford Giant'; 'Oregon Thornless' and 'Himalayan Giant'.

Hybrid berries: 'Loganberry'; 'Thornless Loganberry'; 'Japanese Wineberry'; and 'Tayberry'.

Other fruits: See August, November and January.

Vegetables

Work among the vegetables this month consists mainly of carrying on with the clearing and digging, aiming to have the whole plot tidy by the end of the year.

Check roots in store and if any are showing signs of rotting remove and destroy them.

Redcurrant 'Jonkheer von Tets'.

Redcurrant 'Red Lake'.

Roses

As with herbaceous or shrub borders, try to leave everything neat and tidy before the end of the year.

If not already done, cut back very long new growths on hybrid tea and floribunda roses to 2-3 ft (61-91 cm) high to save them from being blown about in gales.

Rake up and burn all fallen rose leaves and petals which may be carrying disease spores.

Check ties on all climbing and rambler roses.

Alpines

Plants in the rock garden or in sinks or raised beds outdoors should be happily resting for the winter.

Those in a frame under a cloche or in a cold house should be looked at once a week to see if they need water – give it very sparingly in winter.

Check also that they are not being attacked by slugs – if so put down slug bait.

Cold greenhouse

From now on cold severe weather must be anticipated, so the golden rules with unheated greenhouses are:

1. Keep watering to a minimum.

2. Remove dead flowers and foliage regularly.

3. Ventilate if and when possible.

4. Spread newspaper over plants when frost is threatened.

5. Increase the protection of plants in tubs with polythene bags propped over canes.

Pot lilies arriving from bulb merchants for early flowering.

Bring in bulbs from the plunge bed as they become available.

Cool greenhouse

If zonal pelargoniums are to be overwintered in the greenhouse keep the soil on the dry side and the pots in a good light.

Many flowering and foliage plants are bought or received as presents at this time of year. Most of these will be accustomed to more heat than can be provided in a cold greenhouse, so keep and enjoy them indoors or in the cool greenhouse. The following tips may help you to keep them healthy.

Azaleas: Stand pots in saucers and water into these each day. Any water left in the saucer after 2 hours should be thrown away. Keep in a good light.

Standing the pot in a larger container of moist peat and keeping the latter damp helps to maintain adequate humidity.

Bulbs: Keep out of draughts and in a good light or leaves will collapse. Water carefully and pick off faded flowers or they may rot.

Cyclamen: Water carefully – too much causes leaf collapse. A cool light place, for example indoors on a window sill, is best. Use soft water in preference to hard water.

Poinsettias: Need light and careful watering. Allow the soil to get rather dry between waterings. Keep in one place and away from direct heat.

Pot chrysanthemums: Need light and only enough water to keep the stems and leaves turgid. Remove dead leaves regularly. Keep cool.

Primulas: Keep cool and give plenty of water. A light place is essential.

Cyclamen decora 'Pastel Mixture'.

Greenhouse *Chrysanthemum* 'Rydell'.

Primula pubescens 'Rubus'.

Christmas hyacinth 'Ann Mary'.

Chrysanthemums

Keep an eye on the plants, water them sparingly but do not let them dry out entirely. Deal with greenfly or other pests if necessary.

Bulbs

Any late lilies arriving from bulb merchants should not be planted outside unless the weather is very mild and there is no frost on the ground.

Instead plant them in pots and plunge these in peat, soil or ashes outdoors in a cold frame, or else keep them in an unheated greenhouse until April or May. They can then be carefully planted in the garden.

Early flowering tulips for Christmas should be removed from plunge beds on the first of the month. Keep them in the dark for a time in a warm place (65°F [18°C]) until the shoots are about 2 in (5 cm) high, then transfer them to the light, providing a constant temperature of around 68-70°F (20-21°C).

Other bulbs in plunge beds should also be examined. Christmas forcing hyacinths for example should have their pots full of roots by now and be showing strong white shoots. Lift and take these into a light but cool place and leave them there until the leaves and flower spikes are well up, then transfer them to the living rooms to flower. Treat narcissi similarly.

Trees and shrubs

Sooner or later most shrubs and trees need pruning or cutting back. There are various reasons.

1. Limbs may require taking out because they have been damaged by storms or from other causes.

2. There may be dead branches due to dieback or other diseases.

3. The centres of trees may have become so congested that they take much of the light from lower branches. Crossing or rubbing branches should also be removed or cut back; also weak growths and branches which trail on the ground.

4. Cutting may also be necessary to remove any sucker growths at the base of grafted plants, or sprouted watershoots higher up the tree, while a particular specimen may need judicious cutting in order to improve its shape or balance.

5. Finally, and for shrubs in particular, pruning may be necessary for a specific purpose, perhaps because they take up too much

room or to ensure finer crops of flowers or fruits.

Pruning or cutting back

There are no specific rules about these operations; everything depends on how and when the plants flower. Those that bloom on wood produced during the current year for example need a long season of growth beforehand, so these are usually dealt with in late winter or early spring.

Others flower on wood made the previous year and may need pruning after flowering (see p 106). In some cases little or no pruning is required at all.

While dead or damaged wood should be removed whenever seen and at any season, most cutting back of a general nature is undertaken when the trees have lost their leaves, mainly in December and January. Exceptions include members of the plum family, ornamental as well as culinary, as well as flowering cherries and almonds.

Although the principle of removing dead and diseased wood remains these should be spared the knife as much as possible between July and mid-August, because of the risk of contracting silver leaf disease via the wounds. This disease is extremely active during the winter months.

Similarly all cuts over 1 in (2.5 cm) across made on trees and shrubs should be protected from wet, insects and fungus spores with a coat of a sealing compound or grafting wax.

Handy Hint: One of the cleverest gardening inventions of recent years has been the 'cut and hold' tool. This has a blade which presses against an anvil; and attached to both the cutting blade and the anvil are other metal blades. This assembly is at the end of a 12 in (30 cm) shaft. At the other end is a trigger grip.

Using this tool you can reach into a bed or border to cut off, and hold dead flower heads, or reach up

to prune climbers such as wisterias, roses or other shrubs. This is an excellent tool both for the able-bodied or the handicapped. For the able-bodied it often saves the bother of getting out steps to trim shrubs growing against walls or pergolas.

For the elderly or not so agile it enables them to reach into say a rose bed to cut off the flowers fresh or dead without getting tangled up with the thorns.

General tasks

Other tasks this month include forking between shrubs and protecting doubtfully hardy shrubs with leaves or dry bracken. New trees can still be planted if the weather remains kind (see also p 145).

Some plants or shrubs may be protected in winter with a mound of peat or half decayed leaves.

Hedges can also be planted in previously dug and manured soil. Take out a trench the length of the hedge and, using a line to ensure that the plants are kept straight, insert these at the recommended distances. Cover the roots of each plant with about a bucketful of moist peat mixed with a double handful of bonemeal, then return the soil.

Firm the plants and if it seems necessary keep them upright in a straight line with the aid of nylon string or wire strung between supports. This can be removed when the plants are firmly established.

Trees and shrubs

Trees and shrubs with attractive winter flowers

Name	Height	Colour	Season	Comments
Calluna vulgaris Various forms	S 6-36 in (15-91 cm)	Crimson, rose, white	Sept-Nov	'Goldsworth Crimson' 'H. E. Beale' 'Serlei' are good forms. Evergreens
Camellia sasanqua	S 10-15 ft (3-4.6 m)	White, small	Early spring	Evergreen. Grow against a wall
Chimonanthus praecox Winter sweet	S 10-12 ft (3-3.6 m)	Yellow and purple	Feb-March	Grow against sunny wall. Good on chalk. Deciduous
Cornus mas Cornelian cherry	9-12 ft (2.7-3.6 m)	Yellow, before leaves	February	Deciduous. Has small red fruits
Erica carnea Winter cultivars *E.* x *darleyensis* Heather	S 12 in (30 cm)	Red, white or pink Pink or red	Winter	Evergreen. Peaty soil
Garrya elliptica	S 9-15 ft (2.7-4.6 m)	Grey-green on long catkins	Jan-Feb	Evergreen. Best grown against a wall or support
Hamamelis mollis Witch hazel	S 6-10 ft (1.8-3 m)	Golden, richly scented	Dec-March	Deciduous
Jasminum nudiflorum Winter jasmine	C Up to 10 ft (3 m)	Yellow	Nov-Feb	Deciduous
Lonicera fragrantissima	C 4-6 ft (1.2-1.8 m)	Cream fragrant	Dec-Feb	Evergreen, red berries. Shade tolerant
L. standishii	C 4-6 ft (1.2-1.8 m)	Cream fragrant	Dec-Feb	Evergreen, red berries. Shade tolerant
Mahonia japonica	S 6-10 ft (1.8-3 m)	Pale yellow fragrant	Oct-Feb	Evergreen
Prunus subhirtella 'Autumnalis' Autumn cherry	T 20-30 ft (6-9 m)	White, semi-double	Nov-March	Deciduous
Rhododendron mucronulatum	S 6-9 ft (1.8-2.7 m)	Rosy-purple	Jan-March	Evergreen
Sarcococca – several Christmas box	S 3-6 ft (0.9-1.8 m)	White, fragrant	Winter	Glossy evergreen leaves
Ulex europaeus Gorse; whin	S 6-9 ft (1.8-2.7 m)	Golden yellow	March. Intermittently in winter	Evergreen
V. farreri	9-12 ft (2.7-3.6 m)	White	Oct-March	Deciduous, evergreen
V. tinus 'Laurustinus'	7-10 ft (2.1-3 m)	White, pink tinged	Nov-March	—

Trees and Shrubs with Ornamental Fruits

Name	Height	Colour	Season	Comments
Akebia quinata *A. trifoliata*	C	Sausage-shaped violet-grey fruits with dark purple seeds	Autumn	Red purple flowers. Needs mild spring and warm summer to fruit. Usually deciduous

C = climber; S = shrub; T = tree

168

Name	Height	Colour	Season	Comments
Arbutus unedo Strawberry tree	T 15-25 ft (4.6-7.6 m)	Scarlet, round, strawberry-like	Winter	White flowers in winter often at same time as fruits from earlier blooms. Evergreen
Aucuba japonica female cultivars	S 3-5 ft (0.9-1.5 m)	Scarlet or yellow glossy berries	Autumn/spring	Male plants needed to ensure berrying. Evergreen. Shade tolerant
Berberis — most	S 1-10 ft (30 cm-3 m)	Usually pink or red, occasionally black	Autumn	Deciduous kinds best. Very heavy crop
Callicarpa bodinieri giraldii	S 5-10 ft (1.5-3 m)	Masses of lilac purple berries close to stems	Autumn	Lilac flowers
Celastrus orbiculatus	C	Scarlet and gold splitting to reveal seeds	Autumn	Both sexes needed for fruits. Rampant. Autumn leaves turn yellow, then fall
Chaenomeles – most Japanese quince	S 2-10 ft (61 cm-3 m)	Green apple-like becoming yellow. Aromatic	Autumn	Bright red, pink or white flowers in spring. Thorny, deciduous
Cotoneaster – all	Trees and shrubs from prostrate up to 25 ft (7.6 m)	Mostly scarlet	Autumn/spring	Useful in rock gardens, shrubberies and against walls
Crataegus – most Thorns	T 10-40 ft (3-12 m)	Red, coral haws	Autumn	Deciduous, flowers white or red and pink in cultivars of *C. oxyacantha*
Decaisnea fargesii	S 5-10 ft (1.5-3 m)	Metallic blue pods like broadbeans	Autumn	Needs moist but well drained soil. Yellowish flowers. Deciduous
Euonymus europaeus Spindle	S 6-10 ft (1.8-3 m)	Rosy red, winged seed pods	Autumn	Likes a chalky soil. Deciduous
Hippophae rhamnoides Sea buckthorn	T 5-10 ft (1.5-3 m)	Orange berries	Autumn/early spring	Good seaside tree, male plant needed to ensure fruits
Ilex aquifolium varieties Holly	T 10-25 ft (3-7.6 m)	Scarlet, orange yellow berries	Winter	Male plant needed for pollination. Weeping and variegated kinds available. Other berrying species occur
Leycesteria formosa Flowering nutmeg	S 6-8 ft (1.8-2.4 m)	Shiny, reddish purple berries	Autumn	White flowers in drooping sprays with dark red bracts, late summer
Malus – many Flowering crabs	T 10-25 ft (3-7.6 m)	Scarlet, purplish, golden apple-like fruits	Autumn	Some used for jellies. Flowers also attractive in spring
Pernettya mucronata	S 2-5 ft (0.6-1.5 m)	White, pink, red, magenta marble-like berries	Late summer/ autumn	Peaty soil; dislikes lime. Male plants needed for pollination
P. spinosa Blackthorn; sloe	10-15 ft (3-4.6 m)	Black fruits	Autumn	Used to make sloe gin
Poncirus trifoliata	S 5-10 ft (1.5-3 m)	Green orange-like, becoming yellow	Late summer	Deciduous, very thorny. White fragrant flowers in spring
Passiflora caerulea Passion flower	C	Orange fruits	Late summer	Attractive flowers. Needs sheltered position and sun. Usually deciduous

Trees and shrubs

Name	Height	Flower and leaf colour	Season	Comments
Pyracantha cultivars Firethorn	S 8-15 ft (2.4-4.6 m)	Masses of scarlet or orange-yellow berries	Autumn/winter	Thorny evergreen, most soils, tolerates light shade
Rosa moyesii *R. rugosa* and others	S 6-12 ft (1.8-3.6 m)	Scarlet hips. Bottle shaped or round	Autumn/winter	Deciduous
R. spinosissima (R. pimpinellifolia) Scotch rose	12-36 in (30-91 cm)	Black		
Ruscus aculeatus Butcher's broom	S 24-36 in (60-91 cm)	Red, round berries	Autumn	Stiff stems, spine-tipped leaves, minute. All soils. Male plant needed as pollinator
Sambucus nigra and forms Elder	T 12-15 ft (3.6-4.6 m)	Blue-black berries	Summer	Flowers white, scented, various variegated forms. Deciduous
Skimmia japonica and cultivars	S 3-6 ft (0.91-1.8 m)	Scarlet berries	Autumn/late spring	Evergreen, both sexes needed for fruits
Sorbus – most	T 10-25 ft (3-7.6 m)	Pink, red, yellow, white berries	Autumn/winter	Includes the whitebeams and mountain ashes. Deciduous
Symphoricarpos rivularis Snowberry	S 5-10 ft (1.5-3 m)	White spongy fruits	Autumn/winter	Shade tolerant, deciduous
Viburnum opulus Guelder rose	S 10-15 ft (3-4.6 m)	Red juicy berries	Late summer	Deciduous, leaves colouring in autumn; flowers white. Berries golden in 'Xanthocarpum'
V. rhytidophyllum	10-15 ft (3-4.6 m)	Red turning black	Autumn	Evergreen, large corrugated leaves

Variegated foliage

Name	Height	Flower and leaf colour	Season	Comments
Abutilon megapotamicum 'Variegatum'	S 6-9 ft (1.8-2.7 m)	Leaves mottled yellow. Flowers red and yellow	Summer/autumn	Good wall shrub for a south position. Semi-evergreen
Acer negundo 'Variegatum' Box elder	T 20-25 ft (6-7.6 m)	Leaves margined and splashed white	Spring/autumn	Best grown in an island position. Remove plain green shoots. Deciduous
A. platanoides 'Drummondii'	T	Leaves bordered cream	Spring/autumn	Sycamore-like leaves. Deciduous
Aucuba japonica Varieties	S 3-5 ft (0.9-1.5 m)	Gold speckled, blotched or variegated	All year	Usually male forms, but 'Variegata' is female so needs a male plant to produce berries. Evergreen
Cornus mas 'Variegata' Cornelian cherry	S 30-35 ft (9-10.6 m)	White leaf margins; yellow flowers before leaves in February	Spring/autumn	Deciduous
Elaeagnus pungens 'Maculata'	S 9-12 ft (2.7-3.6 m)	Gold-splashed centres of leaves. Small white flowers in autumn	All year	Evergreen. Not for chalk soils
Euonymus fortunei 'Silver Queen'	S 4-6 ft (1.2-1.8 m)	Green leaves heavily variegated cream	All year	Evergreen. Very compact shrub. Does well on chalk

C = climber; S = shrub; T = tree

Name	Height	Flower and leaf colour	Season	Comments
E. japonicus 'Macrophyllus Albus'	S 10-15 ft (3-4.5 m)	Leaves margined white	All year	Evergreen
Fatsia japonica 'Variegata'	S 6-15 ft (1.8-4.5 m)	Large green, hand shaped leaves with white tips	All year	Not as hardy as the green form, but good on well drained soils in mild gardens. Evergreen
Fuchsia magellanica 'Variegata'	S	Leaves margined yellow, red and purple flowers	Summer/autumn	Deciduous, give sheltered site; often cut to ground in winter
F.m. 'Versicolor'	S	Leaves white and green, rosy when young	Summer/autumn	
Ilex x *altaclarensis* 'Golden King'	T 18-30 ft (5.5-9 m)	Gold margins to leaves	All year	Female plant, almost spineless
I. x *a.* 'Silver Sentinel'	T	Cream leaf margins mottled grey	All year	Female
I. aquifolium — many Common holly	T 10-25 ft (3-7.6 m)		All year	Many forms with silver or gold leaf variegation
Kerria japonica 'Variegata'	S 4-6 ft (1.2-1.8 m)	Leaves variegated creamy white. Flowers yellow	Spring/autumn April/May	Deciduous. Most soils
Liriodendron tulipifera 'Aureomarginatum' Tulip tree	T 18-25 ft (5.5-7.6 m)	Leaves margined and splashed yellow. Flowers green and gold	Spring/autumn July July	Deciduous
Pachysandra terminalis 'Variegata'	S 12 in (30 cm)	Leaves white variegations. Flowers white in spikes	All year February/March	Good ground cover plant. Likes moist soil. Evergreen
Pittosporum tenuifolium 'Silver Queen'	S 10-15 ft (3-4.6 m)	Silvery leaf suffusions	All year	Very elegant. Evergreen. Must have mild conditions
Populus x *candicans* (P. gileadensis) 'Aurora'	T 30-40 ft (9-12 m)	Young leaves heavily marked with cream and tinged pink	Spring	Best grown in an island position. Deciduous
Prunus lusitanica 'Variegata' Portugal laurel	S 6-10 ft (1.8-3 m)	Leaves margined white	All year	Evergreen. Large shrub
Viburnum tinus 'Variegata' Laurustinus	S 7-10 ft (2-3 m)	Leaves variegated yellow. White flower	All year Autumn/spring	Evergreen, tolerates shade
Weigela florida 'Variegata'	S 6-8 ft (1.8-2.4 m)	Leaves margined white or cream. Flowers pink	Spring/autumn May/June	Easy shrub, very free flowering, does best in sun

Fragrant flowers or foliage

Name	Height	Colour	Season	Comments
Artemisia aborescens	S 3-4 ft (0.9-1.2 m)	Silvery leaves. Flowers yellow	Summer	Rounded habit, finely cut leaves are aromatic
Buddleia alternifolia	S 10-20 ft (3-6 m)	Mauve	June	Trailing branches, good in isolated position. Needs sun
B. davidii forms	S 9-12 ft (2.7-3.6 m)	Purple, white, violet	Late summer	Flowers fragrant in showy plumes. Deciduous
Camellia sasangua	S 10-15 ft (3-4.6 m)	White flowers	Spring	Fragrant flowers. Evergreen. Give sheltered site

Trees and shrubs

Name	Height	Colour	Season	Comments
Caryopteris – all	S 3-6 ft (0.9-1.8 m)	Blue flowers, grey-green leaves	August/ September	Aromatic leaves. Deciduous. Well drained soil, including chalk
Chimonanthus praecox Winter sweet	S 10-12 ft (3-3.6 m)	Yellow and purple before leaves	February/March	Deciduous. Penetratingly sweetly scented flowers
Choisya ternata Mexican orange blossom	S 6-9 ft (1.8-2.7 m)	White flowers	Late spring/ early summer	Evergreen. Leaves aromatic when bruised. Flowers also fragrant
Cistus ladanifer Gum cistus	S 6-9 ft (1.8-2.7 m)	Flowers white with chocolate basal stains	Spring/early summer	Flowers like single roses. Leaves evergreen, aromatic
Clematis armandii	C Up to 30 ft (9 m)	White flowers in clusters	April/May	Evergreen, flowers slightly fragrant
C. montana	C Up to 40 ft (12 m)	Flowers white, pink	May/June	Flowers sweetly scented. Deciduous
Daphne odora and others	S 4-6 ft (1.2-1.8 m)	Purple pink flowers. Small	Winter/early spring	Flowers very fragrant. Evergreen
Drimys winteri Winter's bark	S 9-12 ft (2.7-3.6 m)	White flowers in umbels	May	Evergreen. Large leathery foliage. Flowers fragrant
Erica arborea Tree heath and others	S 6-12 ft (1.8-3.6 m)	Flowers white	Early spring	Evergreen. Flowers honey scented
Eucalyptus – most Gum tree	T 10-45 ft (3-13.7 m)	Silvery leaves, flowers white or red	Spring	Leaves very aromatic when crushed. Evergreen. Need sheltered site
Hamamelis mollis forms Witch hazel	S 6-10 ft (1.8-3 m)	Golden before leaves	December/ March	Strongly scented flowers
Jasminum officinale White jasmine	C Up to 30 ft (9 m)	White	June/ September	Flowers very fragrant. Semi-evergreen
Laurus nobilis Sweet bay Bay laurel	T 10-20 ft (3-6 m)	Grown for foliage	All year	Evergreen. Leaves aromatic, used in cooking
Lavandula angustifolia (spica) Lavender	S 3-4 ft (0.9-1.2 m)	Mauve in dense spikes	June/July	Evergreen, well known shrub. Flowers fragrant. Well drained soil and sun
Lippia citriodora Lemon Verbena	S 3-4 ft (0.9-1.2 m)	Flowers insignificant. Mauve	July/August	Deciduous. Leaves richly scented when crushed. Needs winter protection and full sun
Lonicera – many Honeysuckle climbers and shrubs	C Up to 20 ft (6 m)	Scented kinds mostly white or yellow	Shrubs late winter/spring	All with fragrant flowers. Some evergreen, some deciduous. Shrubs usually winter blooming
	S 3-6 ft (0.9-1.8 m)		Climbers Summer	
Magnolia grandiflora	T 10-20 ft (3-6 m)	Huge cream flowers	Summer/autumn occasionally early winter	Evergreen. Very large glossy foliage. Flowers smell of lemons. Grow against a warm wall
Mahonia japonica	S 6-10 ft (1.8-3 m)	Pale yellow in long drooping sprays	Late autumn/ early spring	Evergreen, spiny, pinnate leaves. Flowers fragrant
Myrtus communis Myrtle	S 6-10 ft (1.8-3 m)	White	July/August	Evergreen. Aromatic foliage

C = climber; S = shrub; T = tree

Name	Height	Colour	Season	Comments
Osmanthus armatus *O. delavayi*	S 6-9 ft (1.8-2.7 m)	Small white flowers Small white flowers	Autumn April	Evergreens with fragrant flowers. Most soils
Philadelphus – many Mock orange	S 4-12 ft (1.2-3.6 m)	Mostly white	June/July	Very sweetly scented flowers. Deciduous
Populus balsamifera Balsam poplar	T 30-45 ft (9-13.7 m)	Reddish catkins	Spring	Sticky buds in spring and balsam-scented young leaves detectable at a considerable distance
Rhododendron – some especially deciduous azalea types	S 3-20 ft (0.9-6 m)	Mostly yellow orange or salmon	May/June	Ghent hybrids, single very fragrant flowers. Rustica hybrids – doubles. Deciduous
Rosa – many	S 3-6 ft (0.9-1.8 m)	Pink and red have most scent	Summer	See p 123 on roses for recommended scented kinds; also Gallica group of old roses. Deciduous
Salvia – all Sage	S 24-36 in (61-91 cm)	Red, blue, magenta	Late summer	Well drained soil, sun. Leaves pungent. Some have silvery leaves. Evergreen and deciduous
Santolina – all Cotton lavender	S 18-24 in (46-61 cm)	Grey or silver leaves; yellow button flowers	July	Sharp drainage. Needs sun. Evergreen. Scented foliage when bruised
Skimmia japonica	S 3-6 ft (0.9-1.8 m)	White flowers red berries all year	April/May	Fragrant flowers, especially on male plants. Evergreen
Syringa – many Lilac	S 5-12 ft (1.5-3.6 m)	Purple, lilac, white, single and double	May/June	Fragrant flowers. Most soils, including chalk. Deciduous
Viburnum × bodnantense	S 9-12 ft (2.7-3.6 m)	White, rose tinted	October/March	Flowers fragrant. Deciduous
V. farreri	S 9-12 ft (2.7-3.6 m)	White with pink buds	October/March	Well drained soil
Wisteria – all	C Up to 100 ft (30 m)	Mauve, violet, white	May/June often again in early autumn	Deciduous, flowers fragrant. Needs full sun

NB There are many other flowering trees and shrubs such as lilacs, which are fragrant, some more so than others. Moreover some, like the many flowering cherries, crab apples, *Cercis siliquastrum*, viburnums and others are grown for their floral charm and not for their fragrance.

Coloured foliage

Name	Height	Flowers	Comments
Gold and yellow leaves			
Calluna vulgaris 'Aurea'	S 1-2 ft (30-61 cm)	Purple	Leaves turn red in winter
C.v. 'Gold Haze'	2-3 ft (60-91 cm)	White	Use plenty of peat during original planting. All evergreen
C.v. 'Joy Vanstone'	18 in (46 cm)	Orchid pink	
Catalpa bignonioides 'Aurea' Indian bean tree	T 15-20 ft (4.6-6 m)	White, yellow and purple, foxglove-like in bold sprays	Well drained soil needed and sun. Deciduous

Name	Height	Flowers	Comments
Gleditsia triacanthos 'Sunburst'	T 20-30 ft (6-9 m)	Greenish – insignificant	Spineless stems. Deciduous. Young foliage has brightest colouring
Hedera helix 'Buttercup'	C Up to 50 ft (15 m)		Green leaves with golden centres. Evergreen. Foliage very small
Humulus lupulus 'Aureus' Hop	C 15-20 ft (4.6-6 m)	Insignificant	Needs full sun to bring out the colour. Leaves rough, 3 to 5 lobed
Philadelphus coronarius 'Aureus'	S 6-10 ft (1.8-3 m)	White in June	Deciduous. Young leaves brightest; may burn if sun very hot
Robinia pseudoacacia 'Frisia'	T 30-40 ft (9-12 m)	White, but rarely flowers	Deciduous. Bright gold from spring to autumn
Weigela 'Looymansii Aurea'	S 5-6 ft (1.5-1.8 m)	Pink	Deciduous, leaves light gold
Red leaves			
Acer palmatum 'Atropurpureum'	S 10-15 ft (3-4.6 m)		All deciduous. Purple, becoming more crimson in autumn. Leaves lobed
A.p. 'Dissectum Atropurpureum'		Insignificant	Purplish red, very deeply cut
A. platanoides 'Crimson King' Sycamore	30-35 ft (9-10.5 m)		Very rich crimson colouring
Corylus maxima 'Purpurea' Hazel	S 10-12 ft (3-3.6 m)	Yellow catkins	Rich purple leaves. Cut stems hard back in spring to obtain best colours. Deciduous. Any soils
Cotinus coggygria 'Foliis Purpureis' Smoke tree	S 9-12 ft (2.7-3.6 m)	Fawn, in smoke-like plumes	Plum purple leaves, red in autumn. Deciduous
Malus x *purpurea* 'Profusion'	T 18-25 ft (5.5-7.6 m)	Wine red flowers and dark red fruits	Deciduous. Copper-crimson leaves
Prunus x *cistena* Sand cherry	S 4-6 ft (1.2-1.8 m)	White	Deciduous. Red leaves
Silver leaves			
Cistus canescens 'Albus'	S 6-8 ft (1.8-2.4 m)	White with yellow centres	Grey leaves. Evergreen
Convolvulus cneorum	S 2-3 ft (0.6-0.9 m)	White or pinkish funnel shaped. May	Evergreen. Grow in sheltered place. Well drained soil. Leaves silky
Cytisus battandieri	T 12-15 ft (3.6-4.6 m)	Gold in cone-like scented clusters in July	Silky grey leaves. Grow against a warm wall. Deciduous
Elaeagnus angustifolia Oleaster	S 10-15 ft (3-4.6 m)	White and fragrant. June	Grey, silver underneath leaves. Spiny, deciduous
Eucalyptus species	T 10-45 ft (3-13.7 m)		Evergreen. Sheltered site
Helichrysum — all	S 12-30 in (30-76 cm)	Yellow	Will grow in poor soils. Evergreen
Olearia x *scilloniensis* Daisy bush	S 4-6 ft (1.2-1.8 m)	White, daisy-like. May	Grey leaves, evergreen, sheltered site, good near sea
Pyrus salicifolia 'Pendula' Willow leaved weeping pear	T 15-20 ft (4.6-6 m)	White	Silver, deciduous. Needs an island position
Ruta graveolens Rue	S 24-36 in (61-91 cm)	Yellow. June/August	Fern-like, evergreen leaves

C = climber; S = shrub; T = tree

Vitis vinifera 'Purpurea'.

Acer japonicum 'Aureum'.

Cotinus coggygria.

Acer palmatum.

Rhododendron 'Winter Cheer'.

Viburnum tinus.

Viburnum farreri.

Jasmenum nudiflorum.

Winter heathers, *Erica carnea.*

Cornus mas.

Catkins of *Garrya elliptica.*

177

Chaenomeles sargenteae (Japanese quince).

Sorbus 'Pink Pearl'.

Euonymus europaeus (spindle tree).

Cotoneaster horizontalis.

Pyracanthas *(P. rogersiana,* orange yellow and *P. coccinea* red).

Variegated foliage

Euonymus fortunei 'Silver Queen'.

Elaeagnus pungens 'Maculata.'

Kerria japonica 'Variegata'.

Santolina chamaecyparissus.

Drimys winteri.

Clematis montana 'Picton's Variety'.

PESTS AND DISEASES

There are many pests and diseases that may afflict plants in the garden, the greenhouse and the home. Happily there are now many effective ways of controlling them, or preventing them from seriously affecting the plants.

Some pesticides or fungicides are formulated as dusts, some as soluble sprays, others as aerosols which are excellent when only a small number of plants need to be treated.

There are also chemical 'smoke cones' which may be used to fumigate a greenhouse to control many different pests.

Pests

Aphis

These pests are commonly known as greenfly and blackfly although they may be yellow, pink or brown rather than green or black. They feed by sucking the sap of leaves, flowers and young shoots causing distortion and stunting.

Aphis also deposit sticky honeydew on the foliage which later becomes covered with sooty moulds. Not only do they weaken the plants but they also transmit virus diseases. Fortunately aphis are readily controlled by using special greenfly killers or general insecticides or a tar oil wash in winter.

Birds

Birds give added interest to the garden but it must be appreciated that they can cause serious plant damage. Bullfinches for instance feed on the flower buds of both decorative shrubs and fruit trees. Similar damage is sometimes caused by other finches, tits and sparrows.

Tits may also attack the open flowers of rhododendrons and

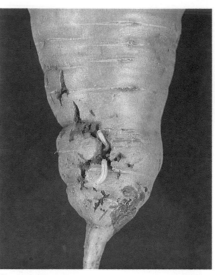

Carrot fly larvae.

Aphids on cabbage.

Caterpillar.

sweet peas whilst hedge sparrows damage the flowers of crocus, polyanthus and runner beans. Sparrows are also troublesome on newly seeded lawns. Top fruit, soft fruit and decorative berries are all liable to bird damage. In the vegetable garden, jays attack peas whilst pigeons and doves devour brassicas.

Bird scarers can be effective in the short term as too can chemical bird repellents. Another method of reducing bird damage is to string black thread over plantings which are at risk and between the branches of trees and shrubs. Complete protection, however, can only be obtained by netting.

Capsid bugs

These very active insects feed by piercing the plant tissue and sucking the sap. The feeding punctures first show up on young leaves as small brown spots but these may later extend into ragged tears.

Capsid bugs also feed on growing points, deforming the young leaves and sometimes causing blindness. They attack a wide range of plants in the flower garden and also damage the foliage and fruits of apples. They can be controlled by repeated sprays with a general insecticide.

Carrot fly

This root fly is the major pest of carrots. The white maggots eat the fine roots of the seedlings and later tunnel just below the surface of the tap root. Not only do the scars disfigure the carrots but affected roots are liable to rot. Eggs are laid in May and again in August so carrots sown at the end of May and lifted during August are usually free from attack.

Earlier or later sowings can be protected from this pest by applying a soil insecticide to the seed drills. Carrots which are not to be lifted until the autumn should also be watered with spray-strength pirimiphos-methyl or trichorphon in mid-August.

Caterpillars

Caterpillars are common pests in all areas of the garden. Most species are foliage feeders but others attack flowers and fruit. They are voracious feeders so it is important to control them in the early stages before they cause serious damage.

Light attacks can be dealt with by hand picking. Indeed this is the only effective way of eliminating those species which protect themselves by spinning webbing 'tents' around the foliage on which they are feeding.

Leaf tying species are also difficult to control by spraying. Most general insecticides are suitable for use against young caterpillars but the larger ones are best treated with sprays based on permethrin or trichlorphon.

Codling moth

The caterpillars of this moth are all too common pests on apples. They tunnel into the cores of the developing fruits, making them inedible. In mid-August the caterpillars leave the fruits to find somewhere to overwinter, so in later picked fruit you see only the mess they leave behind.

This damage can be prevented by spraying the trees with a general insecticide in late June and again in early July. Sprays based on the new synthetic pyrethroid, permethrin, are particularly effective against this pest.

Cutworms

These large, fat, drab-coloured caterpillars live in the surface soil. They feed at night, gnawing the stem bases and causing the plants to collapse. Cutworms attack a wide range of plants being especially damaging to annuals and to lettuce plants.

Careful sifting of the soil near to any damaged plants will usually reveal the culprits. Even so it is good insurance to apply a heavy soil drench of spray-strength general insecticide around the

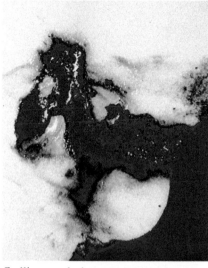
Codling moth damage to apple.

Cutworm.

Raspberry beetle larvae.

target plants to guard against future attacks.

Earwigs

Earwigs, which are readily recognized by their elongated brown bodies and stout pincers, feed on all types of succulent plant tissue. In particular, they can cause serious damage to the flowers of chrysanthemums, cinerarias, dahlias and other plants leaving them ragged and unsightly. They may also gnaw flower buds causing blindness. Since, however, earwigs feed at night and spend the day in hiding they are rarely seen.

The first step in control is to shake open the blooms vigorously to dislodge any hidden insects. Then spray the plants and the surrounding ground with a general insecticide. An alternative approach in the greenhouse is to use an insecticidal smoke. Earwigs can also be trapped in inverted flower pots filled with straw or dried grass and placed on the tops of canes.

Mice

Mice can cause considerable damage during the winter. Indoors they feed on stored seeds, bulbs, corms and tubers whilst outdoors they may gnaw the stems of plants and dig up bulbs and corms. Germinating pea seeds are also liable to attack.

Indoors these pests can be controlled either by trapping or by the use of one of the proprietary rat and mice baits. These baits should be placed out of the reach of other animals in drain pipes or in jars or tins laid on their sides.

Mouse traps or baits can also be used in the greenhouse, in cold frames and under cloches. Bulbs, corms and seeds planted in the open can be protected by repellents such as powdered alum or by laying moth balls on the surface.

Pea moth

Pea moths are on the wing from early June to mid-August, laying their eggs on peas that are in flower at this time. So early varieties escape damage from this pest. Caterpillars hatching from these eggs tunnel into the pods to feed on the developing seeds.

Pea moths are extremely common so it is good insurance to spray mid- and late-season peas with a general insecticide about a week after the plants start to flower.

Raspberry beetle

The small white grubs of this pest, which hatch out from eggs laid on the blossoms, feed on the developing fruit and are often not noticed until the fruit is picked and prepared for eating. Incidentally, this pest, although called raspberry beetle, also attacks loganberries and blackberries.

Until recently the only chemicals recommended for the control of this pest were derris and malathion. Now, however, an even more effective chemical called permethrin is available. This is non-toxic, long-lasting and highly active. Apply when the first fruits turn pink, taking care to spray in the evening to avoid killing bees working on the flowers.

Red spider mites

These tiny creatures, which are only just visible to the naked eye, attack a wide range of plants, both in the open and under glass. They feed on the undersides of the leaves and the first sign of attack is the appearance of a fine yellow speckling of the upper surface. Later the leaves lose their healthy green colour and may become bronzed.

Glasshouse red spider mites spin fine silk webs in order to move to new feeding places. Control by repeated sprays of derris, dimethoate, malathion or pirimiphos-methyl.

Scale insects

Scale insects differ from other pests in that they spend most of their lives firmly fixed to the surface of the plant. They are readily recognized by their shell-like

Effects of red spider attack.

Slug.

White fly.

covering. These insects are sap feeders and not only weaken the plants but also deposit masses of sticky honeydew which becomes covered with sooty mould growth.

Scale insects on vine rods and other woody tissue can be removed by scraping. Deciduous trees and shrubs can also be treated by applying a tar oil wash in winter. Evergreens and herbaceous plants can be cleared of scales by applying repeat sprays of malathion or pirimiphos-methyl in summer.

Slugs and snails

These are particularly damaging pests in the garden. Both slugs and snails feed on the aerial parts of plants making irregular holes in the leaves and gnawing stems and shoots. They are most active in damp humid conditions, feeding mostly at night.

Foliage-eating slugs and snails can be controlled by the use of slug pellets based on either metaldehyde or methiocarb. The underground keeled slugs which can be so damaging to potatoes, do not, however, respond to this treatment. The answer here is to restrict cropping to early varieties and to lift the crop as early as possible.

Thrips

These minute, dark-coloured insects feed on the undersides of leaves, on young shoots and on flowers. Damaged leaves show a yellow mottling whilst affected flowers develop white flecks. Thrips may also deposit small liquid blobs which support brown mould growth. Thrips also transmit virus diseases so infested plants may well become diseased as well as weakened by the pests.

Control by spraying with a general insecticide or, in the case of greenhouse plants, by the use of insecticidal smokes. Since thrips can overwinter on gladiolus corms and on lily bulbs, these should be dusted with HCH prior to storage.

Whitefly

These small white, moth-like insects are major pests in the greenhouse and in recent years they have also become very troublesome on brassicas. They are sap feeders and not only weaken the plants but also foul them with sticky honeydew which becomes covered with sooty moulds.

Whitefly are difficult to control because their eggs and larval stages are resistant to most insecticides. Much the best control is obtained by insecticides based on permethrin or pirimiphos-methyl. Even with these chemicals, however, a programme of 3-4 sprays at 4-7 day intervals is needed for good control.

Wireworms

These soil-living pests are the larvae of click beetles. They are cylindrical creatures with shiny, tough, orange-brown skins and grow to about 1 in (2.5 cm) in length. Wireworms feed on plant roots and also tunnel into tubers, corms and rhizomes, being particularly damaging to potatoes.

They are primarily pests of pasture and wasteland, so are most likely to be found in new gardens. Regular weeding keeps them in check. Where, however, there is a high population of wireworms, the ground should be treated with a soil insecticide at planting time.

Woolly aphid

Woolly aphids are not readily recognizable as aphids because they are covered with white waxy threads. Consequently, colonies of these pests look rather like mould growth. Also, unlike most other aphids, they feed on branches, shoots and pruning cuts giving rise to soft warty growths which may later split open and become cankers.

They are common pests of apple trees and also attack chaenomeles, cotoneaster, hawthorn and pyracantha. Light infestations on dwarf trees and cordons can be brushed

Wireworm.

Woolly aphid.

Rose black spot.

off using a stiff brush dipped in methylated spirit. Heavier infestations on larger trees can be controlled by the use of forceful sprays of general insecticide.

Diseases

Apple and pear scab

This disease shows up as patches of dull olive-green fungal growth on the leaves and as dark-coloured scabs on the fruit. Heavily infected leaves fall early whilst badly scabbed fruit become cracked and unsightly.

Scab normally becomes established shortly after bud burst so it is important to apply a protective fungicide such as benomyl, carbendazim, mancozeb or triforine when the flowers are still green. Repeat sprays are then needed when the flower buds show colour, at petal fall and three weeks later.

Black spot

This common and very damaging disease of roses is easily identified by the large circular, dark-coloured spots which develop on the leaves and sometimes on the young shoots. Infected leaves later turn yellow and fall prematurely thus weakening the plants.

To get really effective control of this disease a general fungicide should be applied when the new shoots are about 5 in (13 cm) long. Repeat sprays should then be given at 14-day intervals. It is also good practice to change the fungicide from time to time as this avoids the risk of a build up of disease resistance to fungicides.

Club root

This soil-borne disease infects the roots of brassicas causing them to become abnormally thick and distorted. Early attacks result in the plants becoming stunted whilst later ones cause discoloration of the leaves and wilting in warm weather.

The club root organism is favoured by acid soil, so a first

essential is to apply lime before planting brassicas. Crop rotation also helps to reduce the severity of attack provided that the ground is kept free of weeds.

Even so, it is necessary to apply a club root fungicide such as benomyl, mercurous chloride (calomel) or thiophanate-methyl to the open seed drills, seedling roots and planting holes.

Peach leaf curl

This fungus disease is all too common on peaches and related *Prunus* species. The first sign of infection by peach leaf curl is that the young developing leaves become thickened and distorted with reddish blisters. Later these blisters turn white as the disease spores develop. Infected leaves fall early, weakening the trees and greatly reducing cropping.

The fungus overwinters on the bud scales so it is best controlled by spraying with mancozeb or with a copper fungicide in late January and again in early February. A third spray should be applied in autumn prior to leaf fall.

Potato blight

Potato blight, which also attacks outdoor tomatoes, is a devastating disease. The first sign of infection is the appearance of yellowish-brown patches on the lower leaves. These quickly turn black and rotten in wet weather which favours the rapid spread of the disease.

In severe attacks the whole of the potato haulm is killed and the disease also invades the tubers causing an evil-smelling rot. Tomato fruits too develop a black rot when infected with blight.

This disease can appear at any time between May and August but is most prevalent in June and July. Spray with a copper fungicide or with mancozeb at the first sign of attack and repeat the treatment at intervals of 10-14 days.

Peach leaf curl.

Powdery mildew.

Powdery mildews

This type of disease attacks a variety of plants but is particularly effective on roses, apples and gooseberries. Powdery mildew infections are easy to recognize since they result in the leaves and shoots being covered with a greyish-white powdery growth of fungi. In some plants the flowers and fruits are also affected.

Once the disease is established it is difficult to control so the plants should be sprayed at the first sign of the disease using a powdery mildew fungicide such as benomyl, bupirimate, carbendazim or dinocap. Repeat sprays at intervals of 10-14 days are then needed to protect newly developing foliage.

Rusts

Rust fungi can attack a range of garden plants but this disease is most common on antirrhinum, geranium, hollyhock and roses. The first sign of infection is the appearance of pale-coloured pimples on the undersides of the leaves. These soon burst open to display a mass of powdery orange or brown fungal spores. Later-formed spores of some rusts may be blackish in colour.

Light yellowish patches also develop on the upper leaf surface above the spore clusters. This yellowing gradually extends over the whole leaf surface and there is premature leaf fall.

The usual method of control is to spray with mancozeb or triforine at intervals of 10-14 days, starting at the first sign of infection. Rust-resistant antirrhinums are, however, available and these should be chosen in preference to other varieties.

INDEX

Picture Credits

A-Z Collection 101-2.
Baco Ltd. 24.
Harry Baker 112 (all); 139; 152 (all); 153 (all); 154 (all); 164 (all); 165 (all).
Walter Blom & Son Ltd. 144 T,B; 166BR.
Bulb Information Desk, Maidenhead 67CL; 86; 109 TL,TC,TR,CR,BR; 142T; 143TL; 149 (all except TL); 160 (all); 161 (all.
K.A. & G. Beckett 29 (all); 39TR; 40b; 46 T,C; 47 TR,BR; 64TR; 67T; 83TL; 114; 135.
Linda Burgess 1; 12; 42-3; 78-9; 136-7.
Philip Damp 88 (all except BL,BR); 89 L,TR.
Samuel Dobie & Son Ltd. 27 C,BR,BL; 55 CL,BR; 56CR; 57CR.
S. Gosling 75 (both); 105; 130; 166CL.
Florapic 39B; 40T; 46B; 47 TL,CR, BL, BC; 55TL; 56 CL,TR; 57TR; 61BL; 63 (both); 64TL; 65; 67 CR,B; 74; 83 TR,C; 84; 87; 94; 95; 96; 99 TL,CL,C,TR,CR,BR; 106; 109 CL,BL,C; 118 CL,BL,TC,C,TR; 119 CR,BL; 131;133;138; 159 TR,BR; 175 TC,TR; 176 (all); 177 L,CR,BR; 178CR; 180 (all); 181TL.
Jenny de Gex 27T; 110-11; 124R.
Granada 4; 18; 56 BL,BC; 57 L,BR; 72; 82; 88 BL,BR; 89 CR,BR; 113; 123; 128BL; 141.
R. Harkness & Co. Ltd. 61 TL,BR;124 TL,CL; 125TR; 126 CL,BL,BC; 128 TL,BR.
Jerry Harpur 70-1; 90-1; 120-1; 150-1.
J.D. Main 39TL; 119BR; 147; 166BL.
John Mattock Ltd. 125 L,BR; 126 TL,TC,C; 126-7; 128TR.
Angela Murphy 159L.
Harry Smith Collection 107; 142B:143 TR,B: 146; 146-7; 149TL; 181B.
Suttons Seeds 30 (all); 31 TL,CL,BL,TC,BC,TR,CR: 56BR; 64 BL,BR; 81; 103; 122 (all); 129; 166TR.
Tessa Traeger 2.
Unwins Seeds Ltd. 31 C,BR; 56C.
Michael Warren 11;13 TL,BL,BR; 34-5; 45; 49; 55 BL,TC,TR; 56TL; 92; 97; 99BL; 102; 109BC; 115; 118TL; 118 CR,BR; 119 TL,TR,BC; 158; 162-3; 175 TL,B; 177TR; 178 L,TR,BR; 179; 181TR.
George Wright 6; 13TR; 19; 58-9.

Illustrations by Hussein Hussein and Rosemary Wise